Author Prof

Maxine Handy was born next to a wood in Kent, with a view of the River Thames from her bedroom window. However, she spent her formative years in a small village beneath a wood (Birchanger) on the Herts/Essex border. From there she attended school in antique Saffron Walden where she joined the choir, giving performances of works by Benjamin Britten. Lucky enough to encounter an inspirational English teacher she won many prizes before reading English Language and Literature at the University of Leeds, completing a dissertation on Henry James' short stories of the literary life for her MA. University also gave her an opportunity to study Classical Civilisation and enter the elite seductive atmosphere of the Greek Department. She is also increasingly fascinated by, and drawn to Jewish history, culture, and literature. The author now lives in a tiny village in rural Cheshire, enjoying writing, countertenors, and the company of her two beloved cats and two adult children. She visits mainland Greece and Italy at every opportunity. Having published *The Life of Bosworth – A Cat* in 2007, described by Julian Clary as 'A charming and surprising read'. Maxine is now working on the novelisation of a countertenor memoir, to be published next year.

Also by Maxine Handy

The Life of Bosworth
A Cat

Published by Maniot Books 2007

The Wishing-Well and Other Fantasies

Published by Lulu, 2010

The Siren of Social Services – a factional memoir

Published by Lulu, 2010

Triple Portrait of a Countertenor

Published by Lulu, 2010

Burning in Blueness
The Dark-Light of a Countertenor

MAXINE HANDY

Copyright © Maxine Handy 2010
First published in 2010 by Lulu

Distributed by Lulu

The right of Maxine Handy to be identified as the author of the work has been asserted herein in accordance with the Copyright, Designs and Patents Act 1988.

All rights reserved. This book is sold subject to the condition that it shall not, by way of trade or otherwise, be lent, resold, hired out or otherwise circulated without the publisher's prior consent in any form of binding or cover other than that in which it is published and without a similar condition including this condition being imposed on the subsequent purchaser

British Library Cataloguing in Publication Data
A catalogue record for this book is available from the British Library

ISBN 978-1-4466-7031-6

James Bowman in the 1970s

'I first sang on the stage of the Wigmore Hall in November 1967, not in concert, but as part of an audition with David Munrow's Early Music Consort…The audition was a success and the rest is part of musical history. This hall has played a very large part in my life, so I feel it appropriate that it is where I should make my last London appearance…'

A few words form James in his sumptuous programme for his last London recital at the Wigmore Hall on Saturday 21 May 2011.

FOR TAMSIN AND LEON

Grateful acknowledgement to Sonia Ribeiro for reading and editorial advice.

Sweeter Than Roses

Sweeter than roses
or cool evening breeze
on a warm flow'ry shore
was the dear kiss,
first trembling made me freeze,
Then shot like fire all o'er.
What magic has victorious love,
for all I touch or see
Since that dear kiss
I hourly prove,
all, all is love to me.

Purcell, realised by Benjamin Britten
James Bowman, Countertenor
Benjamin Britten, piano
Recording location for Canticle 1V and 'Sweeter Than Roses':
The Maltings Snape, November 1972

'A most important recording.' JB

Burning in Blueness
The Dark-Light of a Countertenor

Contents

Introduction   1

PART ONE
The Voice

Gloriani's Garden	11
Sweeter than Roses	14
An obscure hurt	17
Bach - a loving caress	20
Cambridge and Cycling	24
Connections	27
The Holy Ghost	37
The Fairy King	41
Erbarme dich	64
Flowers	72
The National Gallery	84

PART TWO
The Man

Ripon	91
The Library	104
A Day in Kent	107
Childhood and Privacy	114
The Commission	133
A Living Flame	153
Sacred Stones	157
Withdrawal	166

PART THREE
The Memory

Soliloquy	175
Orlando	177
Suicide Notes	184
David Munrow and James	189
The Most Beautiful View in the World	191
Ten Blake Songs	195
The Orante	199
'My face is all covered with shaving foam, Maxine'	202
The Sepulchre	208
King's Hall, Newcastle	211
The Opened Mouth	214
'We shall never be again as we were'	221
Finale	226
Coda	228
The Critics	232
'Thy Sun is Sinking'	237
'Thy Day is at Evening'	239
Postscript November 2010	241
Afterword 2011	241
James Bowman Discography: **CDs**; **LPs**; **Videos**	247

INTRODUCTION

> Classical voice instructors describe the optimal balance of clearness and darkness in the voice tone as chiaroscuro, a combination of brilliance and resonance, with warmth and depth. The 'dark-light' tone should always be present.
> Giovanni Battista Lamperti, singing instructor

Leonardo's painting *The Virgin of the Rocks*, and the song 'Sweeter than Roses', anticipate and express my entire relationship with James Bowman, the Man and the Voice. These two great works set the tone of this whole memoir in which music, painting, and the written word are commingled. Britten's realisation of Purcell's 'Sweeter than Roses' was recorded by James in 1972, in Snape Maltings. This was the year in which I first heard him sing, and the Maltings, Snape, was the place where, in April 1998, we said goodbye: 'Maxine, give me a kiss before you go.'

This Purcell/Britten song is deeply personal and very beautiful; it belongs to James alone. His unique voice possesses both coolness and warmth. He himself would often describe his performances as 'a loving caress, like a velvet-gloved hand around the throat' and I would describe them using Milton's words, 'with an individual kiss'.

In his *Notebooks*, Leonardo records a moment when, standing before the mouth of a cave: 'Suddenly two things arose in me ... fear of the menacing darkness ... [and] desire to see if there was any marvellous thing within ...' Leonardo's four figures create an open triangle, and are in rapt communion. The Virgin's protectiveness is conveyed through her blue cloak and hand gestures. The facial expressions are introspective and enigmatic. The dark cave is threatening but also a place of sanctuary for those who sit in their place of concealment:

Burning in Blueness

> I feel as lit by fire a cold countenance
> That burns me from afar and keeps itself ice-chill.
> Michelangelo, Sonnets

My own magical, risky and mysterious journey into another, into what W.H. Auden called the 'cave of making', was just such an encounter with Chiaroscuro, 'light-sensitive darkness'. Leonardo's painting reveals a delicacy of modelling in which gradual transitions 'veil' the steps from darkest shadow to highlight, like the 'veiled' register change between James' chest and head voice, or the male alto voice veiled with the sound of baroque instruments, which James so adores. In the painting, in the words of Erica Langmuir, from *The National Gallery Companion Guide*, 1994: 'The infant John the Baptist sheltering under Mary's cloak, venerates the Christ child in a cool, watery wilderness…in the candlelit Chapel the glittering frame and the painted rocks from whose shadows the figures emerge would have combined to suggest a mysterious cavern.' James Bowman describes his bass-baritone speaking voice as like a cavern in which his alto singing voice resonates.

    I offer an unconventional, partial portrait of a turbulent, charming, melancholy, and unique genius who gave me the greatest sense of ecstasy, intimacy, and empathy with another that I have ever experienced. This relationship is perfectly communicated by J. S. Bach's Cantata 140, *Wachet auf, ruft uns die Stimme*, which contains a mystical and yearning duet between Jesus and the Soul. It is one of the most beautiful love duets ever written, ardent yet relaxed, in which heavenly and earthly love merge into one: '*Komm, liebliche Seele!*'

    I shall eulogize James' great artistry and enumerate his varied but specialised repertoire, which has such intelligence and exquisite taste. This is 'physical beauty and left-handedness' (Freud's description of Leonardo da Vinci in his monograph on the artist) as seen through my eyes and almost solely from my point of view. 'You see what I am, Maxine!' James said. 'I do my work for people like you who truly appreciate what I do. Seen through your eyes, Maxine, I am Leonardo's beautiful *Virgin of the Rocks*, and yes, I agree with you entirely. But I can't say that! And anyway, it sounds much lovelier coming from you.'

Admittedly, there are many gaps in my retrospective, so my narrative, although luminous, will appear incomplete and perplexing, with a sometimes confusing chronology, but I prefer it to emerge in that form. Lyndall Gordon wrote on letters: 'Letters…are a form of narrative that envisages no outcome, no closure.'

The following chapters or 'scenes' might have taken the form of an epistolary 'biography' of an invisible correspondent, with the mystery of his identity remaining, or an imaginative work of fiction, the more effective because it is documented fact. As it is, my memoir deserves to stand alongside James Bowman's legacy of recordings, which he insisted were his biography: 'I frequently refuse and will continue to refuse to have my biography written, because it doesn't interest me. I think my biography is in the recordings I've made. I'm very happy for there to be so many and I'm very proud of it,' James wrote to me, and repeated these words some years later in an interview on Radio 3.

James Bowman himself has continued to resist any suggestion of a conventional biography, and told me on the telephone of this dislike: 'I don't want a biography, Maxine. I don't want people fingering my private life.' Like his own dear Handel, James Bowman is 'a consummately private man in an extremely public role'. Handel had a similar aversion to personal revelations and refused to write an autobiography; also, he remained largely in control of his paper-trail – carefully destroying almost all private papers.

This memoir, or fragment, is a cherished private story, the transfer of recollection into writing. It is a work of memory and mourning, supported by documentation and research. Henry James, author and man, appears throughout as a kind of mentor and inspiration; his presence haunts this piece. He was obsessed by the fate of private correspondence, and would probably believe that 'These are secrets for privacy and silence'. (Henry James, 'On the Letters of George Sand', *Selected Literary Criticism*.) The story also unfolds through the voice of my singer in the form of conversations, letters, and cards, providing a sort of commentary, whereas my large handwritten correspondence to him remains concealed and locked away in the privacy of his study.

Thousands of my private letters to James Bowman tell the story and paint the picture, of this unique period of exalted receptivity during which not a detail was lost. In many of his Tales and short stories, not least *The Aspern Papers*, Henry James conveys his understanding of the dangers of publishing private letters. Thus the Letters, here, which 'trace each herb and flower', to use Handel's evocative phrase from *Solomon*, as in the idyllic countryside he expectantly awaits his new bride, are reconstructed in part as a first person narrative. In the end, I destroyed nearly all copies of my letters to this singer, but a few are still with me, and I have an exceptional verbal and visual memory. During this story I have included some direct extracts from them. At other times references to documentation or other sources will remain oblique. So to quote Henry James on Leonardo's *The Last Supper* (before restoration): 'A shadow is all that remains, but that shadow is the soul of the artist.'

However, the great artist to whom my original letters

were addressed has kept them all: 'They are all placed in a large box in the privacy of my study,' James Bowman wrote to me. 'I keep all your correspondence separately, Maxine, including the envelopes. It is very beautiful and always so interesting...I can't wait to see what you've written about me.' He has promised to use my unique correspondence to edit and compile a beautiful 'book', to be left after his lifetime: 'You have a corner of a room in my house, Maxine, and my desk is named after you ... I keep all your correspondence, Maxine,' James said to me. 'It is very beautiful. One day, when I've finished with all this, I'm going to compile a book from your Letters, to be left after my lifetime. It is to be front-covered by Leonardo's *Virgin of the Rocks*.'

In compiling the 'book' to honour his memory, James Bowman would license for posterity a disclosure of our strange bond, guarded with discretion during his lifetime. So in his compilation of my letters for public viewing, I would at last be acknowledged as I perhaps wished, and certainly deserved, to be.

As to the fate of the correspondence which I received from my artist, that is extant, but almost wholly concealed. The reader must imagine the 'voice' and create the 'other', in this, my narrative of three decades of unconditional devotion, of which James wrote: 'Thank you for your kindness and devotion to me; I'm deeply grateful for it.'

As so much of my source material is now unavailable, it is of course, difficult to convey the detail of my developing obsession and fascination with this 'falsettist'; 'unique spirit and my mind's sole tendance'. As I have said, all the documents exist in a large box in the house of the singer, but he will probably leave instructions for them to be destroyed after his death. They will probably never be made into a book to be left alongside his recorded legacy. He may wish to keep the past to himself, as a prized and private possession, or decide to reveal this 'living, breathing responsiveness to himself' that he so valued.

In Peter Ackroyd's *Albion – the Origins of the English Imagination*, he has a wonderful chapter entitled 'The fine Art of Biography'. Ackroyd believes biography to be an extension of imaginative literature and that we are drawn into autobiography by the pressure of biography; memoir and biography intersect, moving towards fiction.

Biography is a collection of fictional or dramatic episodes united by a commentary. Interestingly, mediaeval biography resembles a lament, and included constructions of conversations and anecdotes, as are also found in ancient classical 'Histories'. In the 18th century, Boswell was concerned with what Johnson 'privately wrote, and said, and thought', and wished to cast Johnson's biography in 'scenes'. The narrative must be fashioned to accord with the personal vision of the biographer; I must construct a James Bowman answering my private needs.

In this narrative, I quote from James Bowman's written and spoken words, and include extracts from documents and conversations contemporary with the events recorded. I am but one of his many possible chroniclers, but I can be trusted to represent him faithfully from my decade of letters and cards and reconstruct 'all this', a phrase James used to describe his career, and my correspondence to him. In E. F. Benson's *Final Edition* there is a warning to writers of books of reminiscence: one must depend on memory and documents, although 'In setting their scene no one will grudge them a reasonable license in decoration...'

In a sense I have been working at this strange book for the last thirty years and within it there is so much beauty, poetry and death, 'ghosts and spirits, doubles and hauntings, metamorphoses ... '

Perhaps it is significant that the first James Bowman live

recital in which I heard him sing centred around the National Gallery's quest to save Titian's *The Death of Actaeon*. In gazing at Diana in her grotto, Actaeon saw: '...stillness and grace/in the space of one heartbeat/then he saw his own death.' Once again, the marvellous and the frightening are in combination. A place believed to be miraculous – like Leonardo's cave – or Tytania's bank - suddenly and unexpectedly becomes dangerous. Epiphany turns to destruction.

James' transformation into Leonardo's *Virgin of the Rocks* came to me in a vision, and the title, *Burning in Blueness*, in a dream, what Peter Ackroyd describes as 'the English penchant for the dream and the vision'.

The following words are the most beautiful ever spoken to me, and will resonate within me for the rest of my life. They illuminate the dark subject of this small book, and I keep them inside my handbag in memory of a *cosa mentale*:

> Maxine! Show me where you're sitting and I'll open my mouth very wide and sing to you … My live performances should leave you in suspended ecstasy, waiting for the next time … They live and then die like a flower, but there should never be any sense of anti-climax.
>
> James to Maxine

▲   ▲   ▲

Burning in Blueness

James Bowman iin the 1960s

PART ONE
The Voice

Gloriani's Garden

It was the cerebral Henry James who said that the most rarefied love affair was that with an artist. This great and adored writer was indeed there, at the beginning and conclusion of just such a 'rarefied' and charming journey, which was to finish in trauma and the desolation of separation.

My deep attraction to Henry James' work, and a fascination with his account of an 'obscure hurt', recorded in his autobiography *A Small Boy and Others*, coincided with my broken ankle and the dawn of a musical obsession with the male high voice. H.J.'s enigmatic references to his 'obscure hurt' gave rise to the Hemingway fantasy that Henry James 'castrated' himself in an accident, and was thus secretly eunuchoid, perhaps like the castrati singers in Handel's operas 'a Sex without Name'.

To go back to my first enchanted meeting with 'Gloriani's Garden' in Henry James' *The Ambassadors*, I must cross three decades, to my period of postgraduate study at Leeds University. An eminent Jamesian academic told me, in confidence, that it had taken him five years to read *The Ambassadors*, Henry James' favourite novel and his greatest work. Having commenced the struggle my lecturer had wrestled with H.J. until his exploration was triumphant. What did that magical, ambiguous encounter between Gloriani and Lambert Strether in the garden, mean to me then, in the early 1970s? The scene is played out in a high walled garden, a *hortus conclusus*, an ancient symbol of Mary's virginity, but also, as in Baroque theatre, the garden is used symbolically to represent erotic love. Gloriani's eyes in *The Ambassadors* are Henry James', and we remember how Strether is 'held' by them, as 'the penetrating radiance, as the communication of the illustrious spirit itself'. He thinks of them as 'the source of the deepest intellectual sounding to which he had ever been exposed'. Strether has a cherished vision of Gloriani that he will never forget but always struggle to understand: 'Was what it had told him or what it had asked him the greater of the mysteries?'

What was the meaning to me of the work of 'The Master' in those far off student days of immersion in so many, many books, (a plethora, ranging from seventeenth century prose to the picturesque in the 18th century novel and travel literature) under the guidance of Dr Alexander E. S. Viner, a literary aristocrat, like Virginia Woolf's *Orlando*. Alexander's doctoral thesis at Leeds University had been on Anthony Trollope, and when I studied Jane Austen with him, he told me that his favourite novel by her was *Persuasion*. He was fascinated by what he termed 'the theme of love renewed after long delay'. Dr Viner said that I was a 'delight' to teach, and that he'd always known I'd continue at Leeds as a postgraduate because I had 'such flair'.

I loved the diverse taught courses which contributed to my MA but Henry James was special because I felt deeply attracted to his work, and his short stories of the literary life and artists were the subject of my MA dissertation, *The Theme of the Literary Artist in Selected Short Stories of Henry James*. My conclusion reads as follows: 'In depicting the artist, Henry James tells mostly of frustration or deprivation, ignoring the joy of artistic creation which he himself felt so keenly. All that is so enormously attractive about Henry James, both as man and artist, finds insufficient reflection in the literary heroes of the short stories.' Thus I felt it necessary at this time to re-read all Henry James' work, including those last three poetic novels.

But in the midst of this intellectual excitement came the repose and mystery in Gloriani's Garden, and the beginning of everlasting obsession. 'The celebrated sculptor had a queer old garden ... the tall bird-haunted trees ... and the high party-walls ...

spoke of ... a strong persistent order ... Strether had presently the sense of a great convent ... of scattered shade .... and chapel bells ... he had the sense of names in the air, of ghosts at the windows, of signs and tokens ...' At this very moment of a first meeting and apotheosis, Strether knows that despite his liking for Gloriani, he 'should never see him again; of that he was sufficiently sure'.

Gloriani showed him 'A face that was like an open letter in a foreign tongue. With his genius in his eyes, his manners on his lips, his long career behind him and honours and rewards all round, the great artist, in the course of a single sustained look and a few words of delight ... affected Strether ... with a personal lustre almost violent ... with the romance of glory ... Strether, in contact with that element as he had never yet so intimately been, had the consciousness of opening to it ... all the windows of his mind...' Privacy, longing, love, and loss are prefigured. Henry James described Trinity Hall, Cambridge as having 'the most beautiful small garden in Europe'; he was probably remembering it when he described that of Gloriani.

I often likened James Bowman to the 'tree of life', and he responded by sending me a card of a solitary golden-leafed birch tree, everything around it dark and lifeless. I have a wonderful photograph of James Bowman, a 'believer', standing beneath a tree in his old walled garden in Surrey, the brick turned russet with age and weather.

> And all amid them stood the tree of life,
> High eminent, blooming ambrosial fruit
> Of vegetable gold.
> Milton's 'Tree Of Life' in *Paradise Lost*

Gloriani in his 'garden inclosed' ('The Song of Songs', 4:12) offered that combination of and contradiction between cerebral energy, eroticism, and severity. But in its ecstasies and melancholy, the epiphany in the garden, 'a spacious, cherished remnant', anticipated a personal and private story in which all my emotional intensities ended in anticlimax. In youth, I too saw the Blakean tiger in the great Gloriani's secret garden 'the glossy male tiger, magnificently marked', and three decades on suffered, like Strether, the terrible realisation that it was now 'too late' to re-enter the paradise which for so long had called to me. In a Notebook entry for February 1895, Henry James reflects on the theme which came to dominate *The Ambassadors*, 1903 'what is there in the idea of *Too Late* – of some…passion or bond…formed too late?…Its love, its friendship, its mutual comprehension – its whatever one will.'

Sweeter Than Roses

> A cry of enchanting sweetness, yet with a deep and overpowering authority. It invited the very soul. Then withdrawn deeper into the night – floating higher – a summons and an entreaty – the appeal in it is irresistible. The beauty and splendour of that far voice passionately summons the yearning listener.
> Algernon Blackwood, *The Centaur*

In May 1972, I was living in a small stone cottage, next to a copse, in the Meanwood area of Leeds, where I remained until late September, 1976. I almost always worked upstairs as it was much brighter, with a charming view over the elderly Miss Grimshaw's garden smothered in flowers. Also, it delighted me to look over towards the new houses where many lines of baby clothes fluttered in the breeze, increasing my sense of apartness, and delicious withdrawal from the everyday world. The large-windowed bedroom became my inner sanctum where I could devote myself to the writings of beloved Henry James, and remember his own 'garden room' at Rye, sadly destroyed by a German bomb during World War II.

E.F. Benson, author of *Final Edition,* was, for many years, a tenant of Lamb House, and claimed that he was haunted by the ghost of Henry James, who appeared to him in the garden.

My supervising Professor made an annual pilgrimage to Lamb House. Like most James scholars he was absolutely in love with his enigmatic, 'severely celibate' subject and kept a photograph of him above his desk. He liked seeing Henry James' personal artefacts, and told me that Henry had not owned the sort of sofa on which one might enjoy a cuddle; H.J.'s caressings were almost exclusively verbal. The great James scholar and biographer, Leon Edel, underwent extensive travel to all the many places Henry James had visited.

'Some of Edel's friends joked that his passion became not merely a love affair but a marriage. He wore a ring that once belonged to the writer. He guarded his beloved against rivals, insisting upon his privilege. He sometimes identified with James as though he were his reincarnation.' (From *The Times* Obituary for Leon Edel, September 18th, 1997.) Edel's obsession mirrors mine with James Bowman.

Having thrilled to Professor Douglas Jefferson's description of Lamb House, I thought, one day very soon, probably in spring, 1973, I'll visit Henry's house, 'releasing shades of days gone by'. Undoubtedly, like E. F. Benson, I'll see his ghost, probably in the walled garden by the dripping laurel and fragrant blue wisteria.

Upstairs in my sunlit room in early summer, I felt like Thomas Hardy at his writing desk at Higher Bockhampton Cottage, which I'd visited and lingered in at the age of sixteen, eating an apple from a tree he had planted, or Vita Sackville-West facing an antique tapestry landscape in the private world of her tower study at Sissinghurst. A little statue of an angel is fixed above the arch to the entrance of Vita's tower writing room, as if he were a messenger from the world she was seeking. At that time I didn't have a study, and certainly not my own tower. But the upper floor of my old cottage conveyed the same sense of a hiding place, removed from intrusion. 'Solitude nourishes creativity,' said the great pianist Glen Gould.

While I was engaged in doing literary research upstairs in my seventeenth century cottage in Meanwood, Leeds, I'd left Radio 3 on downstairs in the lounge, when I suddenly heard what the early music specialist, David Munrow, had called 'the most wonderful noise in the universe'. James Bowman was singing Britten's very personal and beautiful realisation of Purcell's *Sweeter than Roses*, with Britten himself on piano.

This performance marked the commencement of my passion, and also included the miraculous Canticle II, *Abraham and Isaac*, and Britten's wintry Canticle IV, *The Journey of the Magi*, of which James was the dedicatee. It was broadcast on May 28th, 1972 from the National Gallery, as part of a concert in aid of the Save the Titian appeal. James Bowman was muse to both Benjamin Britten and David Munrow, having met them in the same year, 1966, and lost them both a decade later in 1976.

James worked closely for a decade with Munrow, singing mediaeval and renaissance music. For the next ten years after their first meeting, Britten was to play a pivotal role in James Bowman's career. The ghost of David Munrow appeared many times during my friendship with James, especially on my visits to his old music club at Hinckley.

Those years seem dreamlike now, a vanished miracle... I quote from my letter to Nicholas Kenyon, then controller of

Radio 3, written over twenty years later, imploring him to play this particular recording from his BBC Sound Archives:

9th September, 1993

Dear Mr Kenyon,
The National Gallery recording is uniquely special, as it was the first time I heard James sing ... Through love of his voice the marvellous world of Baroque music was gradually revealed to me, and his work with Benjamin Britten has inspired my passionate enthusiasm for 20th century music for the countertenor.
Purcell's 'Sweeter than Roses' in the Britten realisation, belongs solely to James!

Yours sincerely,
Maxine Handy

An obscure hurt

> For your bounty, although
> The end is now before,
> Me to myself won't restore
> Nor damnation of such pietà rid me;
> Habit of years a day doesn't make free.
>
> Michelangelo, *Sonnets*

My own pilgrimage is now concluded; I've served my purpose and disappeared.

Sometimes, I feel that my ten years of Letters to James in which I conveyed my innermost thoughts, is something that others might only laugh at or misinterpret. I made so many journeys to see my singer and wrote so many letters, for his eyes only. 'You are an addict, Maxine,' he said to me. But in truth it was an addiction to writing, and an all-important link with

Burning in Blueness

London.

Indeed, James' singing has inspired all that I have written with my beautiful burgundy and gold Cross fountain pen, which has a bishop's mitre engraved nib. My leather Mont Blanc pen case is embellished with the symbol of a solitary snowflake. I remember writing the following words to James, a memory he promised to preserve forever: 'I am delighted to discover that you love the stillness and silence of snow at night.' I was unprepared for the sudden cessation of contact; it is now more than five years since I heard from him. How do I remember my time with the King of Shadows? Was he Adam's Angel Guest in Milton's *Paradise Lost*? 'Gentle to me and affable hath been thy condescension, and shall be honored ever with grateful memory.' Or John Marcher from Henry James' *The Beast in the Jungle*: 'She had loved him for herself; whereas he had never thought of her but in the chill of his egotism and the light of her use.'

I'm writing this shortly before Easter, in a top floor apartment at ghostly Fountains Hall, an Elizabethan mansion, and gazing out through a vast mullioned window. The Fountains Estate, which includes Studley Royal and the great Cistercian Abbey, is a place that obsessed Alan Bennett as 'a thing free from imperfection'.

But at that time in May 1972, my ecstasy was such that I ran downstairs to be closer to that cool yet warm androgynous sound, 'A paradox of chilly fire,' to be ultimately admitted, perhaps, like Virginia Woolf, to the 'warmth and intimacy of another soul,' something that James constantly quoted back to me, as something he, too, desperately wanted.

Virginia Woolf, like Rainer Maria Rilke, believed in the essential androgyny of the creative mind. 'Androgyny,' Rilke wrote, 'is the pull inward, the erotic pull of the other we sense buried in the self.'

In this season three decades later, my mind returns to that faraway 1972 Meanwood summer in Fosse House when I first heard James sing with Peter Pears in Britten's *Canticles* II and IV, and then alone in Purcell's 'Sweeter than Roses', a piece originally created by Britten for Peter Pears. This was everything; my love was truly in flower! Like that of his colleague and friend the great English tenor, Peter Pears, his voice was 'the instrument of his soul'. James told me that he loved singing with Peter: 'He was a wonderful duettist.'

At the time of this *Sweeter than Roses*, my CD booklet was as yet not inscribed by him 'A most important recording'; there were no letters to treasure or compile as a legacy. The correspondence, communication and exchange had not begun. In running so quickly down the narrow twisted staircase in Fosse House and falling at the final bend, I had broken my ankle, which quickly turned green and became badly swollen. But such was my ecstatic state that after the broadcast I returned to my writing-table, my view, and 'Gloriani's Garden', knowing that I'd undergone a Jamesian apotheosis: 'a love-philtre or fear-philtre, which fixes for the senses their supreme symbol of the fair or the strange.' (Henry James' dream/nightmare, in the Napoleonic Galerie d'Apollon in the Louvre.) Crossing the threshold of the Galerie d'Apollon in the empire of his own creation was for Henry James the crucial passage of his life and death. The Gallery of Apollo was his true 'home'.

After his The Raptured Soul recital in the King's Hall at Ilkley, in February 1998, James said to me: 'We have something very beautiful, Maxine, why let other people spoil it?' James wished to isolate me and my response to him, to place my focus solely on himself. This is what he demanded and enjoyed.

Ehue! Quam tenui e filo pendet
Quidquid in vita maxime arridet

Anxious griefs, grievous anxieties, are not to be
Sublimed through chiaroscuro. Knowing this,
                    you framed it, clearly.
To mourn is to mourn; the ancient words suffice,
Latin or English, worn channels for the rain.
                    Charged and electric.
We suffer commonly, where we are qute alone,
not the real but the actual natures of things;
and there is now, assuredly, no telling
how spirit readied the hand to engineer
a perceptible radiance – arched and spectral –
the abrupt rainbow's errant visitation.
                    Geoffrey Hill, *To John*
                    Constable In Absentia

Slowly, I entered the shared solitude of the cave and took possession of an atmosphere like the twilight of a night vision.

Bach – a loving caress

I love singing Bach
                    James Bowman

I cannot now understand why my early overwhelming passion lay dormant so long, from its commencement in 1972 to its re-awakening in the late 1980s in Manchester, by a recording of Bach's solo *Cantatas for Alto*. During this lengthy interval, I listened almost exclusively to Beethoven's late Quartets and Schubert's song cycle *Winterreise*, especially the very 'English' version with Peter Pears and Benjamin Britten on piano. Bach believed the countertenor to be the voice of the Holy Spirit, and

I remember James saying that in performance he gave Bach's *'Vergnügte Ruh'*, a 'loving caress'. In the words of Norman Lebrecht, 'The art of interpreting Bach is a book of seven seals that only immortals have unlocked.' James is indeed godlike. Bach is his most difficult but deeply satisfying repertoire. Years later in his live performance of Bach's *'Ich habe genug'* (preserved in BBC archives), he rises to the challenge of making something familiar sound very different. 'I think putting the piece (*'Ich habe genug'*) up an octave and singing it in a different tessitura, in its own way makes the piece sound different to the listener – and you can do more things to the text often at that pitch ... the first movement can be wonderfully plangent up the octave in the countertenor voice. I love singing Bach.' Not only does James remind us of his application of the unique counter-tenor tessitura, but also that he is very much a text man. He works on every syllable to give a dramatic intrerpretation; something he learned as an Ely chorister under the great Michael Howard.

Before that time, after seven years in Leeds, in the autumn of 1976, (after the famous heat wave of that year), I moved to Cambridge, and after five years there, lived on the Leicestershire/Warwickshire border for a further five. It was James who eventually reunited me with dearest East Anglia, ('Where ghost has haunted/Lost and wanted', from W. H. Auden's 'Lunar Beauty', set to music by Geoffrey Burgon, performed by James Bowman and recorded by him in June 1987), and with my childhood there, especially the enchantments of Saffron Walden and Audley End. 'I only like people from East Anglia, Maxine!' I teased him by saying that I could discern his 'fenland' accent and 'linear mind'. This amused him greatly. We discussed our shared love of the unique atmosphere of East Anglia, its remoteness and austerity.

James said that he could imagine me there, in the

Jacobean Mansion Park of Audley End, lying down beneath the trees and meditating. Many years later I'd return to all these places in triumphant and glorious pursuit of my beloved singer, feeling that, like Strether, I had found a paradise for which I'd searched all my life. His overwhelming presence was concentrated now on me alone. I was set apart, and I felt drawn to him by a strength and magnetism that I had never yet in all my life experienced with anyone. I was the chosen one, like Mary in the Bible and the Koran, so it was an equal relationship.

I remember James coming to sit beside me and respectfully touching my arm with his fingertips, whilst quoting from the Nawab in Ruth Prawer Jhabvala's *Heat and Dust*: 'There are certain people who, if they are absent, life becomes hard to bear... These are the people who once sat close to you in Paradise.'

Cambridge, where I'd suffered a miscarriage and a series of personal crises, became the place where I gave birth to my beautiful daughter, and subsequently returned to in order to see my great artist sing to me, giving me the *Agnus Dei* from Bach's *B Minor Mass* – and, like the Archangel Gabriel, bending down to speak to me in King's College Chapel: 'The *Agnus Dei* is for you, Maxine.' All else and terrible memories disappeared to become a light shining in the darkness. 'Total obsession, night and day. When I see you, James, you look *alive* and everything else – fades.' This was one of his favourite comments by me. He treasured it and said it showed that I truly adored him. In response to my remark he sent me a card of a beautiful golden tree the sole living thing in an otherwise dead and desolate landscape. I said to him that out creative contact was not unlike the decade-long relationship between King Philip V of Spain and the great castrato Farinelli. By singing the same four arias nightly for ten years, Farinelli was to bring solace to the depressive King

Philip of Spain. Eventually, in old age, Farinelli fell victim to the same depression which had afflicted his royal master. On Monday, November 8th, 1993, returning home after hearing the B minor *Mass* in Cambridge, I told James in a letter that he had from me the response and focus he desired:

Dear James,
    Thank you so much, for the beautiful 'twin' of 'I know a bank'…How very kind and courteous of you to come over to me at King's; I greatly appreciated those few delightful moments of seclusion behind your score! Thank you, above all, for singing to me, for the absolute Paradise of the '*Agnus Dei*'. I was reminded of a visit, long ago, with my brother, to see the body of a still-born child, a tragic and deeply moving contemplation of death, so very different from the desolation of the old and diseased bodies in the human dissection rooms… Your Isaac with Peter Pears' Abraham completed a perfect week; it is a piece and a performance for which I have a boundless love. Brian Kay has promised me more James Bowman, starting on Sunday November 21st, with '*Scherza infida*' from *Ariodante*; he says there is more to follow in January! I have booked for your *Dream* in Tourcoing, on Saturday April 2nd. My visit will not be quite like *A Little Tour in France*, but never mind! Perfect experiences come only from Art!! I also look forward, very much, to seeing you on December 29th, at the Wigmore Hall, and hope to include the 31st as well!. So glad the Roses were beautiful, and gave you pleasure. I am sorry the book, which should have accompanied them, is a little late, but the order was delayed. I apologize for the slight alterations in the following dedication, but I am sure Purcell will not mind!

    By beauteous softness mixed with majesty,
    An empire over every heart he gains;
    And from his awful power none could be free,
    He with such sweetness and such justice reigns.
                                             Maxine

Cambridge and Cycling

I remember a last exhilarating cycle ride over the Gog Magog Hills in the autumn of 1979 with my unborn baby girl, and a heavily pregnant walk in the snow after a slight blood spotting. I inserted my fingers into my vagina to see if I was still bleeding; after my miscarriage I'd been afraid to use white toilet paper during pregnancy. This time all was well, and several months later, in 1980, I pushed my daughter's pram into King's College Chapel to see the Rubens *Adoration of the Maji*, and then walked back home across Parker's piece. On another occasion during Tamsin's first blissful summer, and just before the operation on her Talipes, ('the innocent fault' in her foot, to use Byron's words on his own deformed foot about which he cherished a morbid sensitivity and antipathy towards those persons who looked at it with curiosity), we had emerged from the world-famous Museum of Anthropology. The exhibits had included a fascinating collection of American-Indian tribal artefacts, and shrunken heads from Borneo and Sumatra.

    I felt an intense loneliness when carrying Tamsin in my arms in the pouring rain. A kind man saw that we were becoming soaking wet and offered us a lift home in his car. Part of me wanted to run away with this compassionate stranger, and never return home. I desired to be seen differently, to come back to Cambridge and experience the deepest empathy. By James, I was highly favoured and blessed, singled out, exalted, and invited to respond: 'I think we're very alike, Maxine, we have an empathy. You are an exception. You are a pearl amongst swine.'

    The horror of the past, betrayal, the isolation and the

deprivation and repression no longer existed or mattered; a Jamesian loneliness united us: 'The port from which I set out was, I think, that of the essential loneliness of my life – this loneliness – what is it still but the deepest thing about one? Deeper, about me, at any rate, than anything else; deeper than my "genius", deeper than my "discipline", deeper than my pride, deeper, above all, than the deep counterminings of art.'

During the early months of my second pregnancy my state of mind was best expressed by a visit to Stratford-upon-Avon to see Shakespeare's *Othello,* and in the Olivier auditorium of London's National Theatre, Harold Pinter's *Betrayal.* These two plays were like a prophecy of the events soon to engulf me, and also recall Henry James' kind action when, seeing his friend Constance Fenimore Woolson alone and sombre at a performance of *Othello*, he came to her in true friendship.

All these locations, including Claybrooke Parva, a small village in the Midlands, near Hinckley, and Rugby, where my adored son was born, came to have the deepest associations with the special occasions and venues, (the topography) of my singer. I would come to him whenever I was called. 'You come to me, Maxine,' he said, quoting from the *Notebooks* of Henry James, 'not I to you – I am the great artist.' Finally, I'd moved my children into Leonardo's cave. 'I like the sort of Chiaroscuro feeling, of one moving from darkness into light all the time through a sort of twilight.' (James on Radio 3, discussing his live performance of Elizabeth Lutyens' *The Tears of Night*.) James Bowman's singing voice was the light within the darkness; his alto voice emerging from his baritone, resembled the figures gradually emerging from the dark rocks of Leonardo's cavern.

My daughter Tamsin and her little friends often played in the school field at the back of our house in Claybrooke Parva. One day, they said that they had seen Arran's ghost in the field, and played with him. Two-year-old Arran had been killed in a recent tragic accident. The entire event as described by Tamsin was just like a poem from Blake's *Songs of Innocence and Experience*, or Shelley's vision of Byron's dead daughter Allegra, coming to him in the moonlight at sea.

On the Friday preceding Arran's death, we had been on a toddler group visit to the zoo and I'd sat next to his mother on the return coach. He had fallen asleep on the journey home, his golden curly head cradled on his mother's lap. I remember him waving to me from an upstairs window on the day before he died at Nuneaton bus station. His mother had omitted to strap him into his pushchair, and as she turned to embrace her mother and kiss her goodbye, Arran jumped out of the pushchair and ran in front of a bus coming out of the station. He suffered severe head and chest injuries and a broken back, but did not die immediately. His mother, Jenny, held him in her arms and, knowing that hearing is the last of the senses to fade, continued to tell him how much she loved him, until he died in hospital later that same day.

They were an Irish family, so kept Arran at home in an open coffin for several days for his 'wake'. I went to see him and kiss him goodbye. The undertaker was said to be 'heartbroken' because the boy was so unbelievably beautiful: 'He looked like an Angel.'

Afterwards I quite often visited Jenny. In her grief she had lost about three stone and resembled a ghost. But one day, I was walking home with Tamsin in a snowstorm, when her son Luke ran towards me to tell me that 'Mummy is going to have another baby.' I was so pleased for her, and a few months later Luke had a beautiful new brother.

Arran will never be forgotten. In time his family moved away – they were army people and used to moving home – but a tree was planted in his memory in Claybrooke Parva Churchyard, where his ashes had been scattered. There is a memorial plaque beneath the tree: 'To Arran – he gave us so much joy and love.'

The following comes from Richard Lattimore's edition of Greek lyric poetry, a book I inscribed and gave to James in May, 1996, to commemorate the twentieth anniversary of the death of his friend, David Munrow.

> Epitaph for Timas
>
> This is the dust of Timas,
> who died before she was married
> and whom Persephone's dark chamber
> accepted instead.
>
> After her death the maidens who were
> her friends,
> with sharp iron
>
> Cutting their lovely hair, laid it upon
>   her tomb.
>   Sappho of Mytilene, 620 to 550 BC

Connections

> There is a kind of sanity that hates weddings
>   Geoffrey Hill, 'In Memoriam: Gillian Rose'
>   *A Treatise of Civil Power*, 2007

Eventually, and with great reluctance, I moved to what James disparagingly and correctly termed 'the Wilds of Cheshire', (mockingly known as the Surrey of the North), feeling very far away from my roots and all I valued in the South-East and East Anglia. I was born in Belvedere, Kent and could see the Thames from my bedroom window; a special delight was to walk on the frozen marshes with my father. This early experience sealed my identification with Pip, the boy in Dickens' *Great Expectations*. Years later, I was to learn that Henry James had spent his final days watching the boats on the river Thames, believing that he was voyaging to Rome, or in Paris as a boy awaiting the arrival of his brother William.

Woods were always of immense significance to me. I was born next to one and when at six moved to Birchanger, on the Herts/Essex border, once again there was a wood at the bottom of my garden, beyond a boundary stream fringed by primroses. My school was in delightful, antique Saffron Walden, and lunch-times were spent on the Adam bridge feeding the ducks, or lying on the top of the old red-brick wall which enclosed Audley End Mansion, one of the most wonderful Jacobean palaces in the country. I used to pretend that it was Bly, in Essex, the great haunted house in Henry James' *The Turn of the Screw*. Like Bly, Audley End was set in rural bliss, deep in the English countryside. When I returned there as an adult with some American postgraduate friends from Cambridge University, they fell in love with those sweeping lawns leading down to the river. Even in the winter, the 'Capability' Brown park was beautiful, entered through wonderful, high wrought-iron gates, and there was the little tuck shop in the village for treats.

I grew up with mediaeval and Elizabethan architecture, lath and plaster, thatched roofs and pargeting, the ornamental plasterwork unique to this unspoiled area. Shopping took place in Bishop's Stortford, a favourite venue – with its associations with Britten and Pears. They were seen by the music department at school as 'local' artists, and we often performed pieces by Britten. Also, whilst still at school and in the choir I was taken to see Benjamin Britten conduct in the lovely old church at

Thaxsted, home of Imogen Holst. Henry Moore, the sculptor, lived only a few villages away, in Much Hadham, and I often walked or rode there to look at his work, visible above his garden wall. And on another occasion our Art teacher took us there on a visit to his workshops. As a child I went to Aldeburgh, but only to the seaside. In early adolescence I saved enough money to go and see Peter Pears, by then quite old, in a National Trust recital at Farnham.

So, even though my children were still quite small, I'd reconnected with the singer who disliked singing with a piano, but who had performed like a god with Britten as his accompanist in the ice-fire of that most personal and beautiful of Purcell realisations, 'Sweeter than Roses'.

Referring to Britten's realisation of Purcell's 'Sweeter than Roses' performed at London's National Gallery, May 1972, James said, 'I like the "Sweeter than Roses" he did with me. I think that's very beautiful. It has a curiously, almost Schubertian charm about it.'

To this day, I have never heard any other singer perform this piece satisfactorily, not even Michael Chance or Andreas Scholl. It belongs to that one voice alone, so that, as Henry James says of Venice, 'You desire to embrace it, to caress it, to possess it; and finally a soft sense of possession grows up and your visit becomes a perpetual love affair.'

The burnings and freezings of this song are precisely the contradictory characteristics and austere juxtapositions within James Bowman's unique voice. And surely, the association of flowers with music is universally cherished. When sending flowers to James I was always most careful to exclude anything he disliked, especially carnations: 'They remind me, Maxine, of cheap, Northern working class weddings, and we don't like weddings do we, Maxine! I mean, I'm not saying I'm upper class, but really...!'

He also said that because hydrangeas abound in the Lake District – and 'they look dead' – he was put off the whole area, despite its connections with his beloved Beatrix Potter. This irrational aversion to the Lake District came up again in a conversation about Lewis Caroll, another author James greatly admired, but one who also had problematic origins in Cheshire. Thinking that James would be interested in Carroll's birthplace in Daresbury, Cheshire, and the 'Alice' stained-glass memorial window in Daresbury Church, I asked him if he had ever visited the village and seen this memorial to Lewis Caroll and his Wonderland characters. James replied that he was attracted to Carroll's 'strangeness and fascination with going down the dark rabbit-hole', but only enjoyed his Oxford connections, not those with the 'loathsome, wide expanses of the flat Cheshire plain'.

The view of the great Cheshire plain is usually admired, especially from Alderley Edge, but James could find nothing complimentary to say: 'It is all so inexpressibly melancholy....'

James' contempt for weddings reminded me of Handel's *Nero* (an opera now lost), the only openly homosexual character in the composer's entire output, Nero himself, like Orpheus, became an important symbol for the relation of music and homosexuality. Handel's Nero particularly enjoyed singing and despised marriage, regarding it as a 'punishment'.

Like Shakespeare's Coriolanus, James was not at ease with the plebeian. 'Most people, Maxine, are perfectly ghastly,' he said to me. He seemed surprised when I told him I had not, as he assumed, attended private school and Girton College, Cambridge. Once when I telephoned him, forgetting that he was away in recital, a workman answered the phone. I asked him if he knew when Mr Bowman was expected back, and he replied, 'I don't know. I'm no one important, as I've been told. I'm just the man doing Mr Bowman's kitchen.' On another occasion, James was talking to me when he was interrupted, and said with irritation, 'Excuse me, Maxine, I'm having to attend to two men tuning my piano.'

This particular setting of Purcell by Britten heralded a revival of interest in Purcell's work. More than anything else, Purcell and Britten shared a reverence for the text; they were both 'text men'. James Bowman has always appreciated the work of composers whose emphasis is on the 'word', but acknowledges that aside from Britten's wonderful 'realisations' of Purcell songs, it was Robert King's approach to Purcell that he found 'so exciting'. In working with the King's' Consort, from the mid 1980s, James was repeating things he had done before, but seeing them in a totally different light: 'I had performed his [Purcell's] music many times before, including performances with Britten and the ECO. I was always amazed that his feeling for Purcell wasn't that great; in comparison with Robert's for example, it was very old-fashioned.'

Dowland, another of Britten's pantheon, is also often named with Purcell and Britten as one of the greatest English song writers, and remains one of James' dearest early composers, even now, in the twilight of his career.

In the twentieth century, Benjamin Britten was celebrated for his ability 'to revitalise older elements in the musical language'. Peter Ackroyd sees this as yet another example, in its ancient sense of preservation, of 'a connection between antiquarianism and conservatism'. In his chapter 'English Music', he cites Ralph Vaughan Williams' *Fantasia on a Theme by Thomas Tallis*, and quotes one critic who observed that 'it seems to lift one into some unknown region' where 'one is never quite sure whether one is listening to something very old or very new.' This piece, in its embrace of present and past time, new music awakened by old, had a special appeal for James. He once said that his idea of Paradise was to sit facing the great East Window of his favourite cathedral, Gloucester, and listen to Vaughan Williams' *Fantasia on a Theme by Thomas Tallis*.

James' love of the East Window of Gloucester Cathedral and of contemporary music which is inspired and animated by antique music, found personal expression in his work with the composer Geoffrey Burgon.

On Saturday October 18th, 1997, I attended at All Saints Parish Church, the world premiere of Burgon's *Merciless Beauty*, written for James, and just such a combination of the mediaeval and modern. The programme notes read as follows: '*Merciless Beauty* is conducted by the composer, who will give a 30-minute pre-concert talk with the countertenor soloist James Bowman, at 7.00pm.' James was late! I overheard ironic mutterings from some musicians: 'late again' they said. As James entered the church, he dashed over to me to say that his lateness was due to having enjoyed an excellent meal before his pre-performance talk, and he apologised to me for 'reeking of garlic', and breathing it all over me.

This piece holds a special meaning for me. Twice, I travelled a very long way to hear it, in High Wycombe and ten days later, in Grantham. I spoke to James several times at home whilst he was preparing his performance of it, and received the inscribed East Window card as he sat beside me in the flint church during the interval. Also, it was on this occasion that I had my vision of him transformed into Leonardo's *Virgin of the Rocks*. Later, I described this to him in a letter: 'When I was sitting close to you, a miraculous transformation took place, in which you changed into Leonardo's *Virgin of the Rocks*. The painting became a living thing and its watery wilderness moved...'

Vaughan Williams is also linked to Brentwood in Essex, where, on Saturday 2nd July, 1994, I travelled to hear James sing Scarlatti's *Salve Regina*, a favourite piece of mine, and one of the engagements he particularly asked me to attend. It was in Brentwood in the winter of 1903, that Vaughan Williams first heard the folk song 'Bushes and Briars', and was affected with the force of revelation, as though he had known it all his life, like an ancestral voice. 'In one aspect,' Vaughan Williams wrote, 'the folk song is as old as time itself; in another aspect it is no older than the singer who sang it.' Vaughan Williams had other close links with James. He had been organist at Gloucester Cathedral and in old age composed one of my favourite song cycles, the *Ten Blake Songs*. These settings of Blake's *Songs of Innocence and Experience* were to prove very significant during my times with James Bowman. They were originally set for tenor, but are rendered much more plangent when sung by a countertenor. My CD of James' recording is inscribed in red ink: 'For Maxine – with best wishes from James Bowman 26.10.96' (a rare date). He never dated anything, which seems very odd for a History graduate, but is part of his very strange sense of time. In *At the Mind's Limits*, Jean Améry writes: 'The experience of terror also dislocates time, that most abstract of humanity's homes. The only fixed points are traumatic scenes recurring with a painful clarity of memory and vision.'

The recording of Vaughan Williams' *Blake Songs* with music by Warlock, Howells, and Ridout, was very much James' own enterprise and a project very dear to his own heart. Vaughan Williams' compositions often echo the melancholy of Dowland, and the plangent sadness of Purcell, a yearning for some lost and precious thing. Byrd and Tallis and Purcell were part of Vaughan Williams' living past, and through James, they became part of mine. As a member of the Choir of the Chapel

Royal, James has recently returned to singing Byrd and Tallis. I was touched to learn that James also loved Gloucester Cathedral (he wanted to perform the Blake songs there) because it is the setting for his favourite childhood story, Beatrix Potter's *The Tailor of Gloucester*, with its charming illustration of Simpkin the cat on a snowy Christmas Eve, walking towards the ancient archway in College Court, a feature which remains unaltered to this day. Indeed, 9 College Court, the tiny house of Beatrix Potter's Tailor of Gloucester, has recently been restored. The house and the alley leading to Gloucester Cathedral can be seen in her illustrations for the story, first published in 1903. In 1897, Beatrix Potter came to stay with her cousin nearby and was told the story of the real Tailor of Gloucester, John Pritchard, who had been commissioned to make a suit for the new Mayor. He left the work unfinished and returned to find the suit beautifully completed, but for one buttonhole to which was attached a little note that read 'no more twist'. The tailor put a sign in his window: 'Come to Pritchard's where the waistcoats are made at night by the fairies.' Inside the house, the kitchen has been recreated just as it is in the book, and one can look across to the Tudor tower of the historic Cathedral from where, in the story, the clock strikes midnight. I wonder if James has visited the restored house. Outside, a letterbox allows you to post a card to be franked with a special Tailor of Gloucester postmark.

On the occasion of the Brentwood (Catholic) Cathedral recital in 1994, it was a red-hot summer's day. James in a short-sleeved blue shirt and sandals walked across the car park towards me; he is a large clumsy man, with the height and build of a rugby forward, huge hands and feet, and an awkward gait, his walk a combination of grizzly bear and Paddington from darkest Peru. Two fingers of his left hand were slapping against the right hand; James is left-handed and sensitive about being so.

When once I noted it as he was using my pen, he defensively said, 'So what?' and I replied I only noticed it because my daughter is also left-handed. At Brentwood, he looked moody and irritated, and gave me a telling off for sending him too many books and letters.

Looking back, I can see that I overdid the Henry James collection: poor James B! I expected him to find the time to read Henry James' massive *Autobiography*, *Prefaces* (in the difficult 'late' style) and *Notebooks*. James Bowman said that he was beginning to understand Henry James as a creative artist, but he hadn't at first realised that his output was so extensive! He liked Henry James' travel literature and letters, stories about children, such as *What Maisie Knew*, *The Awkward Age*, *The Pupil* and *The Turn Of The Screw*. James told me that being superstitious, he enjoyed Henry James' tales of the supernatural. Certainly, my literary cards and letters inspired him in performance (he always read the appropriate one beforehand), and he was touched and flattered by all the books he received as long as he wasn't questioned on them too closely. This elusiveness made James Bowman both charming and frustrating; like Britten's fairies, I was 'following darkness like a dream'.

Nevertheless, at Brentwood I was so hurt that I couldn't fully respond to his performance, even though James turned to sing to me in a wonderful programme of music by Purcell, Vivaldi and Handel. He gave me a brooding glance before leaving. However, after his angry comments, and seeing how upset I was, he relented and said, 'It was the recorded delivery that was the problem. I must have my beauty sleep.' He'd been disturbed very early in the morning and had to open the door in his pyjamas to the postman. Thus he'd been deprived of his sleep by a literary 'inundation' that he didn't really want. 'I usually receive at 9am – not before. Please don't send anything

Burning in Blueness

before 9am.' But having softened towards me, and modified his formidable and frightening tone, he told me that 'All is arranged for the commission'; my piece written especially for him in celebration of his 50th birthday was at last about to receive its first performance in September of that year. 'Continuity with the past' had triumphed for the moment: 'I'm loved, I'm adored, Maxine – don't stop adoring me.' On occasion James set aside his reserve and allowed me to know that he knew how much I loved him. He said that he found me 'wonderfully remote from all other people'. The male florist who personally arranged the flowers and delivered to James commented admiringly on my sublime combination of bouquet and quotation. 'Someone loves and adores you, Mr Bowman.'

The entire occasion at Brentwood in Essex on July 2nd, 1994, reminded me of a day in childhood in 1960, when I had cycled to meet my mother from work one lunchtime. It was during the summer holidays so I felt wonderfully happy and free. I arrived early at our meeting point, and standing astride my bicycle waited patiently in the glorious midday heat-haze. The bees were humming on the nearby flowers and luscious vegetation. It was an indescribably idyllic place, known locally as Tottles Lane. Adam, the carthorse, lived in the field just around the corner, and the farmer's donkey grazed in a tree-shaded field just over the hawthorn hedge. I often made solitary visits to them on my bicycle, bringing treats of carrots, peppermints, and lemon bon-bons!

The silence of the empty lane made me aware of my aloneness, and I began to be fearful of my mother's delay. All at once the atmosphere felt oppressive and slightly menacing. I suddenly felt very small and lonely – a little girl waiting for her mother in a drowsy lane with the tarmacadam surface melting and glistening beneath my feet. Everything seemed so close and yet so distant.

Just at the moment when joyful expectation was turning into apprehension my mother appeared over the rise, smiling and wheeling her bike, its wicker basket laden with groceries. I felt absolutely content and we cycled home together, the moment of intensity, when time stands still, already vanished into the past.

This childhood need for aloneness followed by closeness was a very important aspect of my attraction to James, for James himself is both social and reclusive.

> When the Ear heard Him
> Then it blessed Him.
> And when the Eye saw Him
> It gave witness of Him.
>
> From Handel's 'Funeral Anthem for Queen Caroline' sung and recorded by James Bowman

The Holy Ghost

Looking backwards to the time when in Forsyth's, I lifted up his recording of Bach's *Cantatas for Solo Alto*, I had no thought of initiating a lengthy, almost continuous correspondence. Little did I realise that the journey begun in Leeds had only been temporarily interrupted, and was about to recommence, and develop profoundly: it became 'a feeling so intense, in letter after letter, that it verged on a sort of ecstasy, strange and extraordinarily sustained.' (Lyndall Gordon, on the letters of Minny Temple to Henry James.)

Initially, I merely felt re-attracted to this unique voice from the past, like Henry James in *Italian Hours*, remembering his youthful horse-rides in the Roman Campagna. So I bought the

Burning in Blueness

exquisite recording of Bach's *Cantatas* and returned home to immerse myself in them, especially '*Wiederstehe, doch der Sünde*'. Some years later my treasured recording was inscribed by the great man himself: 'To Maxine from James 5. 97.' This disk is now discoloured and unplayed, forever silent. How I loved these three sacred Cantatas for alto soloist; and listened to them endlessly. I was not alone in my addiction. 'I have lost my recording of James Bowman singing Bach Cantatas. I am going to look for it. If I don't find it, I am going to kill myself.' (The words of a French critic cited by Robert King in his James Bowman Twenty-Fifth Anniversary Programme.)

The opening aria of *Vergnügte Ruh, beliebte Seenlenlust*, is a pastoral mingling of oboe d'amore, strings and solo voice. I remember James on Radio 3 speaking of these pieces as emotionally unsuited to a boy's voice, even that of a 'well-developed' boy, and of his love for singing with the oboe d'amore. The Baroque oboe is always soft and loving, symbolically influencing toward beauty and repose – a piquant juxtaposition. In '*Stirb in mir*' from *Gott soll allein mein Herze Haben*, solo organ, voice and strings combine in an enchanting siciliano:

> Die in me earth, and all your empty pleasure.
> Give me hope and faith in thee, and of love abundant measure.
> Die in me, glory, riches, vanity, evil things that mortals treasure,
> earth and all thy empty pleasure.
> Die in me.
> BWV 169, *Stirb in Mir*, from Bach's solo Cantata '*Gott soll allein mein Herzehaben*', performed and recorded by James Bowman, September 1988, in Wadham College Chapel, Oxford.

Soon I was to move on from just hearing him, to seeing him regularly in performance, and gradually coming to know him.

My contact with James Bowman was very limited, but also unique and profound. Quoting Janet Frame, I said to him: 'For my true thoughts have spent more time in your company than in anyone else's...'. I came to adore his 'Singer's Face' as Janet Baker has called it: the huge, full-lipped, moist, athletic mouth, telling of perfect health in its muscular pink tongue, the large nose and dark-blue eyes from which a deliberate glance let fall, as blue as a ray of sunlight that had penetrated the East Window of Gloucester Cathedral. His mouth, his tongue and even his teeth were extremely seductive, which he knew.

In many ways, James resembles the beautiful opera singer in Ann Patchett's *Bel Canto*, a novel about the 'deep and nourishing love of beauty'.

He is an unpredictable and impulsive performer, audaciously different, and pushing forward the boundaries of what is possible and acceptable for the male alto. It is a rich voice with a life enhancing brightness. James enjoys the challenge of new repertoire but his choice is always guided by impeccable taste: 'I would never do anything to bring the countertenor into disrepute. It's all too easy to sound ridiculous.' When asked by me in 1995 whether or not he was doing a Prom at the Albert Hall, he said no, and was 'glad' not to be, as a populist programme of Lennon/McCartney arrangements was to be performed. 'Ugh,' he said. 'I'm not being a part of that sort of thing!'

James claims that in France, he is seen as too 'populist': 'I think they see me as a male Lesley Garrett.' Despite this, France is a country where he loves working, because of the remarkable Baroque movement there. Although he mostly works within the EEC, more recent, interesting and unusual tours have included Israel, working with the Jerusalem Baroque Orchestra, 'who were excellent', said James.

I remember him refusing to perform a so-called

'Valentine's Day Concert' of Handel's love duets, until Robert King, the director of the King's Consort, agreed to change the title to Twelve Stages of Love and remove the words 'Valentine's Day'. 'That's Robert King looking into the gutter again,' said James; he had utter contempt for populism. In 1970, the television series, *The Six Wives of Henry VIII* and *Elizabeth R* had made David Munrow a household name. When I asked James Bowman about the projects, and expressed surprise that he was involved in anything smacking of 'showbiz', he agreed with my reservations and explained that he had performed for these programmes but 'only behind a mask, Maxine, behind a mask'. After this comment, James suddenly flashed his watch at me, a beautiful gold one, with a brown leather strap, (it looked very expensive) and asked me if I liked it.

Along with my two children, James was to become the most important person in my life. My encounter with his favourite and most famous operatic role, Oberon in Britten's *A Midsummer Night's Dream*, was to mark the beginning of almost daily letters, and my realisation that James himself was as unstable as a dream. I suppose that at times I identified with Janet Frame in her autobiographical *An Angel At My Table*, feeling that James was my solace and inspiration – the Angel guest – and that her devotion to Bill Brown mirrored mine for an artist who was incapable of reciprocal feeling. But eventually Frame's Grand Passion came to an end: 'I'm sorry,' she wrote, 'that I embarrassed you by anything I said, say, did, do, imply or desire.' James described himself to me as someone who never apologized and was 'unembarrassable'.

Maxine Handy

The Fairy King

> I know a bank where the wild thyme blows,
> Where oxlips and the nodding violet grows,
> Quite over-canopied with luscious woodbine,
> With sweet musk-roses and with eglantine;
> There sleeps Tytania, sometime of the night.
> Lull'd in these flowers, with dances and delight;
> And there the snake throws her enamall'd skin,
> Weed wide enough to wrap a fairy in;
> And with the juice of this I'll streak her eyes,
> And make her full of hateful fantasies.
>
> 'I know a bank', from *A Midsummer Night's Dream*,
> Opera in three acts by Benjamin Britten, opus 64
> sung and recorded by James Bowman, 1993

Oberon, the King of Shadows, was to determine my course of getting to know this fascinating Man and Genius. But before discovering the venue for what was to be his last fully-staged performance in England of Britten's *A Midsummer Night's Dream*, I did my homework on the countertenor and through interested friends and illustrious members of an esoteric and sometimes arcane musical circle, acquired my collection of tape recordings of Alfred Deller, his few contemporaries and many heirs. I read his out-of-print biography *A Singularity of Voice*, by Michael and Mollie Hardwick, and learned the history of his relationship with the role of Oberon, written especially for Deller by Benjamin Britten. Alfred Deller worked and recorded with, and was highly respected by, David Munrow and Gustav Leonhardt. He was virtually discovered by the composer Michael Tippett who needed that 'authentic voice' in order to resurrect the music of Purcell, the English Orpheus.

In 1991, I became a friend of the author, scholar and countertenor, Dr Peter Giles, who had many wonderful photographs of the great Alfred Deller, had seen him in performance and worked as a senior lay clerk at Canterbury Cathedral where he told me of having twice seen Deller's ghost. 'A seemingly supernatural presence.' Deller could float sounds in a very beautiful way. 'To do this,' Peter Giles writes, 'a singer uses not merely a frontal-sinus focus, but almost an "out-of-skull" focal image: a "halo sound".' (From *The History of the Countertenor,* Peter Giles, Scolar Press, 1994.) I thought this an equally apt description of James' suspended ecstasy, and reflection of Mary's halo in Leonardo's *Virgin of the Rocks.*

It is the quality of the very greatest artists to 'unsettle'. Alfred Deller's voice was exceptional, a voice of crystalline purity, which 'seemed to belong to a world of weightlessness, and which could effortlessly be spun out to the limits of the possible, without vibration, giving the impression of belonging to another universe, where the spirit sings free from the weight of the flesh.' (Jean-François Labie, on Alfred Deller.) Without the total belief and passion of Seymour Solomon (the producer of the Vanguard recording label), Deller would never have been so extensively recorded.

Deller used to sing lullabies and folksongs to his children; he had two sons and a daughter. By all accounts, he was a loving husband and father, but it was his voice that was the focus of his existence. The best countertenors are very tall, have broad chests and large necks and facial features, like Alfred Deller and James Bowman. Their natural speaking voice is a baritone in which they cannot sing at all, as James once demonstrated to me on the telephone. He only uses his bass range when warming up. On another occasion, in conversation on the telephone, in July, 1995, he suddenly lost control of his voice and it slipped upwards with the menacing falsetto of the Fairy King.

Oberon was to be a central symbol in my decade of

correspondence to my singer; time and again we returned to him. James sent me several inscribed thank-you cards, inspired by Britten pieces, two being of his most famous arias in the *Dream*, the Purcellian 'I know a bank' and its twin 'Now until the Break of Day'.

These depictions inspired many of my bouquets to him, and his written responses. These postcards were of watercolour paintings by the artist and doctor Jane Mackay. They were inspired by the music of Benjamin Britten, and the performances of James, who owns the originals in The James Bowman Collection. Further cards from the Britten Series include 'The river flows between two kingdoms' from *Curlew River*, Op. 71, which James sent to me in appreciation of 'the exquisite Yellow and Blue':

> Dear Maxine,
> Thank you for the lovely Roses – a memory of 'Midsummer Nights'.
> Best wishes,
> James

and:

> Dear Maxine,
> Thank you for the Midsummer Flowers! They still look lovely, even after ten days.

Also, at his request, I wrote him a thirty-page critique of Humphrey Carpenter's newly published biography of Benjamin Britten, which he deeply appreciated, and which greeted him on his return from a concert venue in Italy:

> Many Thanks for the Flowers. I read your comments on Carpenter with great interest. Thank you for sending them.
> Best wishes,
> James (Redhill, 15th May 1993).

I was fascinated by his description of singing his favourite role of Oberon and his special lifelong relationship with that complex creation, a mesmeric mixture of seduction, sadism, and solitude. James Bowman, talking to *Times* critic Hilary Finch, *The Times* music critic and Radio 3 presenter, about playing the role of Oberon in a revelatory production by Elijah Moshinksy, said, 'He [Elijah Moshinksy] really crystallised the role for me. He emphasised Oberon's menacing, all-pervading influence.'

His successful audition for the role (in 1966, the year he met David Munrow) is a marvellous story and really made his career. In 1966, it struck James 'almost as a sign from heaven' that he should write to Benjamin Britten and ask for an audition for his opera *A Midsummer Night's Dream*. In 1963, Herbert Sumsion, the then Gloucester organist, offered James the job of alto lay clerk in the Cathedral Choir. Wisely, he rejected the offer, and three years later came the audition for Britten's *Dream*, the first and only audition of James Bowman's career. Having listened to James, Britten wrote on a piece of paper 'This is the Man'. However, the life-changing letter from Benjamin Britten telling him that he had been given the part did not come until weeks later while James was on holiday in Lake Garda and in his absence his mother opened it. James was 26 years old and still teaching in a boys' preparatory school in Oxford, desperate to escape into music. James' art enabled him to 'enter at will a world of undefiled purity'. (Soseki.)

It is a strange fact that James Bowman's interpretation will bring to perfection a piece of music, whether or not it was specifically conceived for him, and even when he has often arrived slightly late on the scene, after a seemingly definitive performance by his predecessor. The part of Oberon was written for Deller, not Bowman, and Britten made only one change to the score, with James' voice in mind and in consultation with him; James keeps secret the details of this tiny alteration. Another of his favourite roles is that of Isaac in Britten's Canticle ll, yet the part was originally written for the contralto Kathleen Ferrier, not the countertenor James Bowman. And James is, of course, not on the 1961 commercial recording of this piece; his two 1972 versions are preserved thanks to the BBC sound archives. Even the Britten/Purcell 'Sweeter than Roses' was first intended as a love-offering to the tenor voice of Peter Pears, and only subsequently transposed for James. That he was given the opportunity to record it in Snape Maltings truly made 1972 my *annus mirabilis.*

During his time at Oxford University, reading Modern History, he had been singing in two choirs; exquisite New College, where he had obtained an academical clerkship, and Christ Church Cathedral. James has kept up his long association with music at Oxford, performing and recording regularly with both choirs. In November 1998, James was made an Honorary Fellow of New College, Oxford, and his 2003 recording of Bach's *St John Passion* with the choir of New College is recommended as 'an outstanding period performance that can stand comparison with any in the Catalogue'. Male voices only are used, with even the soprano arias sung by a boy treble. But although James would no longer want to sing the standard repertoire of church music, he occasionally goes back to his roots in choral music which led him to New College, Oxford, and then on to Westminster Abbey as a lay clerk: 'I like singing a Palestrina Mass, or taking part in the festivals of the church, so it would be terrible to shut myself away in an ivory tower and behave like a diva.'

There is a well-known anecdote about James' time at Oxford University in the 1960s, when he was singing in both

Burning in Blueness

New College and Christ Church choirs. 'Bowman coped with both appointments by perfecting a running speed of less than ten minutes between New College and Christ Church.' It is possible to *walk* the distance in less than ten minutes; I have done so.

In the ante-chapel of New College is Epstein's disturbing statue of Lazarus, swaddled 'in the bands of death', like a milk-white linen cocoon. In the Cloisters 'There are memorial tablets on the walls, some graves beneath the flagstones, an ancient ilex in one corner, and an atmosphere of peace.' I greatly regret never hearing him sing in the ante-chamber of his former college; it would have been an unforgettable experience, but James told me that he was touched I'd visited it. During a May visit to New College it was a pleasure to walk in the garden quadrangle and then on through the elaborate wrought-iron screen into the garden, which is dominated by the Mound. 'Although this area was a place of burial at the time of the Black Death, the Mound was not used for that purpose. It is a later creation and was simply designed to be decorative. The garden is enclosed on two sides by the ancient City wall of Oxford.' The college, its cloisters and garden quadrangle reminded me of Walter de la Mare's poem of Sun and Moon in opposition, 'Two Gardens':

> Two gardens see! – this, of enchanted flowers,
> Strange to the eye, and more than earthly-sweet;
> Small rivulets running, song re-echoing bowers;
> And green-walled pathways which, ere
> parting, meet;
> And there a lion-like sun in heaven's delight
> Breathes plenitude from dayspring to the night.

When, in 1993, James' long-awaited recording as Oberon in *A Midsummer Night's Dream*, in the role he has made his own, at last appeared, he so sweetly inscribed it for me: 'To Maxine, in remembrance of past enchantments.' During the preceding months, he had spoken to me several times in a state of heightened anxiety over the issue of this seminal recording. Referring back to the October/November 1991 production itself, he said, 'It was a long time ago wasn't it, Maxine? A very long time ago.' He had an irrational fear that the delayed recording would never appear.

I've always regarded Oberon as James' saviour and alter ego. The *Dream* was the work which, in Peter Hall's Glyndebourne production of 1981, picked James Bowman up from a four-year professional abyss after the suicide, at the age of 34, of early music's pioneer and pied piper, David Munrow. 'Hall's *Dream* restored my self-confidence. The main thing I learned from him was that, when in doubt, do nothing. Oberon is essentially the still centre, the incredibly calm core of the piece.' (James Bowman in conversation with *Times* music critic, Hilary Finch.) He also said that he had kept the original score from his first performance of the *Dream* under the guidance of Britten, adding a mark for each performance to keep a record. This anecdote, I thought, recalled a childlike habit of ticking off the days before going on a childhood holiday. On Radio 3 on Sunday, 20th June, 2004, Sir Peter Hall recalled directing James Bowman as Oberon in Britten's *A Midsummer Night's Dream*: 'He's an immaculate musician and an extraordinary singer. But he put on acting and my task was to take away the acting and keep it simple. I got him, by not making huge, heroic gestures, to become something very powerful and menacing in his stillness.'

In a later *Performing Britten* programme on BBC Radio 3, on Sunday 8th April 2007, Sir Peter Hall again discussed the Glyndebourne Dream and Bowman's Oberon. According to

Hall the miracle of Britten's Dream as an opera is that he took a particular aspect of the play (the wood) and concentrated on it as a place where people are transformed. Britten's interests are magic, ambiguity, ambivalence and 'shift'. The action of the opera creeps upon you as both gentle and threatening. Peter Hall acknowledged the magical ensemble writing for the two pairs of human lovers, in which they sing 'Mine own, and not mine own'. For Hall, it is a perfect and very beautiful definition of love: 'you belong to me but part of belonging to me is that you don't belong to me.' He described it as pure Britten, not Shakespeare, even though Britten's prime focus is on the fairy court and the forest, 'a dangerous place of strange alterations'.

The musical illustrations in the programme were from the Alfred Deller recording with Britten conducting and Peter Pears singing the part of Lysander. Peter Hall conceded that 'Alfred Deller sang sublimely, but asexually'. It was the voice of James Bowman that truly captured Britten and Pears' erotic intentions: 'He has weight in the bottom of his voice, almost a masculine quality, which Alfred Deller didn't have,' Hall continued. 'Bowman had lust written all over his lower register.' For an opera which is sleep and visions, 'the wonder of lust and the danger of lust', James Bowman's sound is obviously perfect, and Peter Hall preferred it to that of the more ethereal Deller, saying that 'his' Oberon was 'much nicer'.

The aria 'I know a bank' is tense and lyrical, and central to James' identification with the Fairy King. It takes Oberon a lot of time to tell Puck what he has in mind and what he intends to do to Tytania. The aria is a lyrical evocation of this beautiful spot in the forest, in order to create a horrible change and transformation. Oberon evokes the sleeping Tytania on 'a bank where the wild thyme blows', only to 'make her full of hateful fantasies'. As Peter Hall says, 'The more beautiful the place the more horrible the change ... When he [Bowman] sang about what he was going to do to his wife it was slightly disgusting.' As a result of Oberon's magic, Tytania spends a night of love with a donkey, which, says Peter Hall, is 'wonderful and dreadful ... and pretty gross.' In Tytania's doting on the ass and losing control of herself, Oberon is able to humiliate her.

Norman Lebrecht, author of *'The Song of Names'* warns us, 'Never let yourself be overwhelmed by beauty, or some artist will use it to destroy you.' According to James Fenton, the *Guardian* music critic, writing on Saturday, 2nd June 2007, the Greek gods come into the quarrel between Oberon and Tytania in Britten's *Dream* because they are seen as 'grabbing young beauty whenever it moves them.' Just as Apollo and Dionysus both seek to possess Aschenbach in his pursuit of youthful beauty in Britten's last opera, *Death in Venice*, so Oberon and Tyania argue over the 'lovely Indian boy'.

When Puck becomes confused and anoints the wrong people with the love-juice, his mistake meets with a violent attack from Oberon. In the Sadler's Wells production, James kicked Puck and rolled him down the bank. Peter Hall sees this loss of temper as very unpleasant and frightening: 'Oberon is very happy to live in this anarchic wood where people's affections can be changed almost with the throw of a dice, but he wants to be in complete control, and when he is not in control he goes mad.'

James was unable to really let go of the role even when he had decided to 'retire' from the *Dream* on stage. When at Grantham he told me of his forthcoming concert version, he said in gloomy tones, seeking reassurance, 'I've hung up my wings for a while. They'll have to wheel me out again from the cupboard and dust me down!'

Finally, he also gave me the most wonderful large

Burning in Blueness

monochrome chiaroscuro photograph of himself in the role of Oberon, in a marvellous Covent Garden production. His unearthly radiance is centred within an austere equilateral triangle, truly, 'He is the still, calm centre of it all'. I had the photograph splendidly framed in silver, white, and black.

Three times in one week I travelled from Cheshire to London, (on two occasions taking my children with me) to see him in performance at Sadler's Wells.

I'd spoken to him for the first time, on the telephone at home in Redhill, where he was painting his front door green, having recently moved house and out of London.

This followed on from my very first letter to him, in early August, 1991 (a copy of which I have kept), at his old address in Wetherby Gardens, South Kensington, (and thus delayed for six weeks).

Unaware that he had moved, but having received no reply, I wrote to him again, on the 3rd October, at Sadler's Wells, where he was in rehearsal, addressed and posted it to him at Sadler's Wells as follows:

Mr James Bowman, countertenor,
c/o Opera London at Sadler's Wells, Sadler's Wells Theatre, Roseberry Avenue, London EC1R 4TN

Dear Mr Bowman,
　I wrote to you some five weeks ago. My letter was primarily one of celebration and appreciation, but it also asked many questions of you, so please let me know whether or not you have received my letter, and if so, you might perhaps find time in the future to answer my enquiries ... In my previous letter I expressed my love of your remarkable voice, which has excited and obsessed me since I first heard it, with that of Peter Pears, nineteen years ago ... I also mentioned my delight at the prospect of seeing

you as Oberon at Sadler's Wells ... and am totally involved at present in Alfred Deller's recording of *A Midsummer Night's Dream* ... Having recently seen the countertenor Michael Chance as Apollo in Britten's *Death in Venice*, I was astounded by the impact of the two Apollo sequences, but wanted your voice. Somehow, the voice of Michael Chance did not quite convey the terrifying beauty of Apollo's visitation. This visionary dimension seems to come so easily to you ...

Michael Emery of Radio 3 seemed enthusiastic about my suggestion for what he called 'A James Bowman Commemorative Series' next year in celebration of your fiftieth birthday ... He has given my idea to the appropriate department in Radio 3. We are after all supposed to be in the midst of a countertenor revival and to be showing recognition of the greatness of English singers . . .

With every good wish,
Yours sincerely,
Maxine Handy

He responded by sending me a card on October 5th, with his new address and telephone number, and an invitation to phone him at home if I wished.

This was a month before his 50th birthday, and the six performances of the Sadler's Wells *Dream*. He said that he didn't like the production and was finding it all 'rather a strain'. Although he had 'chosen the cast', he was 'fed up with walking up and down that bloody bank'. He would be glad when it was all over. 'I'm painting my front door and my hands are covered with green paint.' Green, a greatly loved colour, was to be important in our friendship or 'brief encounter' as James once described it: 'We're brief encounter, Maxine, that is what we are,' he said, standing beside a pillar in Grantham Parish Church. He regarded the David Lean film as being about 'The dream life of the English, those secret parts of us that are most important and to which we have least access.' He said it was Henry Jamesian in its renunciation and that 'Yes, we must renounce things'.

My very first flowers and letter, addressed to: 'Mr Bowman' with a salutation wishing him 'happiness, peace and repose' in his new home, had intercepted these three performances of the *Dream*, and resulted in the beginnings of trust and tentative correspondence.

> Dear Mr Bowman,
> I hope that you received your roses on the morning of Saturday 3rd November and that they gave you pleasure…Seeing you three times in *A Midsummer Night's Dream* has been a marvellous experience…and will remain with me always. I loved the use of the bank rather than the wood as a central symbol, and loved your costume for its very interesting suggestion of pagan American Indian combined with Christian priestly details. Your anointing of Tytania's eyes made me think of Blake's 'The Sick Rose'.

If James does not trust you he can be horrid. 'His eyes, to those who have achieved understanding, are gentle and friendly and instill joy…to those, however, who are condemned by their own judgement, they are scornful and hostile.' When I first saw him on stage, I overheard comments that were far removed from my own way of looking at James. 'My dear, have you seen him? He's wearing a dress! I think JB is somewhat over-ripe!' From the Dress Circle at Sadler's Wells I made up my mind that I had somehow to come to know this extraordinary being:

> She almost set him wondering if she hadn't even a larger conception of singularity for him than he had for himself… the rest of the world of course thought him queer, but she, she only, knew how, and above all why queer; which was precisely what enabled her to dispose the concealing veil in the right folds… and she achieved, by an art indescribable,

> the feat of at once – meeting the eyes from the front and mingling her own vision.'
>
> Henry James, *The Altar of the Dead*.

To this day, above my writing desk, I keep a small photograph of the Oberon of this production that he gave me at the time; it had been given to James by his photographer friend David, to bring him luck on the first night. It shows James standing barefooted on the high flowery bank, illuminated by the moonlight, and with his mouth wide open, obviously singing 'I know a bank'.

At first he responded to my beautiful flowers with a frigid, suspicious but intrigued, card inviting me to pursue The King of Shadows, and obtain his subsequent engagement list, which was, to quote Celia Ballantyne, like parting him from his soul. 'Thank you for the flowers. I must admit that it's very strange receiving large bouquets from someone I hardly know and have never met! Anyway, they are very lovely.' He was interested in the obsession he had aroused, encouraged it and protected it with secrecy. James was well aware that he baffled and he beckoned.

> Her dotage now I do begin to pity;
> And now I have the boy, I will undo
> This hateful imperfection of her eyes.
>
> Oberon observing the sleeping Tytania

All this was long before the days of internet web sites and discographies; it was personal, exciting and very difficult; one had to be perceptive and persuasive. But he loved the quotation that accompanied the flowers, words from Pindar's last Pythian Ode, which describes the golden light of immortality when man becomes a demi-god. As the florist had copied it out from my telephone dictation, James complained that the sublime quote was in 'an illiterate shopgirl's handwriting, but at least there were no spelling mistakes'. He at once transcribed it into his own handwriting and pinned it up in his kitchen, loving his beautiful flowers on his mantelpiece and the appropriateness to his Fairy King, of Pindar's last song, 446 B.C:

Creatures of a day – what are we, what are we not?
The dream of a shadow is man.
But when God-given radiance comes, there is a shining light for men and a sweet time.

Some years later I gave James a birthday present of a 'Nightblue' bouquet and an inscribed copy of Pindar's *Odes* in a parallel Greek and English text. 'O we love the Greeks, don't we, Maxine?' he said. James told me that he much preferred the Greek multiplicity of gods to the monotheism of Christianity. He appreciated the overriding love of beauty in the ancient world, conveyed by Patrick Leigh Fermor in his writing on Greek temples, and the Greeks' understanding of light and darkness, the realms of the spirit and the flesh which were difficult to reconcile. He also spoke to me of his relish for their ambiguity, whilst being fully aware that English philhellenes, including Benjamin Britten, often romanticised and oversimplified their thought. But it was the Greeks who first enabled me to enter the life of the great singer. I often compared James to the beauty of classical statuary, and said that his face, like that of Tadzio in Thomas Mann's novella, *Death in Venice*, 'recalled the noblest moment of Greek sculpture'. And I once sent James a bouquet of flowers, quoting Aschenbach's words, to 'the entirely beautiful'.

The composer John Tavener is a member of the Greek Orthodox church and has written a number of pieces for James, including a solo in his *Akathist of Thanksgiving*, composed as a 'musical icon to the glory of God'. The first performance was given in January 1988, and then the work was recorded at this second concert performance in Westminster Abbey, on January 21st, 1994. In attendance along with the composer were leading representatives of the Church Of England, and the Orthodox Church. John Tavener's own notes on the piece, (1994), include the following words: 'And so slowly then, in quiet wonder, we are led by experience into the twilight, as in the past, and that which has fallen asleep in our memory returns again ...'

James Bowman's performance was sublime, but the overly reverential atmosphere and church ritual brought out the rebel in him. Everyone, soloists and choir, was in place, except for James. He was late, and unlike all the others, entered by scurrying alongside the nave of the Abbey. In addition to this strange entry, he was 'goldfishing' during the post-performance group photograph. He later told me that he had felt 'too lazy to do anything but goldfish' for the photo. He assured me that he hadn't forgotten the words. After the performance, I sent him flowers accompanied by the last four lines of his solo:

> Make my hearing acute
> That I may give heed each moment of life
> To your secret voice
> And cry out to you, who are everywhere.
>> 'Ikos 7' for solo countertenor, sung
>> by James Bowman

In 1973, James Bowman recorded his role as the Voice of Apollo in Brittten's opera *Death in Venice*, with its 'classical' affiliation to the 'beautiful boy' with whom Aschenbach, the elderly writer, becomes infatuated. His feelings are platonic but also homosexual. Britten believed that Aschenbach's obsession with a beautiful child, a silent dancer, leading to the humiliation and death of the writer/singer happens because he is an artist, not because he is homosexual. This fatal passion is something that can afflict any artistic spirit devoted to the pursuit of beauty.

James Bowman called the boy 'ridiculous', saying to me that he wished 'people wouldn't go on and on about pederasty' in Benjamin Britten, for which he felt an 'absolute distaste'. However, many critics and audiences are still wrestling with the problems of *Death in Venice* and whether or not it is an apologia for paedophilia.

'All that is left of Venice lies in the land of dreams,' wrote Platen, in the middle of the nineteenth century on Venice; Platen was a Romantic poet with strong classical affiliations, and like John Addington Symonds – a friend of Henry James – homosexual.

In *Death in Venice*, Britten uses sinister and contrasting use of falsetto for the opposing characters of Apollo and the lying, elderly fop, a variation of Dionysus, and five further protagonists who fight for the soul of Aschenbach. James Bowman's radiantly beautiful countertenor as Apollo evokes sunlight and eternity, whereas John Shirley-Quirk's 'ugly falsetto' as the 'rouged and wrinkled' elderly fop suggests the effeminate, emasculated and darkly debauched. It is a description of what Aschenbach later becomes in pursuit of the beautiful Polish boy, Tadzio. On Radio 3, recently, on Sunday 14th April, 2007, the baritone John Shirley-Quirk discussed 'that counterfeit, that young/old horror', the elderly fop. During a rehearsal, John Shirley-Quirk had to improvise for Robert Tear, who was unavailable through illness. Shirley-Quirk did the tenor part by singing in falsetto, and on hearing this 'vulgar' effect, Benjamin Britten decided to use it for the antithetic elderly fop.

The chasm between the spirit and the senses is also the great theme of the modern Greek writer, Nikos Kazantzakis; I introduced James to Kazantzakis's work, including his world-famous *The Last Temptation of Christ*, which, as Kazantzakis writes in the Prologue, is a reinterpretation of the Gospels, through 'The dual substance of Christ ... the incessant, merciless battle between the spirit and the flesh. Within me, are the dark immemorial forces of the Evil One ... within me too are the luminous forces – and my soul is the arena where these two armies have clashed and met. The anguish has been intense. I loved my body and did not want it to perish; I loved my soul and did not want it to decay.'

Interestingly, it was Peter Pears' suggestion that the role of Apollo be sung by a countertenor, rather than a boy treble. Britten's letter to Myfanwy Piper, his librettist, on 6th February, 1972, discusses the choice of voice type for Apollo. Piper and Britten liked the idea of a boy's voice for Apollo as Tadzio communicates with Aschenbach solely through movement: 'Peter has had a stranger idea, but possibly a better one – why not a countertenor – colder, not manly or womanly, and a sound that hasn't been used before?' Britten felt this would also underline the essential incompatibility between the protagonists.

James said that he found *Death in Venice* a 'grim and depressing opera', but described his invitation by Britten to sing the Voice of Apollo as 'an offer I couldn't refuse!' especially as the sinister encounter between Apollo and the voice of Dionysus takes place off-stage. Peter Hall has also said 'You didn't say no to Britten!'

Through the boys' games and the voice of Apollo, Aschenbach is transported to the antique Socratic world:

> He who loves beauty
> Worships me.
> Mine is the spell
> That binds his days.
>> James Bowman as the voice of Apollo
>> in Benjamin Britten's *Death in Venice,* 1974

Already, I adored James and felt deeply protective. My love for him was that of a mother, and I'd already placed him with my children in the sanctuary of my cave. He knew that I took the greatest pleasure in his singing, and that only as a singer did he come before my presence. Dorian Gray, in Oscar Wilde's *The Portrait of Dorian Gray*, falls in love with Sibyl Vane because he falls in love with her performances, with her art.

I've kept James' card detailing a huge, final tour of the *Dream*, and saying 'I'm off to Paris for the *Dream*, taking Henry James with me'. James admitted to me that he had little time to read because he had to focus so much on his music, yet he kept his promise of reading all I sent him and incorporating it into his work. His old teacher at Ely, Arthur Wills, said that he was astounded that James was *reading*! But James' cards to me often contained visual or written references, sometimes oblique, to books I had given him. Admittedly, I did most of the literary interpretation for him and he enjoyed literature through me: 'You have opened my eyes to books,' he told me, 'and above all, I love the beauty of what you give me!' He said that the reading had become part of his musical sensibility but he still preferred to appreciate it *through me*. As time passed, the books informed the symbolism in our exchange of cards as well as our conversation.

I enjoyed my literary precedence and his limitations in this area; it enabled me to *give* to him, although not in the way that he *gave* to me as an artist. However, it offered a means of seeming to participate in his performances, a connection with him even when I was not actually in the auditorium. It was especially appropriate that he took Henry James with him for the tour of the *Dream*, as James told me that he was fascinated by Benjamin Britten's interest in Henry James. It was in 1932, when, aged eighteen and studying at the Royal College of Music, that Britten first encountered Henry James' atmospheric and enigmatic ghost story *The Turn of the Screw*. The composer noted in his diary that it was 'an incredible masterpiece'. Britten identified with Henry James in his unfulfilled longing for a family, his love of ambiguity, and his understanding of children: innocence surrounded by corrupt adults.

There is no doubt that Benjamin Britten had immense appeal to children. They enjoyed the fun of working with him and inviting him to join in their games. However, James Bowman expressed to me his astonishment that he and Peter Pears were naïve enough to believe that they would be allowed to adopt two boys. Eventually, they had to be satisfied with enjoying the company of many children of their friends, and sponsoring two boys in India, a country with which Pears for family reasons felt a special affinity.

Many of Britten's theatrical works are moralities centred on the theme of parental or pseudo-parental responsibility. *Curlew River* is a threnody for the loss of a child, and of childhood. Its dual main character of Madwoman and Mother was created for the tenor Peter Pears; some friends of the singer thought that Britten's sadistic side was coming to the fore when he wrote this female part for Peter. Similarly, when Pears said that singing the incredibly demanding role of Aschenbach in Britten's opera *Death in Venice* might finish him off, Britten said 'I hope it does'.

James Bowman endorsed the view of the pianist Walter Klien that Britten was sadistic, most especially to those he loved profoundly. For Peter Hall, the 'lovely Indian boy' of Britten's *Dream* is merely a symbol of the tension between Oberon and Tytania; their quarrel is really about dependency: 'They are dependent on each other and they don't want to be, as everyone in love is dependent on their partner ... This is the true meaning of their dissent.' As so often in Britten there is a possibility of resolving opposition, but then it all goes wrong. The duet of opposing passions between Owen and Kate in Britten's *Owen Wingrave*, in which Owen tries to evoke tender memories of their shared childhood, merely leads to increased tension. Owen remembers the fighting stags in the park, he weeping for the blood-stained loser and Kate championing the victor.

Both Benjamin Britten and Henry James were interested in strange, erotic relationships among adult males and adolescent boys. Henry James' *The Turn of the Screw* and *Owen Wingrave* were both made into operas by Benjamin Britten, and explore the theme of dominance, psychological or sexual. Strange, ambivalent heroes strive to protect their precious companions. These relationships are both innocent friendships and sadistic encounters. His protagonists inhabit a world which is magical and dangerous, and which 'normal' heterosexuals cannot enter. Oberon is associated with the celesta, always an ambiguous tone colour in the music of Benjamin Britten. It is also the instrument of Quint in *The Turn of the Screw*. Both works ravish the senses. And like Henry James in much of his writing, Britten wanted to alternate between being a child and an adult. Peter Hall said that 'Britten loved little boys' voices and he loved and resented little boys.'

Unlike his lifelong companion, Peter Pears, Britten was never comfortable with the written word. He had great taste in literature but a perverse taste in librettists, such as Myfanwy Piper, who came up with meaningless and prim, pseudo-cerebral dialogue. James asked me if I had read the letters of Benjamin Britten, newly edited by Donald Mitchell. 'I'd give them a miss if I were you, Maxine,' he said. 'Ben could only write music. His letters are dreadful – I have some – and not worth reading.' He then contrasted my 'beautiful letters' with those of Britten, dismissed as 'unreadable'.

James Bowman told me that reading Henry James had helped him to understand Benjamin Britten and that he was especially attracted to Henry James and Britten's depiction of and sympathy with outsiders. This was the reason behind James' attraction to my small stickers of a black bat in flight, which I obtained from a wildlife centre in the Lake District. I used to stick one beneath his name at the opening of a letter, and sometimes also on the envelope. James told me that he enjoyed the allusion to Batman and Robin (his own interpretation) because they were akin to Oberon and Puck in the *Dream*. He also admired the bat as Vampire because it is immortal, complex and intriguing, and like Oberon, an outsider: 'The Vampire thirsts for the blood of the one who loves him but cannot consummate their relationship if the object of his desire remains human. Immortal and beautiful as angels, their problems stem from loneliness and a refined sensibility. Vampires stand for the choice between the worldly and the heavenly!' (Sara Wheeler.)

The theme of vampires occurs obliquely in Henry James, as does that of falling in love with beautiful statues; James Bowman empathised with these odd obsessions. I gave him one such story, 'The Last of the Valerii' (1874), in a collection of Henry James' early stories.

He acknowledged that he was having difficulty with Henry James' long sentences: 'I have to keep going back to the beginning, Maxine, which doesn't say much for my intelligence or powers of concentration!'

I was supposed to go and see him in Tourcoing in April, but in the end I decided never to see him abroad, although so much of his career and work took place there, especially in France. Indeed, rather like the poet Milton, 'He was much more admired abroad than at home: 'He was mightily importuned to goe into France and Italie. Foreigners came much to see him and much admired him, and offered to him great preferments to come over to them...' John Aubrey, the 18th century diarist.

James Bowman is famous and adored in France; he is admitted by the French government as Chevalier to the Order of Arts and Letters. In 1992 Jacques Chirac awarded him La Médaille d'Honneur de la Ville de Paris, in recognition of his long-standing contribution to the musical life of Paris. In France, his old recording of Vivaldi's *Stabat Mater* has been used to advertise Elf petrol, baby food and nappies. James has received no fee or royalties for this recording.

James told me that much as he loved travelling and going to France, he could never live anywhere but England. He was grateful to the French for in effect 'paying me for what I do in my own country'.

The conductor Raymond Leppard, with whom James has worked, has highlighted French vulgarity in their preference for Jean-Baptiste Lully over Cavalli: 'Cavalli could not have known of course, that the French as a race do not greatly care for music and infinitely prefer spectacle, ballet and scandal, all of which Lully provided.' Gustav Leonhardt has dismissed all French composers, except Couperin, as worthless. James told me of the French audiences' fascination for castrati: 'I think they think I'm a castrato.'

James said that so many people wore jewels for his

Twenty-Fifth Anniversary Concert at the Paris Opera, that his eyes were dazzled. He expressed his gratitude to the French for their loyalty and said that he didn't want to be rude about them but 'over-ornamentation of any kind' was not his thing. He said to me that he loved the fact that I came to see him with a carrier bag of books: 'Keep coming that way, Maxine,' he said.

Although he speaks fluent French (albeit slowly) he regards it as an awkward sung language, much preferring the beauty of Italian. I preferred to think of James as a solely English singer who enjoyed his fame in Europe, but did his best work in England, sometimes in the great cathedrals, but often in tiny churches and at unfashionable and obscure venues like Hinckley music club, where David Munrow, and his widow, Gillian Reid, had once been President, and James had followed in later years, performing for no fee. A lute song recital there with the late, great Robert Spencer, was probably the finest performance I ever saw him give – sitting down to sing in order to be closer to the Lute – to his co-performer, his 'duettist'. One day, at the zenith of my time with the 'King of Shadows', my very own commission would be performed there in celebration of his fiftieth Birthday and all that his work meant to me – keeping the Flowers of Love alive.

James loved this flower quotation from Emily Dickinson and used to quote it back at me with some amusement:

> We are the flower, Thou the sun!
> Forgive us, if as days decline,
> We nearer steal to Thee –
> Enamoured of the parting west.
> The peace, the flight, the amethyst,
> Night's possibility!

Oberon's narcotic 'flower of purple dye' and 'love-juice' was potent indeed, and I must mention, as I did in my early letter to James, that the first recording of this role I listened to was that of Alfred Deller, much admired by the great English tenor, Peter Pears. It is an absolutely brilliant performance of the ethereal Fairy King; Alfred Deller had single-handedly revived the countertenor as a twentieth-century operatic voice. Sadly, he was awkward on stage and the production was under rehearsed. Anyway, when Alfred Deller was dropped and replaced by Russell Oberlin for Britten's *Dream* at Covent Garden, the shock to Alfred brought on a severe depression. The conventional story is that he was 'unavailable', but this is not the version told to me by a friend of his, who also knows Alfred's sons. In the words of Deller's wife 'It was as though the whole world had been cut from under his feet'. Deller is said to have recovered from the wounding, but I'm told that he never really got over it. The history of the *Dream*, like its central character, certainly has 'a dark side'.

Erbarme dich

> Erbarme dich, mein Gott,
> Um meiner Zähren willen;
> Schaue hier, Herz und Auge
> Weint vor dir bitterlich
> Erbarme dich, erbarme dich
>
> Bach, *Erbarme Dich*, Alto aria

My correspondence would one day come to fill not 'a special drawer', but a very large box, in James' study. Many years of kindness and devotion would precede the ecstatic moment when he singled me out at Hinckley, and stood right in front of me, to sing Dowland's 'Time Stands Still', and Purcell's 'Evening

Hymn'. And eventually at Snape Maltings, one Easter Monday morning, even though I had risen at daybreak to travel to Suffolk and hear him in Vaughan Williams' *Blake Songs*, he would express his grudge against me for failing to attend his concert version of the *Dream* at the Barbican, on Tuesday, 31st March, 1998: 'A magical occasion, Maxine, but of course you didn't come!' By then, there was no late train back to Crewe, and it was becoming increasingly difficult to attend his London concerts. This became more and more frustrating.

Bach's *St Matthew Passion* in Jonathan Miller's brilliant dramatisation in-the-round, at once became a rare setting for James' alto solo '*Erbarme dich*', known as one of the greatest of all arias. Music can be made intensely personal. James Bowman was supposed to 'move round' but instead, just stood facing me alone. My front-row seat was his point of orientation, and he said that for the entire first night performance, he would sing only to me. James added that as there were three more performances to come he could 'skip one in-the-round' and would do those others in the round, but not mine. He also warned me 'The Evangelist does go on a bit, and unfortunately it's not Peter Pears singing the part this time!'

The alto soloist tells you of the distraught disciple Peter's bitter weeping after his triple denial of Christ. Robert King writes: 'He is supported by a glorious string accompaniment and one of the most ravishing violin solos in the entire repertoire.'

The production was conceived by Ron Gonsalves, a friend of Jonathan Miller and a classical agent and producer. The critics loved it: 'Jonathan Miller has produced a brilliantly effective staged version of Bach's great choral work' wrote Rodney Milnes of *The Times*, singling out James for special praise: 'James Bowman's hyperexpressive alto was superb.'

James told me that working with Jonathan Miller – who

referred to himself as a 'Jewish atheist' – had been most intriguing. He said that it was Ron Gonsalves who had provided the funding and that for James, the whole thing had been one of the highlights of his career. Interestingly though, James did not take part in the ensuing DVD release of the production. When I expressed surprise, he simply said that it would not have been 'appropriate'. That James was absent, and replaced by a very ordinary countertenor, is all part of his alluring mystery.

It was in 1996 that James Bowman gave me his compilation recording, *The James Bowman Collection* on the Hyperion label, inscribed 'For Maxine, with best wishes from James Bowman, April 1996'. It was headed by Bach's '*Erbarme dich*', recorded especially for this compilation; he had not told me of it and was a complete Easter surprise, as I did not know then that he had recorded it.

> Have mercy,
> Lord, on me, regard my bitter weeping,
> Look at me,
> Heart and eyes both weep to thee
> Bitterly.

For Jonathan Miller's unusual production in February 1993, in Holy Trinity Church, Chelsea, I was fortunate to be in the front row, and was staying in my London flat so that I'd already had the pleasure of attending his performance of Handel arias at St John's in the same week. James had invited me to join him for a drink afterwards in the crypt, only to discover that he had to give a talk there to the Orchestra of the Age of Enlightenment, wittily renamed by James, 'The Orchestra of the Age of Embezzlement'. He apologised to me that he had to leave me for 'that bloody lot'.

James' willingness to be in close contact at St John's was rather surprising, because I had clear symptoms of flu and a very sore throat. As we shook hands, I gave him the gift of a book, and said, 'I won't come too close, James, as I have a virus.' He stepped back abruptly in mock horror and terror, placing his hands protectively around his throat, and saying, 'I certainly don't want to catch anything affecting my respiratory system.' He then showed concern for me, adding, 'Yes, you do look frightfully flu-ish, how have you managed to get here?' When I told him that I'd taken a taxi, he roared with laughter, telling me that the journey would have taken 'less than five minutes' on foot! This amused him greatly because he knew that I have absolutely no sense of direction, and thus, like David Munrow, went everywhere by taxi. There is the famous anecdote of Philip Pickett being given a recorder lesson by David Munrow in the back of a taxi. After Munrow's death when Philip Pickett formed his own New London Consort, he was occasionally disparaging about David, and I think this really annoyed James. 'Do you drive, Maxine?' James continued, smiling at me. James loved his car and could give the details of any route; he knew all the roads and in this sense had his feet planted firmly on the ground. James could be surprisingly practical. He concluded our encounter by telling me to 'go straight to bed ... do it now!' to ensure that I was well enough to attend his next live performance in a few days' time. Despite my virus James put his arm round me and thanked me for the book. He then gave me an original photograph of himself, as requested from the Heroic Arias disc, saying kindly, 'I suppose, Maxine, that if you are a mystic then it doesn't matter where you are.'

At this time I would see him in live performance as many as four times in seven days, and the diverse repertoire might range from Baroque arias for castrato, to Elizabethan lute songs and contemporary repertoire for the countertenor. Some of our favourite modern pieces contained mediaeval elements; Geoffrey Burgon was especially successful in writing in this way, and showed himself to be Britten's true heir. James is very interested in contemporary repertoire written specifically for his voice – such as the Geoffrey Burgon setting 'Almost Peace' – but admits to having a large file marked 'Declined'. He complains that most pieces written for him are 'too high and too loud, the countertenor voice becomes inaudible and the experience is vocally destructive'. Arthur Wills was initially worried that his *Galuppi Cantata* for James had too high a tessitura, but James assured him that this was not so, telling me that 'the vocal line is fine, just some rewriting needed in the string parts'.

Folksongs tend to be 'rarities and oddities' in James Bowman's recorded repertoire, but he has given some thrilling live performances in this genre. James' favourite folksong is Irish, the ghostly 'She Moved Through the Fair', and he sings it beautifully in an imaginative arrangement by the composer Geoffrey Burgon. It is preserved in BBC Sound Archives. A swan leaving a lake is a commonly used image of death:

> And then she went homeward
> with one star awake,
> like the swan in the evening
> moves over the lake.
>
> The people were saying,
> no two were ever wed,
> but one had a sorrow,
> that never was said.

Also, there is a 1999 recording with John Turner, *Here we come a-piping: Songs and Instrumental Music of Nicholas Marshall*, which includes Scottish folksongs. The disc is very much a

Turner/Bowman project and was recorded in Cheshire. 'Ye Banks and Braes' and 'Ca, the Yowes' are both settings of Robert Burns, performed by James. I once overheard John Turner say of James Bowman: 'When he comes to stay we always put him in the garden room.'

Omitted from James' repertoire is German Lieder, which he has never sung. He does not condemn those who, like the countertenor Michael Chance, have the right voice and do attempt to sing this repertoire, but has said that he would not do so himself as his voice is not suited to it: 'It is easy to sound hysterical if singing Lieder.' James enjoys listening to Romantic music and unexpectedly loves the symphonies of Brahms, but has no wish to perform the music of this period.

James' wisdom in this matter was evident to me when I attended a largely unsuccessful Lieder recital by Michael Chance at the Wigmore Hall. The concert was scantily attended; David Dimbleby, sitting in front of me, was obviously hating it. Listening in to his conversation with his wife and son, it was clear that he had been 'dragged along'. Very unusually for the Wigmore Hall, many of the audience left during the interval.

The critic Michael Church has described Michael Chance as 'patenting a tone peculiarly English in its watercolour timbre'. When singing German lieder this can create a strange sound, akin to what Britten's friend, the great Russian cellist Mstislav Rostropovich termed 'Aldeburgh Deutsch'. Actually, I find this very attractive, as in the Britten/Pears version of Schubert's *Wintereisse*, preferring it to that of Dietrich Fischer-Dieskau, (a singer whom Peter Pears called the 'school bully').

It was just before his first performance in *The St Matthew Passion* that James said the words, which forever conveyed the essence of my time with him, and our unique interaction as artist and audience. Dress was informal, and James asked me if I liked his jeans and jumper; I said that he looked 'beautiful' and he was delighted. It was a very English moment of naming and individuality. As I entered the church he called my name and gestured to me to come to him, with the following words: 'Maxine! Show me where you're sitting and I'll open my mouth very wide and sing to you ... My live performances should leave you in suspended ecstasy, waiting for the next time ... They live and then die like a flower, but there should never be any sense of anticlimax.'

I keep those beautiful words, written on a small piece of paper, in an enclosed centre section of my purse, in my handbag. (Once, at High Wycombe, he asked if he could look inside my handbag, or at least hold it.) These words relate directly to the painting which was to express our innermost empathy – Leonardo's *The Virgin of the Rocks* which might one day give James' book its front cover, and is derived from the most ecstatic twilight vision of my lifetime, 'transformation unsurpassed'. I'll talk about this again later in my narrative, because it returned again and again as a symbol of our closeness and the way in which I uniquely 'saw' and adored him, but also the way in which he looked at me. We came together in the chiaroscuro of Leonardo's cave; it was a very special evening.

> The deepest experience of the creative artist is feminine, for it is an experience of conceiving and giving birth...as though a woman had taken a seat within him.
>
> Rilke

Although James' preference was for Bach's *St Mathew Passion*, rather than the *St John*, he gave many memorable traditional Good Friday performances of the latter, and recorded it in 1993 with Frans Brüggen; he told me that when he rehearsed the *St*

John with Brüggen, he was overcome and began to cry.

I attended his live afternoon performances with the London group, Polyphony, at St John's, Smith Square in 1995, 1996 and 1997. The aria '*Es ist vollbracht,* It is finished,' from Bach's *St John's Passion* is described by James as its 'inner sanctum, the holy of holies'. As this aria is towards the conclusion of the piece, James has been silent since his first aria near the beginning. He told me that it was very easy to become tense before standing to sing; he could not cough, have a drink or clear his throat in live performance. There was no 'build-up'. Just before his commencement of this amazing and dramatic aria, he would give me the nod, inclining his head towards me and gazing intently into my eyes with, in Byron's words from 'Intensities of Blue' in Canto 1V of *Don Juan,* 'his darkly, deeply, beautifully blue' eyes.

Many significant moments of 'suspended ecstasy' occurred at Easter; I sent him the yellow Roses in blue: 'Dear Maxine, The Bouquet of Yellow and Blue is exquisite. It has truly brightened my Easter.' I was the colour of sunlight and James the lovely blue. Through his words and cards he communicated his understanding of my meaning; they were always in both word and image the perfect response to a particular theme which we were exploring and developing. We would then change and begin something new. In this, and this area alone I was supreme and he would follow me. In everything else I was like Miles to Peter Quint in *The Turn of the Screw,* bewitched by the 'wordless wailing' of his melismas, and the mysterious lady narrator in Henry James' short story 'The Friends of the Friends': 'It was the result of a long necessity, of an unquenchable desire. To say exactly what I mean, it was a response to an irresistible call.'

Flowers

> Green was the colour of true love
> Anya Seton, *Katherine*

At first I was always in the company of my travelling companions, but one by one they were eliminated. 'I think we're very alike, Maxine! We're always having to get rid of people.' If James disliked or resented someone he would never use their name or meet their gaze. You had to intrigue him or you didn't exist, and like his own description of singing a Bach cantata, he is 'full of pitfalls for the unwary'.

I have an anecdote from an old friend, Bob, a former French teacher at David Munrow's old school; Bob used to go to James Bowman's performances when he was with David Munrow's Early Music Consort of London. Pauline, the autocratic wife of my friend Bob, who was in her twenties at the time, approached the young, long-haired James Bowman to congratulate him on his startling performance and request his autograph. At first James gave her a wary glance, so she proceeded with a eulogy. At this point James 'pulled a face of absolute disgust' (her words), turned his back on her and walked away. She was so angry and offended that she never again attended his concerts, saying he was 'psychopathic'.

Naming and individuality had particular significance for him. One of my female companions, (who later received the same treatment as the earlier Pauline, but this time in Tourcoing, in France, where, against my advice, she unwisely travelled all alone to see him in the *Dream*, bearing unwanted roses), was described by him as 'your fat friend with the glasses', and a male friend, contemptuously dismissed as 'the other one'.

He disliked being placed in close proximity to these people, and would always move away to stand close beside me. When physically very near to James, I sometimes felt overwhelmed by a terrifying despair; it emanated from him and passed into me. Even in performance, when I was part of the audience, he said that he wanted us 'to be as close to each other as possible'. Once, at Bolton, on October 11th, 1992, he suddenly moved sideways in order to be directly in front of me whilst singing his encore, Bach's *'Erbarme dich'*; to avoid a collision with James, the violinist had to abruptly slide backwards in his chair.

James' scornful words, 'I loathe schoolteachers, small men with beards, and people with skin diseases', encompassed all my friends. My mother was exempted from this censure. He described her as 'lovely Mum', but safely viewed from afar, I felt. Neither he, nor my beloved mother ever indicated any wish to be introduced to each other. My mother greatly admired and enjoyed his work, especially his sacred repertoire, but was quite happy to remain 'at a safe distance, and worship from afar.'

My son, Leon, was benignly acknowledged at the Commission, and included on many Christmas cards, 'To Maxine and Leon'. My daughter, Tamsin, a perfectionist, loved his performances. She had seen him on Sunday, December 2nd, 1990, at the Wigmore Hall in a morning concert, with the countertenor Michael Chance singing Couperin's sombre and plangent 'Leçon de Ténèbres', but her favourite performance was his Oberon in *The Dream*. Tamsin cleverly enjoyed being 'an observer', and looked through her opera glasses to see whether or not the open-mouthed James had any fillings. Even when my children were teenagers, James still thought of me as 'the mother of small children. That is what you are, Maxine, always.' He quickly excluded and disposed of my husband. Very early on,

Burning in Blueness

after a lute recital at Hinckley with Robert Spencer, he said to him, 'I suppose you've been dragged along.' James was deeply suspicious of him as a nuclear scientist. 'I suppose he was part of that dreadful Sizewell B public enquiry at Snape Maltings,' he added.

> Now night is almost over and the dawn about to break. The contours of the Sizewell power plant, its Magnox block a glowering mausoleum, begin to loom upon an island far out in the pallid waters…
> W. G. Sebald, *The Rings of Saturn*

Later on, before a morning lute song recital, on Sunday 5th June, 1994, at Blackheath Concert Halls, James had confronted my husband's car in a most aggressive manner. James' irritation was doubtless increased by the fact that he disliked singing in the morning because the voice had yet to warm up: 'I prefer to be still horizontal at that time' he told me on the telephone.

But also, James wished to remove me from that particular domestic context. 'You are not married, Maxine, because you don't have a husband. I'll never think of you as married. I told you, you are a pearl amongst swine…' James was happy to think of me as being at home, but only with my children and his recordings. He thought that when I was not attending his concerts, I should be writing and listening to his recorded work.

> Once when I remarked that sitting there amidst her papers she resembled the *angel* in Dürer's *Melancholia*, steadfast among the instruments of destruction, her response was that the apparent chaos surrounding her represented in reality a perfect kind of order, or an order which at least tended towards perfection.
> G. Sebald, 'Janine's Paper Universe', from *The Rings of Saturn*.

I became the isolated focus of his scrutiny, amused affection, and attentiveness. My purpose was 'to impart a vision before the strangeness of it fades.' James did not like me to have conversations with other members of the audience, and told me so. He was jealously and possessively observant:

> Give not that which is holy unto the dogs, neither cast ye your pearls before swine, lest they trample them under their feet, and turn again and rend you.
> Matthew 7:6

Throughout this period there was no doubt that I held a special place in his thoughts and affection, and for me alone he sang the arias from his glorious repertoire of the past. For him I felt 'a love as intense as faith; passing through the senses into mystery'. (Lyndall Gordon's description of what Henry James felt for his cousin Minny Temple and expressed in his letters to her.)

We had yet to come into conflict, and as I researched the male high voice and came into contact with musicians, other singers and scholars within his world, including Dr Edward Higginbottom of New College Oxford, I grew more confident in my musical and literary journey. I first contacted Edward Higginbottom to search for recordings of James Bowman as a boy treble. Although unable to help me with information in this early part of James' life as a singer, he directed me to Michael Howard, who had been organist and master of the choristers at Ely, and trained James in the Junior School. He also advised me to contact Arthur Wills, as he had taught James when he entered the Senior School. Edward Higginbottom replied to my letter of enquiry on 7th September 1991, putting me in touch with several distinguished people who were in the choir during James' time at Oxford, and including Sir David Lumsden, who was in charge. 'I share your enthusiasm for JB's talent. We have had the pleasure of working with him on a number of occasions; he retains a lively interest in the choir and its activities. Best wishes with your research!'

I helped Peter Giles in a very minor way, during the writing of his book *The History and Technique of the Countertenor*, Scolar Press, 1994, and he generously acknowledged my background contribution, both in his book and a letter of 24th October, 1994:

> Dear Maxine,
> Thanks for all your help in whipping up reactions for Scolar. It's been a long agonizing business, but things *look* to be on course now! Thank you again! Scolar have been forced to pulp the first 1,000 copies!
> All best wishes,
> Peter

In a card on 15th June, 1995, Peter described himself as 'too much of a perfectionist, I often suspect! I tinker for ever with my written stuff!'

Also, between April 1991 and September 1993, I received three charming, handwritten letters from the countertenor Michael Chance (from London, the Netherlands, and Australia where he was on tour with Britten's *Dream*):

> c/o Australian Opera
> Sydney Opera House
> 5th September, 1993
>
> Dear Maxine,
> I have been here for three months, doing a wonderful new production of *A Midsummer Night's Dream* which may well go to next year's Edinburgh Festival. Before that, from February to the end of April, I was in Amsterdam, including singing in a less successful production of the

Dream, which also toured Holland... before coming to Australia in June, I went to New York to do a repeat performance of *Ulisse* in the Brooklyn Academy of Music ... so well away from dear old London for the year so far. And I'm afraid it continues in the same vein. I am back in Amsterdam for October and November for a new production of *L'Incoranzione di Poppea* which I subsequently record in early December, with two concert performances in QEH on December 8th and 11th. My only other UK performances in 1993 are possibly, *Messiah* with Richard Hickox on December 14th and a small part of the *Christmas Oratorio* in St Paul's Cathedral on December 16th.

In January and February, I am first in Lisbon and then in Holland... The first UK performances in 1994 are, I think, some recitals with Nicholas Daniels and Julius Drake in March, and a *St Matthew Passion* in Leeds on March 26th. And I have supposedly a date for a Wigmore Hall recital in May, and hope to do lute songs, with Christopher Wilson, which we perform on a recently issued CD... I will know more about next year come the New Year.

I am very touched by your interest — sadly, there are no plans at present to do any more concerts with James [Bowman], but I fervently hope that something may be possible, at least in Purcell's year, 1995.

With very best wishes and many thanks,

Michael

Michael Chance continued to send me his engagement lists, and also gave me his London address and telephone number as a contact point for further information about forthcoming UK performances. In my case, he was happy to bypass his agent, and thanked me for my continued support: 'I am most impressed by your seemingly unbounded enthusiasm for us countertenors!'

If I had become deeply involved in Michael Chance's work, I know that I would never have written anything approaching my ten years of letters to James. Michael might have seemed an obvious choice for a commission or correspondence, but much as I admired him, he did not fascinate, challenge, and inspire me to write; perhaps he was just too 'normal'.

A very literary singer, Michael Chance is a disciple of James Bowman, having read English at Cambridge and sung in the choir of King's College and St John's. Contemporary repertoire is one of Michael's interests; he has done a lot in this area and commissioned many pieces, especially from John Tavener. James Bowman regarded him as his successor in the *Dream*: 'I'm not making a thing of it,' he said, 'but the chances are that I won't do the *Dream* again. Michael Chance sings the part ravishingly, and I think of him very much as my successor. Does that sound pompous? What really thrills me is seeing so many wonderful countertenors around and feeling one has had an influence on them.' (James Bowman to Hilary Finch on the eve of his last fully staged *Dream* in England.)

Virginia Woolf observed that Henry James had shaped his art in 'the shadow' and W. H. Auden thought the insight of Henry James into creative acts was unparalleled. 'It's, I suppose, because I am that queer monster, the artist, an obstinate finality, an inexhaustible sensibility.' Henry James

In the end, what is Leonardo's mysterious painting of Mary and an angel, (probably Uriel or Gabriel) with Jesus and John the Baptist? The forbidding, yet protective, sanctuary-like cave, and the cool, watery wilderness recall the river Bronchi and grotto where Leonardo played as a child. As one gazes at the original in London's National gallery – derived from an earlier version in the Louvre – at what is one looking? According to Erika Langmuir in her *National Gallery Companion* guide, it is 'a deeply emotional yet strangely uncommunicative work.' The candlelit chapel would have increased its sense of mystery, the mystery of great art.

'I am amazed not only by the extraordinary mastery of it, but by the renewal of the magic: each time the mystery remains.' (Benjamin Britten, 1964 on Schubert's Song Cycle *Winterreise*)

It seems to me that from deep within the rocks of Leonardo's painting comes a strange and haunting singing, a high-pitched resonance. The plangent song is intensified by the small wreath-like wild flowers growing on the rocks. The interplay of the natural setting and the devotional image disclosed within is scenery fit for a great man of music.

The first time I heard James sing was in a live broadcast performance from London's National Gallery, (unaware at that time that for James also, this was one of his most important and memorable performances), in a recital in aid of the Save the Titian Appeal, and in this James Bowman is again strangely linked to Henry James. Henry was fascinated by the visual arts, especially painting; he had had formal training as a painter and always retained a painterly eye. 'The inward aspects…of the old National Gallery where memory mixes for me together so many elements of the sense of an antique world. The great element was of course that I well nigh incredibly stood again in the immediate presence of Titian…' (Henry James, *The Middle Years*, from his 3-volume *Autobiography*.)

Michael Kennedy, in the *Oxford Dictionary of Music*, 1980, defines the relationship between music and colour: 'It is impossible for music to convey colours, but it is customary to speak of "colouring" or "tone colour" where variations of timbre or tone are produced by different intensities of the overtones of sounds. "Shade" is perhaps a more accurate term, since the differences are often those of "darker" or "lighter" sound.'

But it is possible that like many musicians, James is Synaesthetic, seeing musical sound (notes) as distinctive colours.

Burning in Blueness

Synaesthesia is defined as 'the production of a mental sense – impression relating to one sense by the stimulation of another.'

Colours were very important to us; he always left the choice to my 'exquisite taste', but would sometimes request yellow and blue, white and blue, blue alone, or for Christmas flowers 'a touch of red'. He described himself to me as 'blue…that is what I am, Maxine', and he had a special love for yellow in blue, 'in austere chiaroscuro juxtaposition'. Many of the bouquets I sent him expressed this idea. He confided that I was the only person in England who sent him flowers, and he was always deeply appreciative of them. 'Dear Maxine, Thank you for the most exquisite Flowers. They are a great Joy. Best wishes for 1998 – James', and on a beautiful card of Florence Cathedral beneath snow: 'Thank you for the most beautiful Yellow Roses – they are giving me enormous pleasure.' James has a Swan fountain-pen, described by him as 'blue, beautiful and very old'. He told me 'I'm never happier than when holding my pen!' 'Um,' said my mother. 'Add two more letters and I think we'd be closer to the truth.' I reprimanded her for this base interpretation.

James sent me a postcard in response to this favourite quotation from the reclusive American poet, Emily Dickinson:

> A Voice that Alters – Low
> And on the Ear can go
> Like Let of Snow –
> Or shift supreme –
> As tone of Realm
> On Subjects Diadem –

The postcard depicts a light snow covering on the Duomo in Florence. The Dickinson poems, (which I had given him), had accompanied him on his recent recital in the great

Cathedral.

Always, with his cards I enclosed a quotation, often of words that he was singing on the specific occasion they were celebrating. During his five-year period performing and recording Purcell's complete *Odes and Welcome Songs* in eight volumes, and for his Purcell Tercentenary celebrations, I always used something from Purcell's *Odes* as a heading for James' birthday flowers. Amongst his favourites were 'Now does the glorious day appear', Queen Mary's Birthday Ode of 1689, and 'Celebrate this Festival', which contains the quietly ecstatic setting for solo countertenor over a ground bass, of 'Crown the altar, deck the shrine', sung by James Bowman and recorded in 1990, with Robert King and the King's Consort. James loved these references to his work, calling me 'charming and witty' for using them. When Queen Mary died of smallpox, Purcell wrote the music for her funeral, and less than a year later the same music was performed at his own funeral. Perhaps the one James loved the most and which I repeated, was the 'Welcome Song' for James 11, 1687, which accompanied his birthday flowers on his return from a recital in Geneva:

> Sound the trumpet, beat the drum,
> Caesar and Urania come.
> Bid the Muses haste to greet 'em,
> Bid the Graces fly to meet 'em
> With laurel and myrtle to welcome them home.

James' favourite among all Handel's English oratorios was *Theodora*, (1749-50), written for a public that above all adored the virtuoso singer. Didimus is the Roman Captain, in love with Theodora, a noble convert to Christianity. Didimus makes his way into the prison where Theodora is captive, but his attempts at rescue and the pleas of each for the other are unavailing. They die in martyrdom. 'Sweet rose and lily' is Didimus's air when he comes upon Theodora in prison, and the love duet 'To Thee thou glorious son of worth' follows.

For two of James' bouquets I used the aria and duet for his character Didimus; but addressing him as Theodora, myself assuming the role of Didimus:

> Sweet rose and lily, flow'ry form
> Take me your faithful guard:
> To shield you from bleak wind and storm
> A smile be my reward.

James loved the gender reversal of so many of my cards sent with his flowers; he thought it 'delightfully Handelian'.

I gave him flowers when he was happy, and flowers when he was 'brooding', upset, or melancholy – nothing was too much trouble in serving him. Once, when he had made 'a slight slip' in a Wigmore Hall live performance of the incredibly difficult *Blake Songs*, which Radio 3 were recording on the 25th January, 1997, I sent him a bouquet of yellow to cheer him up, before he left for a short holiday. In fact, he re-recorded the passage and so the mistake did not appear in the subsequent Radio 3 broadcast, which I recorded at home, having also attended the original live concert. I had also sent him a bouquet *before* the performance, as the recital was so special and the programme so thrilling, including Howell's 'Full Moon' and 'King David', and Warlock's 'My Own Country' and 'The Night', the words of which accompanied the flowers. Because of the rift between us which had arisen from my absence at Chester Cathedral, on July 20th, 1994, and my subsequent failure to attend his concert in Gloucester Cathedral on August 23rd, 1994, I had not seen James for three years.

Dear Maxine,
Thank you for the most beautiful yellow roses – they are giving me enormous pleasure. They go with my current concentration *on* and rehearsals *for* 25 January at the Wigmore Hall.
Best wishes for 1997,
James

James was deeply touched by my charming gesture: 'I'm loved and adored! Thank you for your kindness and devotion to me, Maxine. I'll endeavour to deserve it…I don't care about the world, Maxine, not while I still have you.'

> And the many flowers, which you have touched,
> have fallen in love with your beauty.
> *Tanti Strali al sen mi scocchi,*' from Handel's *Italian Duets,* 1710-11 for soprano and alto recorded by James Bowman, April 1990

'How beautiful yellow is,' he said. James loved the resonance and intensity of my warm yellow flowers and complementary blues; they lightened his mood. And of course, the *Ten Blake Songs* by Vaughan Williams, include 'Ah, Sunflower' from his *Songs of Experience,* (1793). Yellow was the colour on which Van Gogh's search for emotional truth converged. Painted after a period of relative loneliness, *Sunflowers* expresses the radiant warmth and joy felt by a man whose melancholia had been banished, 'Why should those points of light in the firmament…be less accessible than the dark ones on the map of France? We take a train to go to Tarascon or Rouen and we take death to reach a star.' (Vincent Van Gogh, letter of 1889.) During moments of sorrow in Timothy Findley's novel *The Wars*, Barbara d'Orsey always carries yellow flowers, especially roses.

My own daughter, when recovering from an emotional

crisis and depression, bought herself a large print of *Sunflowers* and placed it in her student residence. I was often deeply concerned by James' low spirits, personal crises, and manic-depressive temperament, including flashes of paranoia and aggression. His high yellow note resounds with a plaintive call. 'I often sound insane when I'm singing!' he told me.

> 'The idea that he was slightly mad left her feeling protective towards him…It is a terrible thing to be lonely and unprotected.'

The National Gallery

> To do a concert with Benjamin Britten and Peter Pears was a rare, and wonderful irreplaceable experience, and I'll never forget it…It was one of the great moments in my musical life. I remember it very well. I can remember the whole occasion. I mean it was a dream come true – I'd always loved the piece and to sing it [Britten's *Abraham and Isaac*] with the two people who conceived it was an honour beyond words…It's a wonderful bit of vocal writing.
>
> James Bowman, in conversation with Brian Kay, 2002, referring to The National Gallery Concert: Songs for Three Voices, May 1972

Henry James publicly willed his portrait to the National Portrait Gallery where it hangs today. As Peter Ackroyd points out, we are the one nation to have a National Portrait Gallery. Henry James posed for Sargent in his studio near Tite Street. Sargent's 'masterpiece of painting,' writes Leon Edel, in his *Biography* of Henry James, 'fades into chiaroscuro; the full highlight accentuates the great forehead, the eyes half-closed but with all their visual acuteness; and the lips formed as if the Master were about to speak. Henry James is caught in one of the moments of his greatness – that is, a moment of "authority".'

In almost my last letter to my singer, in 1998, I alluded to 'The story of a Masterpiece', by Henry James, the idea of an Old Master suspended there, and slowly fading; to underline this theme, I'd given James a copy of Henry James' 'The Story of a Masterpiece' and also his novella *The Madonna of the Future*, which also explored the meaning of 'old masters'. James responded to me with a phone call and a beautiful card of an intently gazing jewelled man, the first Duke of Buckingham (1592-1628), in cream silk, lace and red velvet, painted by an unknown artist, but reminding me of Henry James' description in *The Ambassadors* of 'one of the splendid Titians in the great gallery of the Louvre – the overwhelming portrait of the young man with the strangely-shaped glove and the blue-grey eyes'.

In April, 2002, in conversation with Brian Kay, this idea of the 'old master'; had been the theme of one of his Radio 3 five-day retrospectives, *Morning Performance*, 'Artist in Focus: James Bowman', in which the countertenor likened himself in late middle age, to an 'old painting fading…an old masterpiece hanging there'. The personal highlight of the musical illustrations in this series, cleverly mingled with his personal observations, had been his 1972 National Gallery recital with his one-time voice teacher Peter Pears, and Ben Britten, taking me back, yet again, to the commencement of my passion when I first heard him sing in that very recital.

In *The Madonna of the Future,* Henry James writes, 'It may hang somewhere, in after years…and keep the artist's memory warm. Think of being known to mankind after some such fashion as this! Of hanging here through the slow centuries in the gaze of an altered world, living on and on in the cunning of an eye and hand that are part of the dust of ages, a delight and a law to remote generations; making beauty a force and purity an example!'

'It's so perfectly true,' I wrote to James Bowman in 1998, that 'as you slowly fade and your voice darkens with age like the tones of the "old master", you become an ever more beautiful Masterpiece.'

In her small book, *Portraits in Fiction*, 2004, (based on the Heywood Hill Annual lecture 2000 at the National Portrait Gallery, London), A S Byatt explores the writer's preoccupation with the painted image. Referring to *À là Recherche du Temps Perdu*, she describes Odette's reaction to being perceived in terms of a Botticelli work of art: 'Swann idealises the woman he loves by conflating her with the great art of the past. Eventually, precious and adored, the painting on his desk replaces the photograph of Odette. In Henry James' *The Wings of the Dove*, Milly Theale is shown, by Lord Mark, a striking resemblance between her own face and that of the Bronzino portrait of Lucrezia Panciatichi. By seeing her resemblance to a great work of the past, her admirer assimilates her into the world of art, and bestows on her a kind of immortality. As Milly gazes 'through tears' at the wonderful and mysterious portrait 'fading with time', she reflects on its paradox: 'The lady in question, at all events, with her slightly Michel-angelesque sadness, her eyes of other days, her full lips, her long neck, her recorded jewels, her brocaded and wasted reds, was a very great personage – only unaccompanied by a joy!' A S Byatt's authors include Iris Murdoch, and the 'impulsive and sensual Dora in *The Bell*', fleeing the intensities and abstractions of a religious community (as well as a manipulative husband) finds herself in The National Gallery, looking at Gainsborough's painting of his two daughters and finding it a moving experience.

'It occurred to her that here at last was something real and something perfect. Who had said that about perfection and reality being in the same place?'

Either consciously or unconsciously, in his BBC interview with Brian Kay in 2002, James had used the idea in my 1998 letter to him, of his resemblance to an 'old master'.

But James Bowman's shrine is my print of Leonardo's *The Virgin of the Rocks*, framed deep inside an arch of holly green and reeded brown wood. I need no other.

▲   ▲   ▲

Burning in Blueness

James Bowman in the 1990s

PART TWO

The Man

Ripon

> My master and myself and all
> those souls
> That came with him, were deeply
> lost in joy,
> as if that sound were all that did exist.
>
> Dante Alighieri, *The Divine Comedy*,
> 'Purgatory' Canto II

On March 2nd, 1991, James was to perform Vivaldi and Britten in Ripon Cathedral; he had sent me this engagement through the post, as, following a quarrel with his agent of many years, he had decided never again to leave arrangements to such a person, but to do everything himself, with his newly acquired fax machine. He had, by this time chosen to do very little opera, with the exception of Britten's *Dream*, and concentrate on recital, but his agent from Harrison and Parrott continued to make many lucrative opera bookings on his behalf, without his permission, thus overworking the voice and putting it at risk. Apparently, this turning point in James' life came in the mid-1980s, with a performance of Handel's *Semele* at the Fenice in Venice: 'It was so depressingly awful that I thought, I can't bear this any more; there were wobbly singers, everything was loud, there was no caressing of the phrases ... so I decided to give opera up.' James had come to believe that working in large opera houses with modern orchestras was straining his voice 'which I didn't want to ruin,' he said, 'since there was so much other music I wanted to sing.'

We had spoken on the phone a number of times, and I had sent flowers, but we had yet to meet. On that rainy and sleeting Saturday in March it was so cold in the Cathedral that the breath froze. Unique archive film footage of Alfred Deller singing Purcell's 'Music for a While' in an English cathedral in winter came to mind, but like Dante in Purgatory, listening to his singer friend Casella, I was in love with a Voice and physical discomfort mattered little.

That afternoon in Ripon I attended the afternoon rehearsal, or preparation would be a more accurate term. When I first entered into the cold stones of the Cathedral I observed him at once, looking like a god, immensely tall in a long green gabardine coat and tartan scarf, but with touchingly childlike red shoelaces on his huge feet – 'a touch of red' which I would later explore with him in exquisite Christmas flowers. I surrendered to his amazing live performance of Vivaldi's *Stabat Mater*, and remarkable 'mouse' solo from Britten's *Rejoice in the Lamb*. During the latter, he put his fingers to his lips to quieten the overly loud playing of the organist. James had to sing quietly but his was still the loudest voice there. Two days later, I wrote to him:

> I had the pleasure of attending your concert at Ripon Cathedral on Saturday 2nd March ... The whole experience was greatly enhanced by the unforgettable moment when upon entering the Cathedral in the early afternoon, we heard your unique and wonderful voice singing the Amen sequence from the *Stabat Mater*.

On this memorable occasion I was with my friends, including Bob, who had also noticed the red shoelaces but saw them in quite a different way from myself, saying sardonically, 'They're the come-on!' By the end of the evening performance we were all shivering and ghostly white. The Dean of Ripon was extremely kind to us, 'the people from Cheshire', as was the organist, and fearful young tenor who would have to sing with the Great Man; he almost fainted away when at last the performance took place, his face as grey as his grey eyes. Afterwards, several choirboys received a telling-off from the Master of the Choristers; they were threatened with the dormitory if there was any more undisciplined behaviour.

A rather delightful relationship existed between my Singer and the Dean, the Very Reverend Christopher Campling, in that the Dean had been Chaplain at Ely Cathedral when James was a Chorister there. In the Dean's address he paid charming tribute to James for having given his precious time to Ripon, when the very next day he was off to Venice for six weeks to sing in an opera! Obviously, despite his vocal anxieties, James was still involved in occasional opera performances.

What added even more to the special magic of the occasion was that my request to Radio 3, to hear him in Britten's *Abraham and Isaac*, from the original 1972 *Songs for Three Voices* recording, had been successful, and was to be broadcast on the following day (Sunday morning). I was informed by the Master of the Choristers that James knew of this, 'he knows he's on tomorrow', and was highly pleased.

For the next decade I made numerous requests to illustrious personages and presenters, both at Radio 3 and in the wider musical world, for more broadcasting and recording of the voice of James Bowman. They were always wonderfully responsive, especially Michael Emery and Nicholas Kenyon of Radio 3. I enjoyed a lengthy and most fascinating correspondence with Michael Emery on the subject of a Radio 3 Fiftieth Birthday tribute to James. At this time James was moderately hostile to Radio 3: 'They're not interested in me, or in anything I do. You have to be Joan Sutherland – and we won't go into that – the less said the better; a woman of mesmeric vulgarity, all right I suppose if you like "wobbly" voices, and if Handel's notes aren't there, she just invents them

Burning in Blueness

for him!'

But when Nicholas Kenyon, a passionate devotee of James Bowman, took over as Controller, there was a far greater interest shown in the countertenor and Baroque music. Anyway, my requests were played on countless occasions; I always asked for something special for Midsummer, and on his birthday: 'Dear Maxine,' James wrote, 'Thank you for the beautiful Roses. I was away in Basle giving a Recital on my Birthday'.

Nicholas Kenyon enjoyed and praised my 'wonderful card' expressing appreciation of his Purcell 300 Concert, a rare televised event: 'The highlight of the evening was seeing and hearing James in "Hosanna to the Highest" and Purcell's "Evening Hymn", standing sublimely alone before the high Altar in Westminster Abbey.'

As part of the Purcell tercentenary celebrations, 'Welcome, Welcome Glorious Morn' was broadcast on BBC 2. It was a live concert from the Banqueting House, Whitehall, featuring the King's Consort with soloists James Bowman and Robin Blaze, countertenors. This event was again organised by Nicholas Kenyon, Controller of Radio 3 at that time, and was another of James' precious television appearances.

In a much less successful ITV appearance James looked uncomfortable. The Princess Royal introduced a Christmas Eve celebration in words and music, Christmas Glory, from St George's Chapel in Windsor and nearby Eton College. Featuring the tenor Jose Carreras and the actress Maggie Smith, (who were deemed the 'stars') it was a typical ITV glitzy affair, not suitable for James Bowman's tender performance of 'A Babe is Born', (Anon.) and 'The Drummer Boy'.

On October 27th 1993, Ted Perry of Hyperion Records wrote, 'I salute your enterprise and championship of James . . . that's devotion and I respect that.' Ted made me a gift of

Purcell's Complete *Odes and Welcome Songs*, Volume 4, which includes 'Ye tuneful muses', 1686, a welcome song for James II. The jewel of the *Odes* 'With him he brings', is sung by James Bowman. In the Booklet Notes, 1991, Robert King writes: 'Over a wonderful four-bar ground bass the Queen's beauty is praised, with especially delightful writing for "There beauty its whole artillery tries", before the ground bass modulates up a fifth, and Purcell provides a delicious string ritornello'.

> With him he brings the partner of his throne,
> That brighter jewel than a crown,
> In whom does triumph each commanding grace,
> An angel mien and matchless face.
> There beauty its whole artillery tries,
> Whilst he who ever kept the field
> Gladly submits, is proved to yield
> And fall the captive of her conquering eyes.

Also with Robert King, James Bowman recorded another massive series: Purcell's *The Complete Anthems and Services* in eleven volumes. Interestingly, Purcell employed a famous countertenor, 'Mr Abell', and a 'remarkable' bass: 'Mr Bowman'.

James' ten years of performance and recordings with the Suffolk resident Robert King and his Consort were entirely fruitful and account for some of his greatest work on the Hyperion label from 1985-1995. He has said that meeting Robert in the mid-1980s gave his career a 'kick-start again where I got back a lot of self-confidence'. However, despite this decade of outstanding achievements in baroque repertoire, in which Robert King described James Bowman as 'the voice of the Purcell series, whether in ensemble or singing solo', a recent conviction for King, in June 2007, on fourteen counts of indecent assault against five boys (which took place between

1983-1994) inevitably casts its shadow over James' time with the King's Consort. James Bowman's recorded legacy with Hyperion is safe at present, as the company has decided, in the short term at least, not to delete these discs from its lists, reassuring potential customers that 'Robert King is not on a royalty'. *The Guardian* music critic James Fenton argues that 'whatever the rights and wrongs of the case, a separation could be made between professional matters and personal life'.

Michael Emery, my favourite correspondent in the early 1990s, was charming, sympathetic and erudite. My literary background protected me from all these formidable men with musical training, education, and talent, because in that respect alone I had them at a disadvantage. I've always empathised with David Munrow because although he was in many ways a genius, he was a self-taught musician, who like me, had read English at university, and that had inspired his love of vocal music and obsession with the voice of James Bowman.

Before going to Pembroke College, Cambridge, Munrow had spent a year in Peru (VSO) and acquired a vast collection of wind instruments. James' ability to perfectly imitate instrumental sounds was exactly what David was looking for in his specialist repertoire.

> Voice and Verse
> Wed your divine sounds, and
> Mixed power employ
> …and sing in endless morn of light.
> John Milton, 'At A Solemn Music', 1633

I loved this exciting male world I'd entered; it felt like being Leonardo's companion, Melzi, or going to the South Pole with Captain Scott and his 'Birthday Boys' – 'entombed in ice and wind'. Captain 'Titus' Oates' family home was in Meanwood,

Leeds, where I had lived as a student, and where a memorial plaque uniquely refers to his body beneath the Antarctic ice. Oates' last letters betray a passionate longing for home. According to Scott's diary 'Oates' last thoughts were of his mother…'

On that dark winter's day in Ripon on March 2nd, 1991, I had an opportunity to say 'hello' to James; I decided to defer the moment and we merely exchanged a speculative glance. Another opportunity to meet him presented itself later in the same year, on Sunday, June 2nd, and revealed James as surprisingly insecure when in unfamiliar surroundings. It was a recital to celebrate the life and work of the late George Davies, a friend and colleague of the recorder player John Turner. I'd heard about the concert from James himself. He had told me on the telephone that he was dreading it because of the unknown acoustic, especially as the stage was adjacent to a large Sports Hall. He asked me whether or not I was familiar with the acoustic of the Evans Hall, in Wilmslow, but I told him 'Sorry, no – I'm unable to advise you.' The recital was significant because it featured the 'Soliloquy' for countertenor, recorder, optional lute, cello and harpsichord, by Alan Ridout. Robert Spencer was on lute. During the interval, James was standing in the basketball court behind the stage. As I stood having a drink at the bar above, I noticed that he was staring up at me. After the second half, I received further speculative looks and a smile from James, but again decided to defer our meeting.

It was not until a lute recital at Holy Trinity Church in Hinckley in Leicestershire, on Saturday, September 19th, 1992, after almost two years of correspondence and telephone conversations, that we were at last introduced by the formidable, but always kind to me 'I approve of you, Maxine', Marjorie King. Marjorie had spoken to me on the phone and also written to me on August 26th, 1992, saying that she looked forward to meeting me on September 19th, for the lute song recital. She also provided the programme notes: 'James is the leading countertenor in this country. He has broadcast and recorded extensively. Robert has been performing with James since 1969; with him he has toured many countries and made many recordings. He is lute Professor at the Royal Academy of Music.' After the concert, James signed my programme 'For Tamsin and Leon'.

Robert Spencer, that 'most poetic and subtle of lutenists', described James as 'always affable', even during a lengthy and gruelling tour.

Some years later, I attended Marjorie King's Memorial Concert in Hinckley, on a day of blue sadness. She had been too ill to attend the first performance of my commissioned piece, which took place at Hinckley Music Club in celebration of James' 50th birthday.

After his Ripon recital James stayed overnight with his friend the Dean, before leaving for Venice and Opera. The Dean of Ripon most kindly sent me a lovely informal photograph of James and himself on the evening after the concert:

From the Minster House, Ripon
The Very Revd C. R. Campling, Dean of Ripon
July 30th, 1991

> You seem to be doing well in your Bowman research. I am so glad. I enclose the photograph you asked for...

In fact, it was not the photograph I'd asked for, which was of James with the Cathedral choir. I think the Dean was eager to be featured alongside James. Nevertheless, I liked it and I had it framed in Francis Bacon's unusual combination of gold leaf with monochrome portrait. 'The job of the artist is always to deepen the mystery.' Francis Bacon (1909 – 1992). Upon James' return from Venice, following 'an uncomfortable six weeks working with vain divas' as he put it, I sent him a card and a basket of flowers, which he placed on his desk; I frequently welcomed him home in this way. If he was absent then the florist was instructed to leave them in his porch, upon his threshold. Many of James' cards to me bore the 'Gatwick' rather than the 'Redhill' postmark, showing how often he was flying.

> Let us pray
> Gabriel descend
> as a mood almost
> a monody
> of chloroform
> or florists' roses
> Consensual angel spinning this word's thread
> he descends
> and light-sensitive darkness
> follows him down.
> Geoffrey Hill, from *Psalms of Assize*

Unlike Michael Chance, James did most of his work abroad at that time, and it was such a delight to have him back in England. His acknowledgement of my card and flowers showed him to be surprised and reserved at this time, but so pleased at my request for his performance of Britten's Canticle II, *Abraham and Isaac*, composed in January, 1952. He told me his thoughts on this favourite piece about the father and son relationship and sacrifice, which includes the words: 'Take Isaac, thy son by name, that thou lovest the best of all, And in sacrifice offer him to me Upon that hill there besides thee.'

James enjoyed the ambivalence of sacrifice in Britten's Canticle 11, a setting of a text from the fifteenth century Chester

Miracle Play, *Abraham and Isaac*. He felt that Britten's *Abraham and Isaac* was a perfect mix of the divine and mortal and like 'Sweeter Than Roses', achieved an almost Schubertian quality of tenderness. The farewell duet between father and son declares its relationship to Britten's *Billy Budd*, 1968, another favourite work of James Bowman on the theme of an innocent victim about to be sacrificed.

In thanking Michael Emery in 1991 for playing my request for James Bowman as Isaac in the March 3rd edition of *Your Concert Choice*, I wrote:

> It was made perfect for me, because on the previous evening of March 2nd, I had been to Ripon Cathedral to hear James Bowman in concert there, as soloist with Ripon Cathedral Choir…so by playing my request, Radio 3 made my week-end complete and perfect…I take note of what you say about a possible birthday celebration for James Bowman in November, and do hope so very much, that you will do something to mark this occasion…It is at about this time that his recording of Britten's *A Midsummer Night's Dream*, based on the recent production at Sadler's Wells, in which I saw him, is due to be released; how lovely it would be if it coincided with a tribute from Radio 3, to coincide with his birthday on November 6th 1991.
>
> The poet Pindar is said to sing for those who have excelled in what they do. In his last song, (*Pythian VIII*) his magnificent evocation and celebration of the god Apollo, 'as the one who brings ecstasy and joy to the mind and soul of man…' best expresses for me, the experience of being immersed in the sublime and mysterious voice of James Bowman.

Michael Emery responded warmly to my suggestion for what he termed 'a James Bowman commemorative series' in celebration of his fiftieth birthday, and passed on my idea to the appropriate section within Radio 3. The idea reached fruition in Brian Kay's four-part series *James Bowman: a Twentieth Century Voice*, broadcast over four weeks by Radio 3, to coincide with his birthday on November 6th, 1991.

Also, I felt a deep empathy with Ted Perry of Hyperion and indeed met him on Tuesday, March 3rd, 1992, at James' 25th Anniversary concert at St John's Smith Square, and ensuing party in the crypt. In the early years, Ted had been running Hyperion Records part-time as a labour of love, whilst driving a London taxi (he had the knowledge) at night, and an ice cream van during the day. At this time he was also bringing up a young family.

James' programme on this special occasion was Baroque: Purcell, Handel, and Bach, including his sombre funeral Cantata, *Actus Tragicus*, BWV 106, '*Gottes zeit ist die allberbeste zeit.*' James' aria '*In deine Hände*' conveys the serenity of the soul newly arrived in Paradise. These three composers have always been central in James Bowman's repertoire. I had the best seat in the house, right in the centre of the fourth row. Programme notes by Robert King included the following: 'Since 1967, James Bowman has been acclaimed as one of the world's greatest countertenors.' Despite the intellectual emphasis of the recital, James gave us a few moments of fun when he deliberately over-ornamented part of a Handel aria, in the style of florid American countertenors, and of course, the dreaded Joan Sutherland, known as 'La Stupenda'.

The countertenor Michael Chance and the trumpeter Crispian Steele-Perkins were the complete surprise guests. James Bowman had been told by Robert King that they were both working abroad at the time and so, sadly, would not be present. James looked delighted when they suddenly appeared on stage; they were invited to accompany him in Handel's Ode 'Eternal Source of Light Divine', and the countertenor duet 'Sound the

Burning in Blueness

Trumpet' from Purcell's 'Come ye Sons of Art', part of a birthday ode for Queen Mary:

> Sound the trumpet till around
> You make the list'ning shores rebound.
> On the sprightly hautboy play
> All the instruments of Joy
> That skilful numbers can employ
> To celebrate the glories of this day.

The piece is one of Purcell's most brilliant settings on a ground bass, and in May 1987 James had recorded it with Michael Chance and the King's Consort. The disc was produced by Ted Perry and Hyperion Records as *Countertenor Duets and Solos by Henry Purcell and John Blow*. Handel's ode 'Eternal Source of Light' is one of Handel's most breathtaking settings of any text. For soloists, he had available the famous alto Richard Elford, as well as an obviously fine court trumpeter. This combination of solo alto and high trumpet, accompanied by slow-moving string chords, paints an extraordinarily beautiful picture of dawn bringing about a slow and spectacular sunrise to mark that auspicious day.

> Eternal source of light divine
> With double warmth thy beams display,
> And with distinguished glory shine,
> To add a lustre to this day.
>   alto solo James Bowman,
>   with Crispian Steele-Perkins, trumpet.

During the interval I took the opportunity to say hello to Michael Chance, who told me that he wasn't worthy to be mentioned in the same breath as the great James Bowman.

Like me, Ted Perry loved music, although he had not enjoyed a musical education; my own route to music was indirect, and via literature. 'I fell in love with the voice of Peter Pears, and through listening to a concert in which he sang with the countertenor James Bowman, I heard for the first time the voice which more than any other has possessed my imagination, and inspired my adoration of Baroque music...It has been a delight to discover such an enthusiastic, inspired man behind my favourite and most sought after recording label, which continues to give me the music I love the most. Much of my CD collection is on the Hyperion label including all my recordings of James Bowman with The King's Consort.' Having written this letter to Ted Perry, he asked my permission to use it in one of his advertisements.

One of the Hyperion projects closest to Ted's heart was James Bowman's recording, with the soprano Gillian Fisher, of Handel's *Italian Duets*. They were recorded over three days in April 1990. Ted Perry said that this was possibly James' greatest recording to date; they were '... impossibly difficult, only James could do it,' he said. I asked him if a further live performance was likely, and Ted said, no: 'The duets are technically so demanding it is not possible to do the entire collection live, as no voice could sustain the strain. Three of them, maybe, if you are lucky ... '

For many of James' bouquets I used words from the *Italian Duets* to decorate the cards which accompanied them: From *Tanti strali al sert mi scocch'*, 1710-11:

> Many arrows strike at my breast,
> like the many stars which are in the sky,
> and the many flowers which you have touched
> have fallen in love with your beauty.

and my favourite, *Amirarvi io son intento*, 1711: 'I am absorbed by your beautiful eyes, my beloved.'

In the detailed interplay between the two voices and dramatic use of text, sometimes James' voice follows the soprano, but at other times covers it with such sensuous beauty that one is moved to tears. This is a recording for the connoisseur. Whenever I listened to it I remembered the final line from John Donne's elegy 'To his Mistress Going to Bed: 'What needst thou have more covering than a man.' I sent this quotation to James with his flowers in acknowledgement of his achievement with the Italian duets. James was thrilled by this allusion to Donne. He admired and identified with the poet/preacher and was attracted to his portrait by Anon c. 1595, with its Latin inscription, translated as 'Lady, lighten our darkness'. The ambiguity of the inscription appealed to James, as did the brooding, sensuous and melancholy personality emerging from the shadows. This remarkable portrait of John Donne has recently been acquired by the National Portrait Gallery. A celebratory postcard of the painting has been issued by the Gallery, with words from Donne's 'Song': 'Sweetest love, I do not go/for weariness of thee...' printed on the back.

James loved the works of Raphael, Leonardo, Botticelli, Giorgione, and Caravaggio; his cards to me featured the works of all these artists.

The Library

I gave James a wide-ranging library of books, from children's literature to Primo Levi and Elie Wiesel. Everything was beautifully inscribed, marked a special occasion and extended a theme. James used to send me his engagement list on my birthday:

> Here now is my definitive UK Diary of Engagements as it stands at 20.1.94. I am taking Elie Wiesel with me now on holiday.
> Best wishes for your birthday on the 26th.
> James

A central tenet of my thirty-page piece on Britten, written to James in May, 1993, was that the key to understanding his work was Charles Kingsley's *The Water Babies*, inspired by the black streaks down the white cliff of Malham Cove, in Yorkshire. 'A chimney sweep must have fallen over the edge.' I gave him everything by Henry James, including his *Autobiography*, two biographies, his Notebooks, Prefaces, and even a rare first edition of the out-of-print *Portraits of Places*. He promised to read everything, and especially enjoyed Leon Edel's edition of Henry's Letters: 'I'm gradually working my way through every one of them, Maxine. Don't worry, I'll read it all!' As I went from concert to concert, from Oxford to Hampton Court, to Penkhull, to Cambridge and Bolton, I'd ask him each time how he was getting on with Henry.

The Penkhull concert was a rather shabby affair, a rare appearance with an amateur choir conducted by the dreadful, domineering May Whalley. They kept making mistakes and stopping. James appeared out front to fiddle with his music stand which was not set at the right height for him. It was far too low down, but would not fit in place when he adjusted it. Like the terrible choir, it kept slipping. Then James found that he couldn't see properly to read the music, so he went off to get his glasses, saying that it was a sign of age, he was 'wearing out'. At the end of the concert I said farewell with the gift of a copy of *Henry James*, by D. W. Jefferson, (1960), my old supervising professor.

'Dear Maxine,' James wrote to me in a letter, 'Thank you for the latest Henry James *Biography*. I am now rapidly acquiring a comprehensive Henry James Library. I shall call it the Maxine Handy Library. I will take it to Paris with me when I go for the *Dream*.'

James was also captivated by Elie Wiesel's *Night* because '...it was short and about a father-son relationship which involved the eventual loss of the father'. He said that the book cover (of a face looking down from the starry sky) reminded him of his aria 'Father of Heaven' from Handel's *Judas Maccabaeus*.

James regards his contribution to this oratorio as the summit of his recording career with the King's Consort, describing his single aria thus: 'For me, it is simple and very special,' and the critics agree.

Stephen Pettitt, in *Classical Record Review* on Saturday January 9th, 1993, wrote of being spellbound by Handel's oratorio *Judas Maccabaeus*, '... trumpeting the cause of Judaism ... the lovely hymn-like air 'Father of Heaven' sung by the Priest, his only aria at the opening of Act III ... To my mind, however, King's trump card is the creamy-voiced countertenor James Bowman, who turns the Priest's single aria into arguably the most intense musical point of the performance.'

So James incorporated me into his work abroad in a most endearing manner, and spoke often of how much he enjoyed 'dear old Henry' and how very 'fond' of him he had become. On one occasion he invited me to 'meet up' with him for a London performance of a revival of Jonathan Miller's production of Britten's *The Turn of the Screw* (text by Henry James of course). He was just departing for a recital in Belgium: 'A dreadful place – the only thing they are good at is making chocolates. Do you like chocolates, Maxine? I'll bring some back for you.'

James complained yet again that I lived in 'the wilds of Cheshire'. He said that if I moved to the South East, we could meet up and go to the theatre and opera together.

A Day in Kent

> In the deep shadows of the rainy July, with secret steps,
> thou walkest, silent as night, eluding all watchers.
> Rabindranath Tagore
> 'Song 22' from *Gitanjali*

In every copy of the *Bulletin* of the CDTCC, the Campaign for the Defence of the Traditional Cathedral Choir, there is a reprint of Peter Giles' note that the objective of the organisation was: 'To champion the ancient tradition of the all-male choir in Cathedrals, Chapels Royal and similar ecclesiastical choral foundations.'

I looked forward immensely to my first meeting, in 1991, with Peter Giles, voice consultant, countertenor and author. It was my friend, Owen Wynne, an alto lay clerk at Manchester Cathedral, who has a unique, eunochoid voice, (and five children) who first suggested that I write to Peter Giles.

'I have so many questions I wish to ask you on repertoire, and performing practices, and on opera in particular – but I must wait patiently until August 11th,' I wrote. Peter and I became very good friends and I have a shoebox full of Peter's correspondence to me. He described me as having 'a unique relationship with the countertenor voice'. He also gave me several inscribed copies of his books, and most touchingly of all, perhaps, a booklet plus two-disc set of his marvellous compilation *Les Contre-Ténors Mythes et Réalités*, which included what he called 'Max's piece' (Desprez, *Déploration sur la mort de Johannes Ockeghem*) performed by Dominique Visse, haute contre et direction Ensemble Clément Janequin. Johannes Ockeghem died in 1497, and Josquin paid him homage in this motet-chanson. The poem is by Jehan Molinet (1433-1507) and through it Josquin has threaded the Requiem Chant in long notes as a *cantus firmus*. Josquin also echoes Ockeghem's style in several ways, thus intensifying his act of homage. Peter said that whenever he heard this beautiful lament for 'music's very treasure and master', he always thought of me and my devotion to the world of the male high voice, especially that of James Bowman. Peter was a young alto lay clerk at Ely when James was there at between 18-19 years of age. He told me that somewhere he has an old reel-to-reel tape of them singing together at Ely, and how spectacular and remarkable James Bowman sounded, even then. Peter said that James, at the age of eighteen and a half, had 'phenomenal' breath control. 'I don't know when he breathes – I've never seen it.'

Peter described James as a lonely but rude, arrogant, bombastic character, whom he found it difficult to befriend. 'I've never managed to have a conversation with him in the whole of my life.' At Peter's invitation, they went for a drink together one evening, when James suddenly turned on him with great aggression for being overly familiar (calling him 'Jimmie') and placing himself in close physical proximity (his hand on his shoulder). Peter Giles said he had never forgotten the incident, and although he had come into contact with James Bowman on many subsequent occasions, it had marked the tone of their ensuing relationship. He also said that James never mentioned his family; 'One thought of him,' said Peter, 'as the Son of God!'

Perhaps this is why James said the following aria has a 'special meaning' for him:

> Father of Heav'n! From thy eternal throne,
> Look with an eye of blessing down,
> While we prepare with holy rites,
> To solemnize the Feast of Lights!
>
> Father of Heav'n' from Handel's *Judas Maccabaeus*, performed and recorded by James Bowman in 1997

In a postcard of 24th November, 1995, Peter told me of the wider response to his latest and largest book, *The History and Technique of the Countertenor*, (published at last in August, 1995), and thanking me for some tapes of a recent live broadcast of James Bowman singing Purcell. Peter wrote: 'Lots of people are reported as being very impressed with the book, but with the occasional comment that it doesn't deal enough with the absolute present (i.e. they aren't in it!). They are probably right, but that's the fault of Scolar Press. The German book (if it happens), will deal with that, as will Volume II! ... J.B. OK in Purcell, but not quite on form. I fear he's turning his voice inside out, i.e. belting the higher notes, which weakens the lower range!'

When Peter Giles invited me to join his Campaign for the Defence of the Traditional Cathedral Choir and become its chairman, James dissuaded me. Peter said, 'We'd be really glad to have you aboard, Max, as we go into battle!' James acknowledged Peter's great achievement in writing his book on the countertenor and indeed had written the Foreword, but thought the best place for Peter Giles was America – which James hated – where countertenors are seen as at worst effeminate, at best 'quaint'. 'The Americans like their countertenors to sound like women…they haven't come to grips with the cool, crystalline European sound.' James had eventually come into conflict with David Munrow because David dragged him around America on lengthy, exhausting concert tours.

James dislike of America has endured over his lifetime as a musician. In the autumn of 2000 he said in a feature interview: 'As far as the United States is concerned, I'm not that interested, which is just as well, since they seem to be totally uninterested in me. Everything there has to be so big, and that includes the concert halls which personally I don't like – there's no intimacy, which is important when you are working with chamber music.'

Most of Peter Giles' travelling had been in the United States and Canada, where he had lectured, broadcast and taught White's Technique, an approach to voice production complementary to the now widely known and extensively used Alexander Technique; Peter Giles says that 'Like Alexander's, White's Technique underlines the crucial need to rectify both postural and psychological factors. Ultimately, White's Technique teaches and demonstrates the need to picture voice as emanating from the cranial cavities…. This method is therefore totally free from the mid-nineteenth century obsession with throat-based, power-orientated, imitative teaching which had such a hold over (and often did such harm to), many voices since.'

In February, 1997, Peter Giles wrote to me with details of his recent American visit: 'My tour – or more accurately trip, for I did not travel far – went excellently. I did two university lectures (with no notes!), three workshops for voice, two master classes and 16 hour-long individual vocal/production singing lessons – and all in ten days! I hardly stopped, made some money, saw no sights except from a distance! I was in Washington D.C. and North Virginia, exclusively. A good number of the 16 lessons were with countertenors – one of them a dispirited tenore altino, who had been getting depressed because he wasn't getting enough work!'

When he asked, 'Should I give up?' I said, 'No! For heaven's sake, keep going!' With such a rare voice, he could score very well. He seemed pleased to be told. 'I did a Master Class with the Washington Cathedral CTs, and the Master of Music, Doug Major, sighed for my permanent presence there! Very flattering! The CDTCC continues to develop. There's little time left for the tradition.'

Peter Giles said that the only thing James had in common with Leonardo's painting *The Virgin of the Rocks* was its darkness. He also advised me 'Don't spend all your time with *Orlando*, Castrati and homosexuals.' He said that James was 'a strange one and just not normal', and that although it would be a great shame for us both if our friendship ever faltered, he also warned me 'You'll be alright, Max, I suppose as long as you don't mind what he is, most women would eventually have a problem with that. Peter emphasized that James would never use the word 'gay' to describe himself. Pears and Britten also, never used the term 'gay' because Britten said he couldn't think of a less appropriate word to describe such a difficult, 'confusing and guilt-ridden' condition.

James has acknowledged in conversation on Radio 3 that 'everyone thought Ben fancied me but no, there was nothing like that; we were just friends, no more than that.'

Peter Giles told me that in his opinion, James Bowman secretly just wanted to be 'normal' and have 'a wife, family, and a Christmas tree'. He thought it was sad that James would socialise with 'all sorts of unsuitable people, rather than be alone'. Peter cited some of James' inappropriate drinking chums, and told me, 'He would not want you to see him with his coterie, looking like Oscar Wilde.' I reminded Peter that it was Oscar Wilde who had acknowledged the gulf between the man and the Artist. 'It is through Art, and through Art only, that we can realize our perfection.'

I believe that at some level James yearned for domesticity and children, but knew it was impossible, because as he had said to me, he was an 'odd' difficult and ambiguous personality, probably incapable of a lasting domestic union, even in later life.

I enjoyed a glorious day at Peter's home in rural Kent, listening to his fascinating collection of Countertenors and a Castrato, stroking his cats, and reading the manuscript of his book. We spent most of the time looking over the manuscript, which was spread about in several rooms, including one reserved for the 'castrati' section. Although it was such a hot afternoon, Peter closed the window and curtains before playing me his recording of Alessandro Moreschi, *The Last Castrato*! (Complete Vatican Recordings.)

Professor Moreschi, born in 1858, received the title '*L'angelo di Roma*' because he was possessed of a voice of exceptional beauty. He retired from the Sistine Chapel Choir in 1913, after having sung there for thirty years. In 1903 Leo died; his successor, Pope Pius X banned castrati from the Papal Choir. Fortunately, however, Moreschi was permitted to remain as soloist and made his recordings in 1902 and 1904.

Alessandro Moreschi was the last known castrati and the only one to have made records. Unfortunately, by 1902 his voice was well past its prime, and this fact, combined with primitive early recording methods, and the sometimes sentimental repertoire makes the disc difficult to appreciate. James Bowman told me that when singing Handel arias written for the contralto castrato Senesino, he could work out the sound from reading and studying the score. He said, 'I can hear Senesino's voice in the music, such as in the title roles of Handel's *Guilio Cesare* and *Orlando*.'

According to Peter Giles, the castrati remain in our midst. He told me that he had access to 'a secret index of castrati, both natural and created' and that there are 'dozens in this country, Max, but only a handful are singers.' I have no idea where Peter's information has come from. A countertenor friend of mine suggested that Peter might be performing 'home castrations in his own bathroom!'

> Let not the eunuch say: behold I am a dry tree. For thus sayth the Lord to the eunuchs: they shall keep my Sabbaths, and shall choose the things that please me, and shall hold fast by my covenant...I will give them an everlasting name which shall never perish.'
>
> Isaiah 56: iii-iv

After a pub lunch in the delightful village of Bridge, we sat in Peter's lounge and on to my lap jumped his cat Hawksmoor, named after Peter's favourite architect. Unfortunately, he had a severe flea infestation and as I stroked him, they kept jumping on me. Having three cats myself, I pointed out to him the benefits of Nuvan flea spray. But Peter repeatedly rose from his chair to personally remove any fleas which he noticed on me. This was somewhat disconcerting as we enjoyed endless cups of tea and the fun of conversing on our love affair with the high male voice. He said that never before had he met anyone who listened daily to James Bowman.

The uniqueness of my daily listening was later incorporated into a card given the heading 'Day After Day', to commemorate James' live performance and recording of Frances Grier's anthem, 'Day After Day, O Lord of my Life.' It was specially written for the Rodolfus Choir and James Bowman in

1994, and performed in the beautiful, late-Gothic architecture of Eton College Chapel, magically lit by a mere dozen candles. The Piece is a setting of 'Song 76', from Rabindranthath Tagore's *Gitanjali*, in his own English translation from the Bengali, and described by Grier in the CD booklet Notes, as a 'combination of mystical adoration and a burning energy ... typical of much of Hindu spirituality'. My sole disappointment was that James had only one solo: 'Day After Day, O Lord of my life, shall I stand before thee face to face? With folded hands, O Lord of all worlds, shall I stand before thee face to face? ... And when my work shall be done in this world, O King of Kings, alone and speechless shall I stand before Thee face to face?'

In a further gesture, at his home in Kent, Peter insisted on concluding our time together by singing to me. His choice was Purcell's 'One Charming Night', (recorded by James in April, 1988.) We said an affectionate farewell in the warm rain, Peter telling me how much he'd enjoyed my visit, and have remained in touch, meeting up on many occasions. Indeed, Peter has recently appointyed me his literary executor and written the Foreword for my 2007 book, *The Life of Bosworth – A Cat*.

He thought that James was very lucky to have my devotion, and saw him as a rival to 'avoid wherever possible'. It was through Peter that I came into contact with Alan Ridout's Literary Works Executor, Robert Scott, which led ultimately to obtaining Alan Ridout's remarkable 1985 *Soliloquy*.

Childhood and Privacy

> Set apart. First out down the aisle
> Like brides. Or those boys
> Who were permitted
> To leave the study early for music
> practice

> Privileged and unenvied, left alone
> In the four bare walls to face
> the exercise,
>
> Eyes shut, shoulders straight back,
> Cold hands out
> Above the keys. And then the savagery
> Of the piano music music's
> going wrong.
>
> Seamus Heaney, 'The Bereaved',
> Bodies and Souls, *Electric Light*,
> 2001

From the commission of *A Toccata of Galuppi's* to completion took three years, and an extensive correspondence with Dr Arthur Wills, OBE. He finished the piece on my birthday, 26th January. But before the first performance at Hinckley music club, I was given the opportunity of at last meeting its composer in the vast, cold space of Ely Cathedral. This small, private commission lay at the heart of my entire and special time with James Bowman, this incomparable and irreplaceable artist. It was truly the pearl on the Madonna's cloak in Leonardo's dark Cave, as magical as rippling water in the warm dusk.

It seemed entirely appropriate that I was introduced to the composer of my piece in the austere place where James had passed his childhood and adolescence, having been 'packed off' to boarding school by his mother at the 'age of eight', in Festival of Britain year: 'She couldn't wait to pack me off,' he told me. In fact, at this time, in 1951, he was ten years old, but he always described himself to me as having been eight.

The misery of homesickness whilst at boarding school is beautifully evoked by W.G. Sebald, writing of his friend, Frederick Farrar, who was sent to boarding school at the age of eight: 'The great pain of separation ... was with me for a long time, especially before going to sleep or when I was just tidying my things.'

James was sent to Ely from Jesmond, where he had been a chorister from the age of five at St Nicholas' Cathedral in Newcastle. 'I was a chorister briefly at the Cathedral of Newcastle, and then I moved to Ely where my mother sent me as a boarder.' It was after a period in the King's School Sanitorium at Ely with a throat infection, that his voice (and heart) had broken: 'When I came out again my voice had broken.' Also, it was in Ely that he had his first singing experiences as a senior with Dr Wills, and gave his first public performance as a countertenor under the guidance of Arthur Wills, his debut piece being Purcell's 'Here the Deities Approve'.

I first contacted Arthur Wills for the purpose of attempting to discover boyhood recordings of James, but nothing was unearthed. Interestingly, I've just come across such a piece in a recent entry to *The Boy Choir and Soloist Directory*, which reads as follows: 'Former boy soprano James Bowman has given a private recording of himself singing as treble, to the British Library Sound Archive. No commercial recording exists.' As he grows older, James is clearly becoming aware of the need to document his legacy.

James told me in conversation that Arthur was 'a dear old thing. He was like a father to me at Ely', although Arthur's response to this was surprise and to say that he sometimes felt 'ignored and overlooked'. I have numerous friendly letters from Arthur Wills, including one in which he told me of his struggle to get James through his Grade 1V piano exams. I also have Arthur's book on *The Organ*, which I remember reading on an aeroplane before falling asleep on my way to Rhodes. Also, during the course of our lengthy correspondence, 1991-1994, he sent me a copy of his retirement concert of July 1990, which James had attended, and where he once again performed his first debut piece from long ago:

> Here the Deities approve
> The god of Music and of Love;
> All the talents they have lent you,
> All the blessings they have sent you,
> Pleas'd to see what they bestow,
> Live and thrive so well below.
>
> Purcell, 'Here the Deities Approve', countertenor solo from 'Welcome to all the Pleasures', *Ode for St Cecilia's Day*, 1683

How prophetic an aria! James was to enjoy a lifelong association with this plangent composer, the greatest setter of English words before Britten, (who was born on St Cecilia's Day, November 22nd) and Britten's musical ancestor. 'He also sings a piece by Purcell which he sang on his first public appearance as a countertenor in a King's School concert around 1960 I think,' wrote Arthur Wills in the letter wrapped around the tape that he gave me. (According to James, the debut concert took place in 1957 when he was aged sixteen.) On Radio 3's *In Tune*, on Thursday 12th October, 2006, James Bowman was in conversation with Sean Rafferty, discussing his forthcoming 65th birthday Recital of English Song, 16th–20th Century, at Blythburg Church, Suffolk. It was to take place on October 14th, with Andrew Plant on piano, beneath the famous Angel roof. James mentioned that this celebratory programme would include his debut piece by Purcell, 'Here the Deities Approve'. According to James, 'There is nothing better than to sing a Purcell song in the right venue and with the right accompanist – it is one of life's great experiences.'

According to the singer Guillermo Silva Marin in *My Baritone-Tenor Transition:*, 'Voice is generally defined by colour or timbre rather than by range ... any singer regardless of where they find themselves classified must deal with issues of vocal identity.'

James Bowman told me that his transition from boy treble to male alto at the age of sixteen had been a gradual and relatively straightforward process, but on another occasion, he told me that it had been 'sudden and traumatic'. He had always been happy singing in the upper register and was deeply attached to the repertoire for the male high voice. It seems that from an early age, James took confident ownership of his instrument and was happy with his personal choice.

He likened singing countertenor to playing the viola, as his range is similar, and the role of the alto singer is analogous to that of the viola in an orchestra. The countertenor or alto clef is the C clef, placed upon the third line of the stave for the use of countertenor or alto voices, and the viola. James mentioned that as a chamber music player of distinction, Benjamin Britten's chosen instruments were the viola and piano: 'Ben loved the viola, so often regarded as the "strange and awkward" instrument.'

James has always acknowledged that 'singing high perpetually is odd' and that he was teased about it at school, but for him it was a technical challenge, not a psychological one. He explained when questioned by me that the instrumental quality and expressiveness of his voice is closest to a violin, and when asked how he produces that sound, expanded on this in discussions on Radio 3: 'By using the edge of your vocal cords and neglecting the central part, which is the bass area. It's like playing harmonics on a violin. I can sing bass – I use it to warm up with before I sing countertenor. But I can't keep it up for long – it feels odd.'

Interestingly, Eva Mayer Schay, a violinist, for many years a member of the English National Opera Orchestra, told me recently that she is indifferent to the sound of the countertenor voice, 'except,' she added, unaware of this memoir, 'James Bowman.'

James said to me that technique was solely his responsibility; mine was emotional response. Through my written response I had added new dimensions to his work, and that is what he wished to document in his proposed book of my letters. What he did not envisage is that I would write a memoir of my own: after reading my manuscript, Sonia Ribeiro said, 'I think that James Bowman will come to regret the ending of your friendship, although he will never relent on the matter of your private memoir.'

It was Arthur Wills who first wrote to me and suggested a small commission piece for James' 25th Anniversary Concert at St John's; he sensed an opportunity:

Ely, 15th September, 1991

Dear Ms Handy,

I'm very glad that you like the extracts from my concert recording – it was done simply as a memento for me. I wonder whether you have this BBC Radio 3 concert, a tape of which I enclose? I wrote *Love's Torment* for James many years ago. It consisted of three songs then, and after singing them at a Wigmore Hall concert, he asked me to extend the work by adding a fourth – 'Sweet Angel Devil.' He also sings Rodney Bennet's *Times Whiter* series. If you would like to retain this tape, please do so. James has approached Ted Perry about recording some of this material but without success so far! Nothing to prevent you trying though!

One thought which occurred to me on reading of the projected concert at St John's is: would you like to commission a short piece for James to sing at this? The idea may appeal as a unique way of demonstrating your appreciation of James' art over the years. Let me know what you think.

> With every good wish, yours sincerely,
> Arthur Wills

Arthur Wills was an organist-composer in the Anglican tradition: 'In you come with your cold music till I creep thro' every nerve.' (*A Toccata of Galuppi's* by Robert Browning.)

I was first put on Arthur Wills' trail by Christopher Campling, the Dean of Ripon, who replied to my enquiry with the following letter, including Dr Wills' address, which preceded the letter of July 30th, 1991, from Arthur Wills, and which enclosed the photograph:

> The Minster House
> Ripon
> July 10th, 1991

Dear Mrs Handy,

Thank you very much for your letter of 28th June about James Bowman. I agree with you strongly about his voice; It is unique and very, very beautiful, and indeed, as beautiful as ever as we heard when he gave the concert in Ripon Cathedral.

I am afraid I cannot help you about recordings of his voice in the distant past... None of my cassettes go back as far as him; I knew him in the middle fifties, and of course, cassettes were not being used then, only the old tapes, and I haven't got anything of his on them either.

The only person I know who might be able to help you is the Assistant Organist at Ely at the time James was a chorister – Dr Arthur Wills, OBE ... I know that he is in touch with James....

So that puts you on the trail.

> With best wishes,
> Christopher Campling

By the time of James' *Messiah* performance at Ely, in June, 1998 – 'I shall be singing straight down the nave!' he told me – the enchantment was at its height, enhanced by the glorious summer weather, and always at every live concert he singled me out to sing to me. Just a few days earlier at Hampton Court Summer Musical Festival, he had changed his programme to give me Handel's *'Verdi prati'* aria from *Alcina*, because I'd asked hopefully if it was included. In Ruggiero's aria *'Verdi prati'*, he bids a sad farewell to the paradise in which he was bewitched by Alcina. Originally written for 'first singer' in 1735, the castrato Carestini, it is one of the most glorious of all Handel's arias:

> Green pastures and pleasant woods
> lose their beauty,
> Just as in nature,
> Where the fair flowers
> and the running rivers are transitory,
> So too will your beauty
> Change and disappear.

Talking with me in the wind and rain during the interval, James promised to sing to me at Ely Cathedral in a few days' time, despite the fact that I wasn't to be seated in the nave because the complimentary seats had all been allocated. '"He was despised and rejected'," will be for you, Maxine.' I will always remember the raindrops on his green gabardine, as I stood beside him under a huge umbrella in the great Base Court of Henry VIII's palace, with my mother keeping a respectful distance under her large black umbrella. 'Night's my time,' he said, quoting from his sensual, sacred aria in Vivaldi's *Nisi Dominus*. (*'Cum dederit dilectis suis somnum,* For so he giveth his beloved sleep'.) And he kept his promise – Oh so sublimely – turning to me in the north transept, to give me Handel's wonderful aria and leave me in suspended ecstasy…waiting for the next time. Like St Teresa in Bernini's famous sculpture, I was to await the second arrow from my 'angel guest', both tender and cruel.

Handel's *Messiah* at Ely Cathedral on June 19th, 1993, was a performance to mark the launch of the Cathedral Music Endowment Fund. John Major and his wife had been invited to 'enhance' the occasion and grant it added publicity, but the Dean received a letter from him saying that sadly, they were 'unavailable'. James' ironic comment to me was that their presence would have been a joke, because Mrs Major was a Joan Sutherland fanatic. 'She has actually bothered to write a biography of her, if you can call it that, Maxine'. James had dreadful memories of working with Joan Sutherland in 1986; they were recording Handel's third English oratorio, *Athalia*, when James sang Joad, the High Priest, and 'the vain diva', as he called her, played the title role of the tyrannical queen. James cannot bear what he terms 'wobbly sopranos and woofy mezzos … all singing too loudly. He particularly loathed her 'incompetent' overuse of vibrato: 'In singing the greatest skill is needed in use of vibrato or it becomes wobble.' Michael Kennedy, in the *Oxford Dictionary of Music.*

It was most awkward for James to turn to me in the North Transept as he was supposed to be singing 'straight down the nave'. Nevertheless, he turned directly towards me to deliver his greatest arias – my mother was delighted and amazed – and the rest of the audience, including the front-row ecclesiastical dignitaries and Arthur Wills, were stunned.

Having courteously introduced me to his old teacher and friend, Arthur Wills, he remained in Ely until the early hours of the morning to work on my piece *A Toccata of Galuppi's*, a Scena for Countertenor and String Quartet. 'When you've performed a new piece you've been through earth, fire and water . . . learning new music is very stressful on the voice.' I'd travelled to Ely from London that day, and all the shops were closed in that remote Fenland town. My mother and I had eaten nothing and when, after more than three hours of music we rushed to the station, we found that we had missed our train (or would have done, had the train been running! – it takes Ely people a long time to explain anything!). We then thought that we were stranded in Ely for the night, but a taxi was provided to take us to Cambridge – and thence a train back to London. 'One needs to be keen for all this,' said my patient mother! At 1:30 in the morning we walked through Pimlico and arrived at our flat. This journey was typical of the effort I would make to see James in live performance. At that time I had small children for whom it was necessary to make elaborate overnight babysitting arrangements. I'd spent some of my own childhood in East Anglia and also lived in Cambridge for five years, so Ely and the Fens were very familiar to me. Ely is a place of freezings and burnings, beautifully evoked by the poet Geoffrey Hill:

> Crowned Ely stands beset
> by winds of straw-burning,
> by the crouched run of flame.
> Cambridge lies dark, and dead.
> Geoffrey Hill, 'Dark Land', in the *Canaan* collection

Geoffrey Hill had been Gregory Fellow in Poetry when I was at Leeds University and in my third year as an undergraduate, he was my Shakespeare tutor; Hill shared with us his love and knowledge of ancient languages.

When John Horden, my personal tutor at Leeds, a world expert in bibliography and textual criticism, first saw the newly appointed Geoffrey Hill (decades later to be described as

'England's most important living poet') wandering about in the corridors of the School of English, he said 'He always looks so miserable. That must be because he is a poet.' Hill had a lifelong passion for music and Milton; in 'G. F. Handel, Opus 6' he takes from Milton the title for his 2007 collection: 'each of itself a treatise of civil power'. John Horden so many years earlier also said of Hill, 'He thinks he *is* Milton'.

Peter McDonald, in the *Guardian*, Saturday 18th August, 2007, in his review of Geoffrey Hill's most recent collection, *A Treatise of Civil Power*, emphasises the parallels between Hill and his predecessor Milton, and using Milton's own words, he writes of Hill's admission of the '... inward and irremediable/disposition of man'. Hill's title is taken from Milton, and McDonald continues: 'The poet of *Paradise Lost*, an expert on man's fallen nature, is a pervasive presence in [Hill's] book.'

It always seemed strange to me that the prosaic John Horden, who, along with Geoffrey Hill, eventually took a Chair at Cambridge University, was a descendant of the Earl of Southampton, Shakespeare's patron and possible dedicatee and inspiration of his *Sonnets*. Professor Horden owned a decorative sword which was supposed to have belonged to the Earl. A recently discovered portrait of Henry Wriothesley, the Earl of Southampton, painted in the early 1590s, was originally mistaken for a woman, as Henry is wearing a dress. In England in the sixteenth century being androgynous was considered a mark of aristocratic birth.

I used to call James my 'Fenland flame'; his descriptions of his boyhood in Ely revealed the deeply private to me, on those rare occasions when he confided in me.

I believe that real intimacy or equality of friendship came as rarely to James, as it did to Henry James. Both Minny Temple and Constance Fenimore Woolson looked to Henry James for more than he was prepared to give. He drew them into communion, then left them exposed when he withdrew into the sanctuary of his writing. In his novel *The Master*, Colm Tóibín describes Henry James as 'a man whose artistic gifts made his career a triumph but whose private life was haunted by loneliness and longing and whose sexual identity remained unresolved.'

The occasions when James Bowman confided any fact about his personal life came hardly, and call for special comment. Minor fears about his health, or the state of his voice would occasionally surface, and latterly he excused his occasional abruptness towards me and moodiness by revealing a crisis in his personal life, and the problems associated with his by then, dying mother. He sometimes asked for my advice when suffering from 'emotional problems', as he told me that he found me frighteningly perceptive, highly intelligent, and had a great respect for me. 'I love discourse with intelligent women, Maxine', he said effusively, but there was a pattern of involvement and withdrawal which was sometimes in opposition to my own. He was fully aware that he was viewed by some as a 'careless user', and in my case he tried hard to be an 'attentive soul'. He rarely made promises but at this time the door remained open and there was no sense of finality. Despite his violent and sudden mood swings, I was always left with hope and the possibility of renewal.

It now appears to me that James' concert at Hereford Cathedral was emblematic. It took place on Thursday, 25th August, as part of the Three Choirs Festival, and included James' world première performance of Alan Ridout's *Canticle of Joy*. Ridout was in the audience and died of cancer a few weeks later. It had been written especially for James, with Martyn Hill, tenor; the theme of the songs is 'a profound happiness that could not be rediscovered'. As James came on stage he gave me a slow, intimate smile and proceeded to sing to me. My mother said, 'My dear, his skin is flawless, is he wearing make-up?' I replied that it didn't matter either way. In the following year, 1997, James gave a wonderful performance of Alan Ridout's *Songs of Thomas Hardy*. They were part of the Alan Ridout Memorial Concert, a tribute to Alan Ridout by his friends and colleagues, which took place on Monday, April 21st.

Occasionally, when angry, James accused me of intruding on his privacy, but then apologised for what he thought a most unjust accusation, and invited me to participate in that very privacy, away from the public domain. Indeed, as I came to know him better I felt further and further removed from the public domain, even though I was only seeing him within the context of his audience. Like the Catholic Queen Henrietta Maria, a portrait of whom he had sent me, I lived in the intimacy of my pearls. In his imagination I became his sole audience, precious and trusted, and knew his secret soul. Constance Fenimore Woolson in her stories spoke of the 'sanctuary where each soul waits for its interpreter'.

In Simon Nowell-Smith's wonderful 1947 Compilation *The Legend of the Master* – both public and private, he recounts an Edmund Gosse anecdote in which Henry James appears to reveal inmost tensions and frustrations. Hugh Walpole regarded him as being probably emotionally bisexual. Henry's *The Lamp at the Window* experience can be interpreted in many ways, but Gosse's account is certainly interesting:

> He disclosed to a friend, or rather admitted such a friend to a flash or glimpse of deeper things. The glimpse was never prolonged or illuminated, it was like peering down for a moment through some chasm in the rocks dimmed by the vapour of a clash of waves. One such flash will always leave my memory dazzled. I was staying alone with Henry

James at Rye one summer and as twilight deepened we walked together in the garden ... He spoke of standing on the pavement of a city, in the dusk, and of gazing upwards across the misty street, watching, watching for the lighting of a lamp in a window on the third storey. And the lamp blazed out, and through bursting tears he strained to see what was behind it, the unapproachable face. And for hours he stood there, wet with the rain, brushed by the phantom hurrying figures of the scene, and never from behind the lamp was for one moment visible the face. The mysterious and poignant revelation closed, and one could make no comment, ask no question, being throttled oneself by an overpowering emotion. And for a long time Henry James shuffled beside me in the darkness, shaking the dew off the laurels...nor was the silence broken when suddenly we entered the house and he disappeared for an hour.

Edmund Gosse

To see James in Ely and to be with him where he had lived as a boy, was redolent with atmosphere and meaning for me. It deepened my understanding of the way in which James' voice defines an extraordinary space, reaching backward and upward. It opens out unexpected vistas. It contains morning light, narrow passageways, and dark cavernous pools. He told me of his first night in the dormitory at Ely, listening to the small boys crying and heartbroken. 'I have no affection for the place, it's too big and always cold...The school was a terrible place, Maxine, the bullying and beatings – but one adjusts and adapts, even to the dreadful food.' He enjoyed singing in the Cathedral, 'mostly to the bats', although said that as a boy treble, trained by Michael Howard, he had a very loud voice but was 'nothing special'. Evensong was 'the icing on the cake', and the exquisite Lady Chapel was 'inspirational, Maxine!' Begun by Alan of Walsingham in 1321, Ely's Lady Chapel was completed just before the Black Death in 1349. The sculptures were all 'beheaded' in 1541, soon after the Dissolution, and the decorated gothic Lady Chapel was laid waste. In 1643, the Chapel was stripped of its stained glass and for years it stood open to the elements, further eroding the delicate carvings of the interior. Eventually windowed with clear glass, the Lady Chapel of James' childhood was light, symmetrical and cool, but replete with tragic echoes of its lost past. In 2000, The Dean of Ely commissioned the sculptor David Wynne to restore 'Our Lady' to her chapel. In the words of Germaine Greer, writing in Arts Comment in *The Guardian*, Monday 10th September, 2007: 'The Chapel's austere monochrome was harshly assailed in 2000 by the installation of a life-size effigy of a woman with raised arms ... the carved female figure dominates and dwarfs the whole space.' She is painted in electric blue and gilt. 'The Virgin is here depicted at the moment of Conception, as she utters the words from St Luke's Gospel.' Germaine Greer describes the Marian statue as a 'horror', in need of destruction by modern iconoclasts.

I think that James' preference for smaller venues arose from his years in the great vaulted space of Ely Cathedral. His deep need for intimacy and dialogue found artistic satisfaction through pieces like Handel's Italian Chamber Duets – intimate in mood and composed most probably for the drawing rooms of Italian aristocrats, with Handel himself at the keyboard. James said that returning to Ely was 'like stepping into a dream', and talked to me of his pleasure as he looked across at the rising Cathedral, in retracing his boyhood, driving through the dark Fens, his former cross-country running route, 'I remember when the river froze from Ely to Cambridge, Maxine.' To a small, vulnerable boy at such a remote boarding school, it must have seemed an infinite distance to home in Jesmond.

James loved this quotation from the Book of Ruth, which accompanied his Ely flowers from me:

> Intreat me not to leave thee, or to return from following after thee:
> for whither thou goest, I will go...
>
> Book of Ruth

His most poignant revelation of his years at Ely concerned his mother: 'My mother never visited me, well, hardly ever , because it was too far...' After such moments of introspection he would fall into a sort of trance or disappear to be alone. I believe that James' compulsion to disappear suddenly and be alone goes back to the trauma of the lack of privacy in his schoolboy life at Ely. Like Emily Dickinson's Visitor in Marl, he 'Caresses – and is gone'. Peter Giles once commented to me: 'Just when you think you've got him, he walks away!'

When Celia Ballantyne, Promotions Manager for Hyperion Records, called in at his home to deliver some documents, she told me that for a brief interlude he was very pleasant, and then abruptly disappeared saying that he must go and feed the Abyssinian cats, Max and Maud, his 'little boy and little girl'. Celia had been privileged to work closely with James for nine months and during this time, described him to me thus, in a letter dated 6 March, 1992: 'A nicer and more appreciative man you could never hope to meet'. But some months later her opinion shifted and her warmth towards him evaporated. James had invited her to his 50th birthday celebration recital at Versailles, and then, having taken his companion, completely ignored her. 'Next time,' she vowed, 'I'll take my brother!' James' behaviour, she told me, had shocked her by its rudeness. Also, he had become irritated by her attempt to change his image for marketing purposes, by having him photographed more informally, wearing a 'designer jumper', the colours of which were intended to emphasize his remarkable eyes, which no photograph ever did justice to. It worked for a while until James became annoyed because she was fixated on the 'superficial'. Celia also told me that he has an attic full of scrapbooks with cuttings of his performances, but all undated. 'A biographer's nightmare' she said. When I travelled huge distances to see him he frequently said, with great satisfaction, 'You have come a very long way, Maxine, such a very long way to see me.' I could never forget this image of the lost boy, confined to the sanatorium with a severe throat infection, the aching in his throat like the voice he had lost, apart from him and howling…far away. I sensed that in the sanatorium, he had endured overwhelming loss. My mother and I noticed his facial ticks before the performance at Ely. The pain returned to me at Marjorie King's Memorial Concert in David Munrow's Hinckley when he had sung to me and laid his hand on my arm like a haunting ghost. 'Thou shalt no more be termed Forsaken, neither shall thy land any more be termed desolate.' Watching his performance and grace I had wanted to add my own presence to the beautiful image before me. We discussed his 'blueness' and love of the colour green, the colour of nature, and in the Middle Ages, the 'colour of true love', which signifies life and hope and brought with it in time, these very memories.

> Green how I love you green.
> Green wind.
> Green boughs.
> The ship on the sea
>   and the horse on the mountain.
>   Lorca, 'Sleepwalking Ballad'

I was fascinated by James' absorption in melancholy events and the reversal of fortune. His abiding obsession was with the Tay Bridge disaster of 1879; his preoccupation with it and railway journeys in general went back to early childhood. His mother and stepfather had indulged this obsession by buying him books on the subject. I remember telling him that the old Liverpool Street Station (before work began to rebuild it at the end of the 1980s) had been my frequent meeting place with my father, after visiting my aunt Irene in Edmonton or seeing a play at the Old Vic. I have always thought of it as my father's very own railway station, described by W. G. Sebald, as 'one of the darkest and most sinister places in London, a kind of entrance to the underworld…full of ghosts'. James especially loved the West Highland Line with its high viaducts and wonderful landscape; we sent each other a number of Scottish postcards.

I remember listening to James' poignant exposition on the Tay Bridge disaster, on Radio 3, I think: 'This is a different kind of bridge, pleased if you stop halfway across to take deep soundings, ask yourself if you can count on being alive next day.'

He loves trains, and all model making, especially toy theatres, which he builds and collects. Miniaturisation is a way of being in control. James enjoyed watching Nick Parke's Wallace and Gromit plasticine Stop/Motion animations; I sent him a card of 'Gromit Knitting' which amused him greatly.

According to Freud, the great Leonardo remained like a child for the whole of his life: 'It is said that all great men are bound to retain some infantile part. Even as an adult, he continued to play, and this was another reason why he often appeared uncanny and incomprehensible to his contemporaries.' James sometimes said to me, 'You and I are playing!'

Seated together in September, 1997, on the wooden pew in St Mary's Church, Hinckley, we leaned towards each other and he spoke to me of his feelings, memories and fears: 'And as I leaned, I know I felt Love's face...'

'You have children, Maxine,' he said, 'you have a boy, Maxine, a boy. You would never send your children away, Maxine, you'd go mad without them.' He said that he 'couldn't go back to teaching the boys' and candidly told me that I mustn't think him clever: 'I'm not clever, Maxine. I wouldn't want you to think that. I only got to Oxford because of my voice, not for any other reason. I should have read English; I'd have been frightfully good at it! Or music.' He was slightly flustered because I had asked for a 'Jamesian' inscription in my Britten book. 'Something clever, James, something Jamesian!' I said.

His most moving words on this wonderful but melancholy occasion referred to his earliest moments in relation to his genius, 'I didn't come out of my mother's womb like this, Maxine. I've had to work at it and take care of the voice.' He asked me how my own son Leon was coping with the changes of adolescence and the loss of his 'boy's voice': was he heartbroken? Was he mourning?

For Freud, Leonardo was a 'vulture child'; like James, he had had a mother but no father. In his *Notebooks*, Leonardo wrote: 'It seems that I was always destined to be so deeply concerned with vultures; for I recall as one of my very earliest memories that while I was in my cradle a vulture came down to me and opened my mouth with its tail and struck me many times with its tail against my lips.'

Because of this Leonardo was able to identify himself with the child Christ and his mother, the Blessed Virgin. Leonardo's art is full of mother figures and tender childhood moments. His *Virgin and Child with St Anne* is a dreamlike image of maternal love and divine androgyny.

> The familiar smile of fascination leads one to guess that it is a secret of love. It is possible that in these figures Leonardo has denied the unhappiness of his erotic life and has triumphed over it in his art, by representing the wishes of the boy, infatuated with his mother, as fulfilled in this blissful union of the male and female natures.
>
> Sigmund Freud on Leonardo's painting, *The Virgin and Child with St Anne*

The Commission

> Then they left you for their pleasure: till in due time, one by one,
> Some with lives that came to nothing, some with deeds as well undone,
> Death stepped tacitly and took them where they never see the sun.
>
> Robert Browning, *A Toccata of Galuppi's*

James gave me a moving account of his times at Ely, and his deep love for the small and exquisite Gloucester Cathedral. When he sat beside me in High Wycombe Church, just before his world-premiere performance of Geoffrey Burgon's *Merciless Beauty*, I gave him his birthday present of Pindar's *Odes* and he gave me his picture of *Paradise*, the great East Window of Gloucester Cathedral, which commemorates the fallen at the battle of Crécy (1346) and beneath which he has so many times performed. The tomb of the murdered Edward II is near the high altar. Also, James told me of his love for ecclesiastical architecture and of singing in cathedrals. He said that keeping in touch with his Cathedral origins 'is very good for both my soul and perspective as a singer'. I remember my phone call to him to discuss his 'Nightblue' bouquet. 'Hello James – this is Maxine. Do please let me know when you would like your

Merciless Beauty flowers – especially as a solely Blue bouquet will take some time for thought.' He enjoyed setting me increasingly difficult tasks to give him pleasure.

Arthur Wills' composer's programme notes describe perfectly the meaning of my special piece for James: '*A Toccata of Galuppi's* was commissioned by Maxine Handy to mark the 50th birthday of James Bowman. Browning's poem deals in a superbly imaginative way with Venetian life and music in the mid-18th century, when the countertenor and male soprano voices were at their greatest peak of development and renown.' This first performance took place in holy Trinity Church, Hinckley, at 7:30pm on Saturday 24th September 1994. On the 18th January 1994, Dr Wills OBE had sent me a kind letter with a copy of the score:

> Dear Maxine.
>   I thought that you would like to have a copy of the score you commissioned, so here it is! I'm sure James is most grateful for this very tangible evidence of your admiration for his art, and I'm also sure that he will do his best to programme it as soon as he can. It is indeed gratifying to have a piece which unites our mutual affection for both James and Venice, as well as his earlier singing experiences at Ely, closely associated with myself.
> With every good wish,
Yours sincerely,
Arthur

Peter Giles described Arthur Wills as an enormously tall man, of whom the boys at Ely were terrified, but teased mercilessly because of his prominent front teeth. When Peter became an alto lay clerk at Ely Cathedral, he had for a time studied harmony and counterpoint with Dr Wills. Arthur once confided to me that he had not found the boys easy, and was truly pleased to be retired and enjoying the freedom to lecture, compose, and tour for recital purposes.

To write my piece, Arthur Wills had to go to Venice in order to research some manuscripts of Galuppi's music. The great Venetian composer, Baldassare Galuppi, was born in 1706 on the island of Burano in the Venice Lagoon. In 1762 he became director of the prestigious Doges' Chapel of St Marks. He died on 3rd January, 1785 and was given a lavish funeral, at which the renowned castrato, Gaspare Pacchiarotti, sang. Galuppi's countless vocal compositions were not published and today, his manuscripts are scattered all over the world.

Arthur Wills was consistently courteous to me, but dropped me completely soon after *A Toccata of Galuppi's* received its first performance. On the day of the commission, I sent him a bouquet with a CD of the Galuppi Motets, and he bent down at Hinckley to give me a thank-you kiss. James was listening in to my conversation with Arthur, and James, having overheard his admiration for the 1994 disc of the Galuppi Motets, interrupted us to say, disapprovingly, 'Oh, yes, I take it you're referring to the recording by Gérard Lesne,' and pulling a face, he added, 'I've heard him in France; his voice is so quiet you can't even hear him at the back of a small concert hall. He's no good live!' James was clearly irritated by this French alto, and Arthur's liking for him. We then moved to the topic of Arthur's several compositions for organ. I admit that I have never really cared for organ music, finding it rather boring and organists somewhat frightening, pedantic figures. My young son attended the commission and was pleased when Dr Wills said, 'Hello, "Maxine", let me give you a kiss.'

From James I received a delightful, appreciative card, which made it all seem worthwhile. It depicted him, in a painting by June Mendoza, seated in front of his model theatre and holding in his left hand a miniature of Oberon from the famous Glyndebourne production by Sir Peter Hall:

> Dear Maxine,
> Just a note to let you know how delighted I am with your Commission, *Toccata of Galuppi's*. Arthur Wills and I spent most of last Wednesday going through it, prior to the rehearsals with the string players later this month. It is a marvellous piece, full of piquancy and harmonic twists. He has cleverly incorporated some of Galuppi's music into it, giving it a Baroque/Contemporary flavour. I hope you will be as pleased as I am.
> Best wishes,
> James

At this moment two examples of James' inconsistent behaviour occur to me. When I first suggested a commission for him it was to coincide with his 25th Anniversary concert at St John's. There was so little English or BBC interest in this occasion that James had to partially fund it himself, helped by his mother, and subsidise ticket prices – it was a very different story in France where his fame was renowned. He treated my original suggestion like an unwanted imposition and with some hostility, implying that I was trying to select his programme. 'The programme is chosen – I think I may choose my own repertoire and accompaniment.' At first I was deeply hurt and offended; I was only trying to give him pleasure! But as this suggestion had come from Arthur Wills and James was super-sensitive to any hint of control or domination by another, I forgave him and rose to the challenge of persuasion. When James spoke to Sue Lawley, on the 16th April 2000, on Radio 4's *Desert Island Discs* of his love for the sea, he said that one of his chosen books would be Daphne du Maurier's *Rebecca*: 'If I had been the heroine I'd soon have given Mrs Danvers "what for",' adding, 'and the drippy heroine herself a good slapping.' And when, in the same programme, he said that his chosen object was a Fabergé egg, and Sue Lawley asked him what he would do with it, 'Would you bury it in the sand?' he said no, he would just sit and contemplate it. This apparently trivial conversation struck me as implying an interesting identification with the female, combined with a loathing of domination by women. He always claimed that Handel wrote his greatest arias for female sopranos. 'The women get the best ones,' he said with envy, citing Handel's *Semele*.

James' sometimes nostalgic love of the infinite sea is also expressed by his passion for Britten's opera *Billy Budd* (from Melville's novel), especially the final epilogue of Edward Fairfax Vere, Captain of the *Indomitable* (sung by Peter Pears): 'I was lost on the infinite sea, but I've sighted a sail in the storm, the far-shining sail, and I'm content.'

James had been introduced to E. M. Forster, the librettist for *Billy Budd* by Britten, and had thought him most unpleasant: 'I hope you don't admire E. M. Forster, Maxine. I met him once and he was absolutely, absolutely...' Apparently, Forster was a terrible snob who loved living at others' expense, and a compulsive groper of handsome young men.

In early childhood, James had spent summer holidays in Donegal, a coastal retreat; he stayed with his grandmother in Armagh and enjoyed helping her with the drying after she washed up; this was one of James' favourite memories, once echoed by his amusing words to me when I handed him his very first gift of a book, Henry James' *A Little Tour in France*. 'Is it a tea towel?' James asked.

James, quite rightly did not want a contemporary piece alongside his otherwise Baroque programme, and much to my delight, Arthur's original suggestion for piano accompaniment (which horrified me as I knew that in general James loathed singing to a piano) was replaced by a String Quartet. 'I've always said, rather scathingly in the past, that singing with the piano reminds me of choir practice.' James' recording of solo songs with piano by Betty Roe, *The Music Tree,* has always seemed to me to be completely out of character, and I know that he disliked the disc.   James knew the Quartet players through his teaching work, and my piece was further delayed when the leader of the Quartet was in a road traffic accident, and to quote James 'has broken every bone in her body'. She was in the Radcliffe Infirmary in Oxford for a long time, but eventually made a complete recovery. James did not tell Arthur of this, so that task fell to me. Neither did he tell Arthur that he had moved out of London. James did not want to change the Quartet as he had promised it to his original choice and wished to keep his promise.   A second inconsistency typical of his mercurial temperament was his disdainful reference to Peter Hall as 'nothing but a manipulator, Maxine, moving my body about', and a later discourse on Radio 3 praising him as a great director! I grew used to these contradictory outbursts and often sent him Shakespeare's very appropriate words from *Twelfth Night*:

> Now the melancholy god protect thee, and the tailor make thy doublet of changeable taffeta, for thy mind is a very opal.

I later connected this with a poetic memory of my mother, and a small mystical piece I wrote for him. He once called me his 'sweet and kind little mystic Maxine'.

As I mentioned earlier, James' hobby is making and collecting model theatres. He loves to use his hands. He especially loves the Old Vic, so I generously made a present to him of all my Old Vic programmes from the great days of Laurence Olivier. All my life I'd been addicted to the Theatre and every available moment throughout my teenage years was spent at the Old Vic in Waterloo Road. These 'archive' programmes were associated with some of the happiest days of my youth and James was really pleased to be given them. In my teens, I often visited the National Gallery, and it was at the age of fifteen that I first encountered Leonardo's painting *The Virgin of the Rocks*. Leonardo worked on this painting throughout an epidemic of bubonic plague: in *The Flights of the Mind*, Charles Nicholl writes: 'In Leonardo, the mouth of hell has become a scene of serene benediction.'

On one occasion, James confided in me that he was anxious about a numbness and tingling in his left hand, worried that it might be 'a forerunner of arthritis'. He was inscribing my book at the time and said, 'when I'm holding my pen I suffer a loss of sensation and control…' I tried to reassure him and suggested that it might be repetitive strain injury from holding his score in cold, damp churches. I said that I'd speak to my doctor brother on his behalf. When I did so my brother recommended an excellent aromatherapist in his locality, and felt that James was probably suffering from stress and needed some individual attention. He felt that acupuncture was not advisable as in certain circumstances it could cause damage. James explained to me that his mother was seriously ill and in a hospice. 'She's crippled with arthritis, confined to a wheelchair, doubly incontinent, and totally blind, but her hearing is as acute as ever.' He told me that if they were speaking on the telephone and she heard his television in the background, she would tell him off, and he had to go and switch it off '*at once*'. He asked my advice on whether or not to send flowers for her birthday on the following day. 'And then there's Mum,' he had said to me during our very first conversation. On another occasion when I phoned him, he answered by saying, 'Thank God it's you, Maxine, and not my mother, I'm so pleased that it's you.'

In Harriet Vyner's 1999 biography of her friend the art dealer and gallery owner, Robert Fraser, known as 'Groovy Bob', who died of AIDS in 1986, she wonders whether his ambitious and adoring mother, Cynthia, in spite of the complications of their relationship, 'was able to ignore as unreal the imperfect side to his life and focus on his achievements'.

In the hot summer before the first performance of *Galuppi* I travelled to Brentwood in Essex to hear James in Scarlatti's wonderful *Salve Regina*; the recording followed later. I had once travelled all the way to Snape Maltings in Aldeburgh, and returned the same night – just to hear him sing this piece. The recital was on Saturday, 28th August, and formed part of the 1993 Snape Proms' Masters of the Baroque. It also included Vivaldi's *'Filiae maestae Jerusalem,'* his beautiful setting of the Miserere Psalm. After his performance, I saw James emerge from the shadows at the rear of the hall, just as Peter Pears was said to have done. James was accompanied by his helpers, including the bag-carrying Stephen, employed by Robert King. Stephen, to whom I had spoken on the phone, having been given his number by James, was wearing a Hawaiian shirt in lurid pinks, *and* smoking a Lambert and Butler cigarette; alongside him was Miles, his friend, dressed in motorcycle leathers.

'Put out that filthy cigarette!' James commanded, as Stephen approached to place James' bags in the boot of his car. Stephen obeyed at once. I watched them both walking away towards the moonlit trees, Stephen leading and James following with bowed head, in a reversal of the relationship between Oberon and Puck.

Earlier in my narrative, I mentioned that I incurred James' displeasure at Brentwood, for having 'inundated' him with books and letters: 'Once a week will do, Maxine!' But a few days later when I suggested that I stop writing to him he said emphatically 'Oh no, don't do that.' At this time his recording schedule was incredibly busy, especially during his huge 5-year Purcell series with Robert King and the King's Consort. I collected all his recordings, visited Harold Moore's in Great Marlborough Street, London, for any still only available on vinyl, and taped his every performance broadcast on Radio 3. For someone who has had to 'seek-out' his repertoire and is very careful of what he does, his discography is huge. Nobody even started to record poor Alfred Deller until he was in his fifties, and even James didn't really come into his own until mid-life. From his late forties to fifties was a golden time for James, some of his greatest recordings over a 35 year career come from this period, and include Handel's *Heroic Arias*, inscribed 'For Maxine – A Living Flame' and *English Arias* – 'For Maxine – Tracing each Herb and Flower'. The ravishing 'Yet Can I hear that Dulcet Lay', from Handel's *The Choice of Hercules* is part of the *English Arias* disc:

> Yet can I hear that dulcet lay,
> As sweet as flows the honey dew?
>
> Can I those wilds of joy survey,
> Nor wish to share the bliss I view?

I remember going to the *Ten Blake Songs* at the Wigmore Hall, and then recording the subsequent Radio 3 broadcast. 'He looks very h-o-m-o-s-ex-u-al doesn't he dear' said one elderly lady to another, emphasising and drawing out the word homosexual. Even educated people often thought that countertenors and castrati were synonymous. According to James, his lucrative, but noisy and not very intellectual French audiences were particularly guilty of this. Each attendance by me was preceded by morning Flowers, 'Joy cometh in the Morning', accompanied by an exquisite and appropriate quotation. Each gift contributed to a kind of tapestry or fresco, in which I developed patterns of interpretation which created an intimate and intricate connection with his work. Sometimes my words directly influenced his performances, 'I bring your cards to my performances, Maxine', he said, and there they were inside his wonderful old well-travelled music case. James once signalled to me at St John's Smith Square, to wait for him after the performance. He then came to fetch me 'backstage' where he took off his white tie and tails outfit and opened his small leather case, inside which was his folded blue check jacket and jeans. As he was getting changed, the needlewoman in me came out; my great-grandfather was a master tailor. I commented on the hundreds of tiny crease marks on the jacket, and suggested he have the fallen hem repaired as soon as possible.

Often, after a London concert I'd return home to Cheshire at about 3:30am and by dawn have written my response to his performance, to be posted by the morning – like the words of a favourite female soprano aria, transposed and recorded by James, from Handel's *Theodora*:

> As with rosy steps the morn
> Advancing, drives the shades of night,
> So from virtuous toils well-borne
> Raise thou our hopes of endless light,
> Triumphant Saviour, Lord of day;
> Thou art the life, the light, the way.

All my letters to James are precisely dated, so ten years of his UK performances are certainly documented in great detail – one could relive them through reading my words, just as if he was a painting by Leonardo, come alive, as he was in my vision of him.

The programme for the Commission was most interesting and wonderful, and included some of my favourite songs by Alan Ridout. My seven-year-old son and elderly mother attended the performance, and Leon sat between us, very pleased by James' attentiveness towards me, something he still remembers and treasures. Afterwards I had a few moments alone with James in the vestibule. He inscribed my score, using my Cross signature fountain-pen, which he held for some time admiring its burgundy and gold beauty, and telling me to 'be careful not to smudge the ink.' He understood the meaning of my pen and carefully replaced it in the leather Mont-Blanc case embellished with the symbol of a single snowflake. 'I knew that you, Maxine,' would dislike matching items; to have things that match is so suburban!'

As my little group walked along Vicarage Road in the rain, we saw James drive slowly by in his burgundy BMW. James only likes listening to his own recordings in the car, or so he says. Leon, who had presented some flowers to the quartet, admired the car and said he was hungry. So we found a late opening corner shop to buy some food and drink, and then left Hinckley.

Just before the performance James thanked me for the beautiful Roses which he had received that morning, and for his marvellous *Toccata of Galuppi's*: 'Your enthusiasm, Maxine, has born worthwhile fruit. You have given me a major piece of new repertoire for which I am very grateful. Without you none of this would have come about.' And at the end of the concert he enthusiastically discussed plans for a second performance at the Wigmore Hall or St John's. 'I'd like to do it in front of an audience where the average age is less than ninety!' Arthur favoured the Wigmore but James preferred St John's. 'You Maxine, will have many opportunities to hear this piece,' said James. I had gone to great trouble to make this a truly special celebration for James; I took ages choosing the commission card, Odilon Redon's pastel *Orpheus*.

> But even then that head, plucked from the marble-pale
> Neck, and rolling down mid-stream on the river Hebrus –
> That voice, that cold, cold tongue, cried out "Eurydice!"
> (Cried) 'Poor Eurydice!', as the soul of the singer fled,
> And the banks of the river echoed, echoed 'Eurydice!'
>
> *Nearing the Upper Air* (1988), Dramatic Scena for countertenor James Bowman. Words excerpted from C. Day Lewis' translation of Virgil's *Georgics*, conducted by Geoffrey Burgon. Burgon's setting, written in 1988 for the Stour Music Festival in memory of Alfred Deller: 'The story is given to a countertenor…'

James' emphasis on the drawn out word 'f-l-e-d' in Burgon's piece imitates the sounds of a fading male orgasm and withdrawal. 'Maxine, what is your favourite sensation in the whole world?' James once asked. 'Orgasm,' I replied. 'Quite so,' he said. 'Mine too.' James once described Nirvana as 'a never-ending spiritual orgasm'. He was always able to combine the physical with the spiritual.

My recording is inscribed 'That Voice cried out'.

Orpheus' greatest musical achievement was that of conquering death by winning Eurydice back from the Underworld. The Orpheus legend symbolises the power of music, but Orpheus ultimately failed in his quest to rescue Eurydice from Hades. In the earliest known written version of the myth, the Hellenistic poet Phanocles in 250 B.C. specifically relates that Orpheus was killed because after Eurydice's death, he was 'the first in Thrace to desire men and to disapprove the love of women', thus defining the Orpheus story as an origin myth of homosexuality. Ovid repeats this claim in his *Metamorphoses*, calling Orpheus the originator of male homosexuality. However,

Virgil's version in the Fourth *Georgic*, (which James told me he loved), the one used by Geoffrey Burgon in his *Scena*, avoids a definitive statement about Orpheus' sexuality, saying only that Orpheus rejected the interest and advances of women and was murdered by women because he disdained them (perhaps because he remained faithful to the memory of Eurydice).

An early cantata of 1707 (text by Cardinal Pamphili), specifically compares Handel to Orpheus. According to Ellen T Harris in her book *Handel as Orpheus: Voice and Desire in the Chamber Cantatas*, 'The Orpheus myth runs as a thread through Handel's life, its same-sex implications always available, but rarely obvious.' However, she also adds: 'Handel was a multifaceted personality; his love life remains private and veiled with no defining evidence about his desires or actions.' The same could be said of Henry James.

Harris believes that in the 18th century the image of Orpheus provides a double emblem of musician and homosexual, quoting one 18th century writer who defined homosexuality as 'the passion contrary to nature which the Thracian dames avenged by the massacre of Orpheus, who had rendered himself odious by gratifying it, the inconceivable appetite which dishonoured the Greeks and Persians of antiquity.'

Pamphili's erotic text for Handel's *Orpheus Cantata* abounds with sexual innuendo. All the animate and inanimate objects that Pamphili lists are attracted to Orpheus – including 'rocks', a familiar metaphor for the male sex organs and male sex generally. The musical references also have sexual subtexts; specifically, the verb 'to sing' can mean to have sexual relations.

However, Jonathan Keates repudiates any possibility of a 'gay', (homosexual) Handel and provides him with a long list of female conquests: 'Handel was very well built and lacked nothing in manliness ... the assumption that as a lifelong bachelor he must perforce have been homosexual is untenable in an 18th century context.'

On the 23rd August 1993, I had written to Ted Perry of Hyperion Records in an attempt to persuade him to record my SCENA for James plus String Quartet *A Toccata of Galuppi's* (a setting of the poem by Robert Browning): 'It is expected that it will receive two performances next year, the first in Hinckley, (where James Bowman is the president of the music society) and the second in London. The piece is a major work, lasting approximately 20 minutes.'

James and Arthur had both approached Ted on the subject of recording their SCENA but to no avail, and suggested that I 'have a go'. In the months following on from this first performance I wrote to him many times and asked him to reconsider! He did indeed agree to have a rethink and put it in his 'suggestion box', but ultimately decided that it was not commercially viable. When I met him in the Crypt of St John's, Smith Square, he told me that as my piece only lasted about 20 minutes with what else could he have filled the disc? I suggested some other pieces by Arthur Wills written for James, *The Hound of Heaven*, and a Britten String Quartet – probably the no 3, its theme being Venice. Britten composed the last movement shortly before his death. I think it would have been a most wonderful disc, and an expression of true devotion.

Earlier on I'd received a few warning indications from Arthur of James' temperamental, suspicious, and inconsistent nature, including his violent temper. James was perfectly capable of promising something and then forgetting it completely, although he undoubtedly meant it at the time. In the words of Lyndall Gordon on Henry James 'he sang arias to intention on the edge of action'.

This could be deeply disappointing and hurtful and give rise to disillusionment. On the 24th April 1993 Arthur had written to let me know that he had managed to finish the SCENA, adding 'Keep in touch, and you can gently nag James about putting on the piece!'

Despite all the excitement and glory of that supreme occasion, there was no second performance, or Radio 3 broadcast. How I wish they had been there to preserve the first and only live performance. I'd suggested a perfect scheduling opportunity to Nicholas Kenyon and he had seemed interested. I do not even have an amateur recording as a private memento, as obviously James would never give permission for his voice to be recorded in that way. Certainly I would not have asked him to consent to such a thing, so I must simply treasure the memory, and the moments after his performance when he invited me to join him in a bow, wrapping me in the glittering mantle of his fame. My final words to him that evening, as we said farewell, were from his favourite Gospel of St Matthew:

> For where your treasure is
> There will your heart be also
>
> Matthew

Along with the letters and ghosts of Flowers, I keep that day in the dark of my heart. 'That I may never forget Thee'. The disappointment of no promised second performance at a prestigious London venue, was immense. But true heartbreak and perpetual absence were yet to come; I still seemed to serve a useful purpose. Like Ruggiero in the erotic magical garden of Handel's enchantress Alcina, I was 'held captive in a kind of dream by the promise of endless ecstasy'. (Robert Carson, A director's note.) '*Alcina* concludes when all magic spells are exhausted; it is the heroine who vanishes, and with her, all her cruelty, her beauty, her love, her pain and her mystery.' The ruins of her now deserted palace are submerged by the sea and disappear into a sinister underground cave; nevertheless, 'our compassion, our love, our memories and even our gratitude, are for her alone.' (Ivan A. Alexandre, *A Necromancer Amid his own Enchantments*.)

When things were perfect, James too ascended to a seemingly unattainable realm, so the epiphanies described were not mine alone. 'When things are perfect, Maxine, it is for me just as it is for you, as you describe it,' he told me.

My mind scans these scenes from a vanished past, both ecstatic and anguished, to evoke a series of pictures of James' genius. On Sunday 7th March, 1993, at St Giles' Cripplegate, near the Barbican, James knelt reverentially by me after his performance of Britten's *Abraham and Isaac*, and admired my small Siamese Cat brooch, which I wore at all his performances. It was like the twilight atmosphere of Leonardo's *Annunciation*; I felt truly blessed. However, I was sitting next to a friend and sharing my small carton of orange juice with him. As James knelt beside me, he glowered at my friend and cut him dead when he attempted to exchange a few words. He then pointedly thanked me for Henry James' *A Little Tour in France* and said how much he had enjoyed it, because it included all the places which he too had visited. 'I suppose the Aldeburgh lot are here,' he said dismissively, and aplogised to me for his abrupt departure, saying 'I've got to run across to the Barbican. Rostropovich is playing there tonight and I've got to say hello to him, to that bloody imbecile!' The musically brilliant 'Slava' was one of Britten's closest friends, an irritating man/child who enjoyed dressing up in silly outfits and playing pranks. He once disguised himself as a Russian bear.

An amusing incident had occurred before the beginning of the concert at St Giles. A very large harp was needed for Britten's Canticle, *The Death of St Narcissus*, to be performed later in the concert. This harp was obscuring James' view of me, so despite having taken the platform in black tie and tails, ready to sing, he lifted up the harp and moved it out of his line of vision. The audience looked astonished. On the midnight train back to Cheshire, my friend made no comment on the concert, but said simply, 'He did not like us sharing an orange juice.'

At King's College Chapel, Cambridge, on Monday, November 8th, 1993, he'd given me Bach's *'Agnus Dei'* and contemptuously ignored my friend, seated beside me. During the interval, he came over to thank me for his birthday flowers and tell me that he had sent me a very special card. He used his score to shield us from my friend and other people in the audience, whom he described as 'trying to intrude on us'. As he left, James gave my companion an insulting and dismissive glare.

'I saw him, trying to lean against you … I felt like hitting him, hitting him,' James later told me.

> An intimacy is often intensified by the presence of an excluded third.
> A S Byatt, *The Virgin in the Garden*

After the concert at King's, I watched James walk away across the floodlit quadrangle before I walked in the opposite direction down towards the misty river bank.

> He was very tall, well over six feet, with…black hair, beautifully cut, short and conventional…His lips were large and full…His shoes were beautifully polished…His voice was clear and belling…full of a thick-blooded mixture of confidence and desire…he gave me the impression of

Burning in Blueness

> wanting to eat huge meals with gusto, and fly first class at great speeds.
>
> A S Byatt, *The Biographer's Tale*

His irritation and exasperation with me at Brentwood Cathedral on Saturday, 2nd July 1994, seemed to threaten the impending Commission, but this fear proved unfounded. Instrumentalists irritated by James' occasional lateness included the first violinist of the King's Consort. At Brentwood, when James seemed never to be appearing, he threw his bow to the floor where it clattered as he glared at his watch. But musicians with whom James works closely are generally complimentary; scholars often find him rude and moody. Robert King first encountered the 'terrifying 6ft 2ins James Bowman' in 1972, when, as a twelve-year-old boy treble, he stood alongside him. They were recording the solo sections of the Purcell 'Te Deum' and 'Jubilate' with the choir of St John's College, Cambridge. Robert King later wore out his LP of this recording, listening to James' magnificent singing. According to Robert King, this boyhood worship had changed into adult obsession, and the achieved desire of working with him. In a rather bland but anxious letter to me in 1997, Robert said:

> Dear Maxine,
> I agree with your thoughts about the wonderful James Bowman. We are very lucky indeed to have such a marvellous musician and personality in our midst; indeed, long may it last!
>
> With best wishes,
> Robert

Occasionally, Robert King would push a reluctant James into a so-called 'fully-staged' production, usually for reasons of financial backing. Handel's *Ottone*, with James in the title role, was scheduled for Thursday, 12 November 1992, at the Royal Naval chapel, Greenwich. The next day, it was to be taken to Japan, (the Japanese were sponsoring the production and subsequent recording), and a second 'fully-staged' performance was to be given at the Queen Elizabeth Hall on Monday, 25th January, 1993. James telephoned me during rehearsals to warn me of the under funded, shoddy production. 'It's worse than at school, Maxine, more like Toytown. I'd give it a miss.' When I attended the performance at Greenwich, the singing was wonderful, but the production terrible. The 'costumes' seemed to be anything the singers could find at home, and the opera so under-rehearsed that Jennifer Smith missed her cue. James walked to the edge of the 'stage' and raised his hand to his brow as if looking for her out at sea. As a result of this, he had to repeat his desolate aria, *'Tanti affani'*, written for Senesino in January, 1723. So I was delighted.

James is aware that the pre-performance adrenalin rush can make him difficult and that is why he has always said 'I prefer to work with people I know!'

James told me that when I had upset him by something I'd said, ('Why do you tell me these things?') he would brood on it for weeks or even months. He was deeply sensitive over the way he was 'looked at'. Even at this time some people still found countertenors not sublime but ridiculous and even he, the greatest of them all, was 'terrified of being laughed at'. I made the mistake of telling him that at one of his performances of Scarlatti's *Salve Regina* in the Barber Institute of Fine Arts at Birmingham University, on 5th January, 1995, I was seated behind two female students and their mother who were laughing uncontrollably at the falsetto sound and suggested throwing their roses at him as a token of his absurdity. I had reprimanded them and asked them to be quiet as they were preventing others from enjoying the performance. I told James to let me know if I had inadvertently said anything to upset him, and please discuss it with me, but he said that he preferred to 'let these things lie'.

According to Peter Ostwald, Glenn Gould, the celebrated and eccentric pianist, suffered from a combination of the two opposing impulses: 'stay with me' and 'keep your distance'. Beethoven's biographer, Maynard Solomon, has called this dilemma a 'conflict between a defensive narcissism and a wild thrusting desire to break out of a painful isolation'. Within James Bowman, there existed a paradoxical combination of vulnerability with superiority in his relations with others, a certain helplessness, but also the feeling of being the centre of the universe. Certainly, he did not want to behave like a typical world class artist; he did not play the prima donna. He usually came across as remarkably modest and endearingly unpretentious. 'I can learn as much from young people as they can learn from me,' he said, and he was not interested in the 'trappings of success'.

I need not have worried that the Commission was under threat – he was much too professional for that and we usually overcame our temporary misunderstandings. He willingly conceded that he sometimes 'misunderstood' me, and his off-handedness changed to affability. '…I spoke to Arthur Wills this morning and agreed that I would be the dedicatee of his new piece. All is now arranged for the first performance. It will be on Saturday 24th September at my Music Club at Hinckley, Leicestershire. Midland Arts are subsidising it and are going to give the event suitable publicity. Here now is my definitive UK Diary of Engagements…'

A Living Flame

All that I have written is as nothing to you
Maxine

Tensions reached a climax at James' The Raptured Soul concert in the King's Hall, Ilkley on Wednesday, February 11th 1998. Initially, he had eagerly commanded me to come, especially as for me it was relatively close to home and an easy train journey via Leeds. A few days before the recital he phoned me and told me not to come, saying it would be 'a ghastly occasion, with ghastly people'. It would be much better for me to stay at home with his recorded work and listen to him there. He told me to reserve my 'mystical talents' for his 'special occasions', and that the journey was impossibly difficult for me. In fact it was one of the easiest I'd ever undergone! During the performance he did sing to me, most beautifully but it was an unresponsive very 'northern' audience, largely unsympathetic to James' God-given genius. After the performance a gentleman seated next to me made an unwise comment and James stormed over to me sardonically asking me if I'd heard anything to upset me on this occasion, and making a fist gesture towards the man. As the man walked past us he made a 'thumbs-up' gesture at James, saying 'That were a bit of all right, mate!' – James gave him a wincing nod of acknowledgement. It seemed to me that some sections of provincial Yorkshire were not yet ready for the countertenor voice, especially as a solo instrument. They did not understand it and probably regarded male altos as eunuchs. It was obviously an audience that was much more comfortable with mezzos and contraltos. For James, '...the male high voice has long been out of the ghetto.... Countertenors do belong to the mainstream of Creation. We're not some weird, semi-mythical oddity that people come to peer at in disbelief.'

I intimated that I was surprised to see him perform in such an unattractive, backward place, and he retorted angrily 'I told you not to come.' He then expressed his fury with me for not sitting in the front-row (these seats largely were empty but reserved at all times for club members). I was deeply shocked by his attitude and asked him if he had received his bouquet that morning. He then relented slightly and asked me to walk outside with him to continue our conversation. He proceeded to excuse himself 'I'm sorry Maxine, you caught me at a bad moment...I have a crisis in my personal life at present and my mother is dying'. He explained that he had a lot of problems, psychological and sexual problems and was suffering from emotional blackmail. He touched my arm affectionately, but then as suddenly moved away from me and accused me of bringing him into conflict with himself; 'You bring me into conflict with myself.' I have never understood what he meant by this 'aria of the unsaid'. His turbulence upset and disturbed me, I saw our infinitely precious empathy disappearing before my eyes and I accused him of bearing a grudge and that all my writing meant nothing to him. 'All that I have written is as nothing to you,' I said. He denied this: 'Don't be ridiculous – did I ever say that?' he retorted. 'You've come all this way Maxine, on a sort of pilgrimage, to see me. We have something very beautiful, Maxine, why let other people spoil it?' He was still sulking with me but his defensiveness 'Are you saying that I'm defiling myself? I have to earn my living in places like this, and anyway, I've quite enjoyed it...', had disappeared and he acknowledged with remorse and honesty that I was right about the atmosphere at Ilkley, 'I know what they're thinking when they look at me – what an odd looking man with a peculiar voice.' Indeed, the gentleman seated beside me had said to his wife, 'It's not so bad love, as long as you don't look at his face.' And when James returned for the second half 'Oh no! Not that singer again! It would be alright if it weren't for him.' They had come for the King's Consort and their instrumental repertoire. They had probably never even heard of countertenors! Like America, initially, the North of England had obviously lagged behind the South in its appreciation of the adult male high voice. When Alfred Deller first went on tour in America he was described by critics and audiences alike as 'quaint'. In the 21st century, many homegrown American countertenors have become superstars and gay icons, David Daniels being pre-eminent. He now dominates baroque operatic roles but his voice has been likened to that of Kathleen Ferrier. 'In some ways,' Daniels says, 'it's crazy to talk about femininity in my voice, but it would be ridiculous to say that it doesn't sound feminine at all, because it obviously does.'

When I first heard David Daniels sing, I almost mistook him for a female contralto. Lovers of the countertenor voice have a well documented dislike of the female contralto, finding the sound too emotional. Women especially have an aversion. James Bowman said he was not at all surprised that I disliked Kathleen Ferrier's voice. He has said that when a countertenor is ageing, the voice is at risk of sounding 'bosomy', something to be avoided.

Unusually, the all-American David Daniels (formerly a tenor and still passionate about playing basketball), is openly and flamboyantly 'gay' and says that his gayness colours his singing. But recently he has distanced himself a little from his overtly gay admirers by insisting that the sexuality or gender of the voice is of no interest. Peter Giles has told me of his dislike for the David Daniels sound. When Peter was compiling his French, two-disc *Collection of Countertenors* for Harmonia Mundi, he deliberately omitted Daniels, and received rude telephone calls from 'a number of Daniels' camp friends, who took great exception to this omission'.

Even Alfred Deller, the Elizabethan miniaturist, who always preferred the Cathedral to the Theatre as his performing arena, was defensive about the sexuality of his voice. It is one of the reasons why, despite having a wife and three children, he always kept his goatee beard, to prove that he had normal masculine facial hair and thus needed to shave.

Despite his outburst at Ilkley, James shook hands in a conciliatory gesture and at last acknowledged my morning flowers. When I called him back, saying that I had not finished speaking with him, he returned to me.

The whole scene resembled Britten's *Dream*, in which Oberon torments Tytania for the perceived injury. 'Jealous Oberon', having secured the disputed 'lovely boy stolen from an Indian King', then begins to pity Tytania's infatuation and awakens her from her dream. They celebrate their restored friendship with a dance in the sylvan world of shadows.

> Sound, music. Come, my queen, take hands with me
> And rock the ground whereon these sleepers be.
> Now thou and I are new in amity.
>
> Oberon to Tytania

I quoted these words of Oberon back at him, myself assuming the role of the Fairy King and addressing him as 'Tytania'. This brought a momentary delightful smile to his lips.

He asked me to come to his *Dream* on 31st March, 1998, in a concert version at the Barbican, and his beloved *Blake Songs* at Snape on Easter Monday, despite his loathing for the 'tacky gift shop traders' now occupying the old buildings adjacent to

Snape Maltings and 'despoiling Ben and Peter's concert hall'. He even explained that many of his family members would attend his *Dream* and therefore it was possible that being surrounded by relatives might prevent him from being able to come over to me. I longed for Snape although it felt like the unease of James' own hesitant, *Journey of the Magi*. When I told James that he had made me cry, he said 'Good, you deserve it, you deserve to suffer – Ah! *mio cor*,' using words from one of Alcina's tormented and beautiful arias.

I felt that despite our reconciliation I had become the victim of James' irrational behaviour. Having incurred his displeasure he would be angry with me and then kind. The whole process was terrible and completely unfair and disconcerting. He would tell me that 'it's all becoming a bit much' and then say that he wished me to write to him always, and never stop adoring him. I was simultaneously invited to come closer and then rejected.

'There was something in him that wanted to embrace...and there was something else, stronger, which turned towards denial...She might have been able to move these tiny particles of experience into her memory, place them in a special chamber and make them beautiful.'

Sacred Stones

Oh fatal day!

1997 and 1998 were two wonderful years, although the latter really concluded my time and tenuous relationship with James, 'King of Shadows'. The Marjorie King Memorial Concert on

Burning in Blueness

20th September, 1997, was a sombre yet ecstatic occasion, and marked the end of my association with Hinckley Music Club. Marjorie King had welcomed my 50th Birthday Commission for James, but sadly had by then been too ill to attend 'She'll soon be dead,' said James coldly. Most of all she adored James' lute song recitals with the unique lutenist Robert Spencer, with whom he had worked since the David Munrow days. She preferred them to any of his concerts with the King's Consort, who she felt sometimes drowned him out. Also on the telephone she told me of her deep affection for the late David Munrow, describing him feelingly as 'poor dear David, poor dear boy'. She was devastated by his tragic suicide and James told me how deeply distressed she had been at his funeral; he seemed surprised by the intensity of her sorrow.

Marjorie was a formidable lady and could be extremely rude, but I never saw that side of her. She told me warmly that she 'approved of me', and it had been Marjorie who had first introduced me to James in the autumn of 1992, and invited me back to her house for 'a cup of tea'. At the moment of our introduction, an elderly lady with a stick walked by unsteadily. 'Mind how you go,' said James, with a wicked wink, and emphasis.

For this 'memorial' occasion, on September 13th, 1997, I sent James yellow in blue flowers, a beautiful card with the words of Purcell's 'Evening Hymn', and a telephone message, a copy of which I've kept. 'Hello James – this is Maxine – your bouquet of yellow and blue will now arrive on Saturday morning – September 13th –instead of tomorrow. I have changed the date to give the florist more time to find the most suitable flowers – there is a shortage at present – if this is not a convenient date for you then please let me know.' The reason for the shortage of flowers was the recent death of Diana, Princess of Wales.

During the interval James discussed with me the recent death from cancer, of his friend and colleague, the lutenist Robert Spencer. 'Precious friends hid in death's dateless night'. This had passed unnoticed outside musical circles and had deeply depressed James, who missed him greatly, 'They always mourn the wrong people, don't they Maxine?' he said. 'Bob taught me more about the text than anybody, and to sit down for lute songs. You must sit down to make it a domestic duet.' As a special mark of his respect for me, he changed the programme to include Dowland's 'Time stands still in gazing on her face', and concluded his programme, especially for me, with Purcell's 'Evening Hymn', because I'd written it on his card. James told the audience that he had 'forgotten' his score for his intended encore, so would perform the 'Evening Hymn' instead. This he did just for me, as I loved it so much; his pretence was charming.

> Now that the sun hath veiled his light,
> and bid the world goodnight,
> To the soft bed my body I dispose;
> But where shall my soul repose?
> Dear God, even in thy arms. And
> Can there be any so sweet security?
> Then to thy rest, O my soul,
> And Singing, praise the mercy
> Halleluia!
>
> Purcell, 'Evening Hymn'

I had written the *Hymn* out on his card. 'I bring your cards to all my concerts – and thank you for the exquisite Yellow and Blue bouquet,' James added, and later wrote to me.

During the interval, he sat beside me and kissed his fingertips in a gesture of adoration for his flowers. He emphasised his love of green as a musical colour, and asked me, 'Shall we mingle, Maxine? No I don't think so, not amongst this lot.' When two rather unpleasant female admirers of his, seated behind us, attempted to speak to him, he rebuked them for their interruption, saying, 'Do you mind! I'm speaking to my friend.' He then raised his score to screen us from their jealous and spiteful gaze.

'It's an awkward, brief, odd kiss, and if anyone were to see it, it would provoke a smile. But like every kiss, this one is an answer, a clumsy but tender answer to a question that eludes the power of language.'

He did some of his best work at Hinckley, but regarded it as a horrible little Midlands provincial town full of dour people. But when James performed there he transformed it into Eden. He said 'I am blue Maxine, that is what I am...' I'll always remember the remarkable blue of his eyes as he looked at me. He explained his conviction that women understood and appreciated the countertenor voice much more than men, because 'with women there isn't the problem of masculinity.' He said that 'love for a voice is something very personal; it is a deeply personal thing.' His melancholy mood informed our entire interchange and he expressed his anxiety that once he ceased to perform he would soon be forgotten, 'I've no idea how much longer I've got; it can go suddenly like a boy's voice. When I stop singing you won't want to know me, Maxine! I'll have to disappear and become a mystic memory'. Also, he again discussed his love of singing in cathedrals and of his deep affection for Lincoln Cathedral, where, in the 16th century, William Byrd had been organist. Lincoln Cathedral is the church of the Blessed Virgin Mary; it is full of golden light and spiritual joy. Many people describe the coloured interior as like a person calling to them, (a voice rather like the one in Jane Eyre). The High Altar is in the Angel Choir, built during the Geometric period of Gothic architecture (c. 1255-90), and inspired by the Laudate Psalms, (Psalms 148-150). The carved, winged Angel Gabriel holds the sun in one hand and the Moon in the other, as in Psalm 148, verses 2-3.

'I love the very stones of Lincoln Cathedral, and you, Maxine, are redolent with their spirituality,' said James. His rare compliments were unforgettable.

The small church of Holy Trinity in Hinckley was full of ghosts. The living moment for me was James' performance of Alan Ridout's *Soliloquy in memory of David Munrow*, 'a very Irish piece' as James termed it. Some observers say that James' voice changed forever after Munrow's suicide – certainly he had to reconstruct his voice completely after the four-year vocal crisis – and he never again performed Munrow's mediaeval repertoire, saying that he no longer possessed the technique. He continued to sing and make recordings throughout this period but one can hear that the voice does not sound 'right' at all. In December 1977, he recorded the aria 'O God, Who from the Suckling's Mouth', Handel's 1749 Anthem for the Founding Hospital. It was originally written for the castrato Guadagni. James described his voice in this aria as 'brave, but damaged to the point of disintegration.' It was only through the support of colleagues and friends that he was able to carry on at all; this particular recording was made with the choir of Christ Church Cathedral, Oxford, with whom he had worked whilst at University.

James has said on Radio 3 in 2001, that he had been overworking in the 1970s, but that the vocal crisis was largely 'psychosomatic'. He confessed to me the shock of losing both Benjamin Britten and David Munrow in the same year, 1976: after all, he was Muse to both. He had met them both in 1966 and then lost them in the same year, a decade later. Munrow's

Burning in Blueness

suicide was not altogether 'unexpected', as he had attempted a drug overdose the year before, but Britten had been expected to recover from his heart operation. 'They died in the same year. It was awful, Maxine, awful!'

Certainly, James loved Geoffrey Burgon's *Merciless Beauty* because it combined the mediaeval and contemporary, but Munrow's specific mediaeval repertoire he never resurrected. *Merciless Beauty* was premiered at the Woburn Festival on Saturday 18th October 1997. The unique voice of James Bowman was a major influence on the choice of poems. In his programme notes, Geoffrey Burgon said of James, 'There is a warmth and intensity to James Bowman's singing that marks him out from all the other "falsettists"...' The poets set are Anon, Kit Wright, Chaucer and Blake. It is a setting of seven songs about love, for countertenor and orchestra, and is a very dark piece indeed. James was very defensive when I expressed my surprise at using the words of such a mediocre poet as Kit Wright, (who sat next to me at the subsequent performance), even though he had asked my opinion whilst speaking to me on his mobile phone because he wanted to discuss the subject from 'a high place', the top of his step ladders. He said that I was too critical and analytical and then changed his mind, saying that he totally endorsed my disdainful comments. 'Yes, I shouldn't have to sing about a horrible ice-cream van,' said James, referring to Part IV of the song cycle, a setting of Kit Wright's 'Tune for an Ice-Cream Van'.

On the morning of his performance in lovely old High Wycombe Church in Buckinghamshire I sent him flowers and a card, 'Good luck for your world premiere performance of Geoffrey Burgon's *Merciless Beauty*; I hope the Nightblue bouquet is beautiful and gives you pleasure.' When he sat so close beside me and transformed into Leonardo's *The Virgin of the Rocks*, I knew that this vision would probably never return and was how I would like to remember him. He thanked me *in private* for my Flowers and said that for his forthcoming birthday he would once again like the austere chiaroscuro juxtaposition of just two colours, but this time blue and white:

> Like a flame blown whiter and whiter
> In a deeper and deeper darkness
> Ever more exquisite, distilled in separation

I posted D. H. Lawrence's poem – by which James was inspired and endlessly fascinated – to him on 20th October 1997, promising to search for his 'Birthday white and blue'.

In her book *The Geometry of Love – Space, Time, Mystery and Meaning in an ordinary Church*, Margaret Visser writes of personal epiphanies: 'This was a mystical experience. As such, one of its characteristics was that in it my mind embraced a vast contradiction…One of the consequences of having had a mystical experience is a sense of loss. If only it could have gone on and on, and never had to stop; if only the hardest lesson we have to learn is that we cannot bring about such an experience, any more than we can make it last. Sex can remind us of it because, like a mystical experience, sex is overwhelming, and delightful; it feels bigger than we are…What I have left is the enormous memory, and the fact that it has enlarged all of my experience ever since.'

My favourite Christmas cards from James were Sandro Botticelli's 'Madonna of the Book', 1483, which depicts the Virgin teaching the Christ child to read, and 'Mary with Baby Jesus', by Margaret W Tarrant (1888-1959). It is a blend of mediaeval and contemporary design, yellow in blue, ('Burning in Blueness,' said James) and Blakean in style in its painting mingled with text, 'Thou shalt call his name Jesus, for he shall save his people form their sins' (Matthew), simply inscribed by James 'To Maxine, from James'.

The painting depicts the infant Jesus blissfully asleep in his mother's arms. James said I was Mary and he was Jesus. His exaltation and idealisation of me had reached its climax. Whether it be Auden's poem 'Lullaby' in Geoffrey Burgon's song cycle *Lunar Beauty*; Byrd's 'Lullaby my sweet little baby', (recalling the cradle song to the infant Jesus), or '*Schlafe mein Liebster*' from Bach's *Christmas Oratorio*, James Bowman's singing of a lullaby is unsurpassable:

> Sleep, my Dearest, enjoy Thy rest,
> from henceforth watch over the
> wellbeing of all.
> Refresh the breast,
> experience the joy,
> there where we gladden our hearts.
> '*Schlafe mein Liebster*', from Bach's *Christmas Oratorio*

One of James' favourite pieces is Brahms' tender *Intermezzo* in E-flat major, Op. 117/No. 1. It is based on a Scottish folksong 'Sleep Softly, My Child'. At the top of the score, Brahms quoted two lines from this ballad: 'Ballou, my boy, lie still and sleep/It grieves me sair to hear thee weep.'

It was at High Wycombe that James gave me the inscribed Gloucester Cathedral East Window card:

> For Maxine
> The essence of Mediaeval inspiration and ecstasy.
> James Bowman

The mystical union between James and myself was more like a relationship from mediaeval times. I think it was that which he wished to convey in the inscribed card. This adoration manifested itself on a number of other occasions.

I sat in the front row at Hinckley and James stood right in front of me, inclining towards me – as he had in Bolton on October 11th 1992, when he asked me 'Have you time for an encore?', and I replied, 'I'm dying for one,' and he gave me Bach's *'Erbarme dich'*, opening up the intimate space of his mouth wider and wider still.

> She listened to me as if I were her music,
> Sitting alone by the altar…
> Ovid: *Metamorphoses*

He ran after me as I was leaving the scaffolded church in Bolton, waving to attract my attention, just to say 'hello!' before sardonically dismissing my companions. 'Oh! I didn't see *you* there, behind the scaffolding pole,' he said to my friend, cruelly alluding to his thinness. James said that he wanted to speak to as well as sing to me. He and I stood aloof, for once alone.

> But, when the emotion was at its profoundest depth, the voice rose out of it, yet so gradually that a gloom seemed to pervade it, far upward from the abyss, and not entirely to fall away as it ascended into a higher and purer region.
> Nathaniel Hawthorne, *The Marble Faun*: on the battlements, Miriam's singing voice after she suffers the guilt and evil of having incited murder.

Withdrawal

> O Solitude, my sweetest choice,
> Places devoted to the night.
> Remote from tumult and from noise,
> How ye my restless thoughts delight.
> O Solitude, my sweetest choice.
>
> Kathryn Philips

In May, 1987, James Bowman had recorded Purcell's solo setting of the extraordinary visionary text by Kathryn Philips. When I used it to accompany his flowers, he told me that he adored the words of this poem and that they reminded him of 'us'.

Indeed, an aura of aloneness surrounded James; it was what Henry James called 'the solitude of Genius', and regarded as the dedicated writer's fate. An Oxford postcard James Bowman sent me expressed this exactly, as did a Christmas card of a darkly clothed figure standing alone in the snow.

I'll always remember seeing James in his long green gabardine, walking alone in the night rain at Greenwich. I'll never forget James in the night and the rain, which for me has come to symbolise loss. It was just before his 50th Birthday recital at the old Royal Naval College Chapel, on Tuesday, November 12th, 1991. Trevor Pinnock and the English Concert were his accompanists on this occasion and were late arriving – James had walked towards the station in the pouring rain to look for them; there were raindrops on his green gabardine. The atmosphere in the chapel was so damp that the musicians had problems that evening with some of the early music instruments; the strings kept playing out of tune. Trevor Pinnock said that after the recital, James was sure to want to say a few words on this special occasion; he said nothing. Added to which his usual Baroque trumpeter, the great Crispian Steele-Perkins, was unavailable and the substitute, Mark Bennett, messed up the conclusion of Handel's 'Eternal Source of Light Divine'. James winced.

    Before his Handel and Purcell recital at the Royal Hall on August 3rd, 1994, in Harrogate, we had fallen out yet again and he'd withdrawn from me, 'Life is terrible, Maxine, terrible.' Nevertheless I forgave him and sent him flowers. 'I hope the flowers give you pleasure; roses to remind you of your ravishing interpretations of Purcell's music.' As I approached the evening's venue I saw him walking towards the artists' entrance. Seen from behind without his singer's expressive face he seemed enveloped by loneliness and melancholy. My mother said, 'He looks as if he is going to his own hanging. He is definitely more Moon than Sun. My dear, what are you worshipping?'

    'Success no longer has the colour of the sun, but grows in the light of the moon, and no one has ever said that this second luminary was displeasing to the creator of all things. Jesus himself meditated in the garden of Olivet, at night.'

Like my mother, I felt overwhelming pity for him and was so pleased when he saw me in the theatre and gave me a wonderful intimate smile of joy and gratitude 'his dark face softening to my eyes'. After the recital he'd run after me but I'd already gone – 'I saw you in the Hall looking ecstatic!' he later told me. He had sung David's first aria from Handel's *Saul*:

> O King, your Favours with Delight
> I take but must refuse your Praise.
>   Handel, *Saul*

Years before, in 1972, a critic had written of James' performance of David: 'James Bowman sings the role with considerable brilliance, though his is not a particularly ingratiating voice.'

Burning in Blueness

During the interval of The Marjorie King Memorial Concert, James asked me what I had in my carrier bag, and could he look inside it? I showed him my books on Thomas Mann, and Britten, 'Benjamin Britten's Poets, the poetry he set to music' and he asked to write an inscription in it for me. James said that he wanted to think carefully 'in private', so he took my book to the back of the church and during a break in his performance he inscribed it in private, 'To Maxine – withdrawn for a season, but always attentive and receptive. James Bowman, 20.9.97'. He said that he wanted it to be ambiguous. 'It might apply to either of us,' as at that moment he referred to us as 'we', who had both suffered withdrawal after loss. He once said that I reminded him of David Munrow, and David's hand bells (now owned by the recorder player John Turner) made their appearance at Marjorie King's Memorial Concert.

Probably the resemblance to David Munrow was because of my curly hair, small stature, large eyes and love of literature. As a child my brother told me my coarse curly hair meant that no man would ever fall in love with me. On a tree-shaded bank in the spinney at the bottom of our garden, he used to bury me in damp leaf-mould, sometimes with a covering of ivy and bird bones taken from carrion in a nearby wood. The local farmer shot crows and pigeons as alleged 'vermin', and then left them to hang in rows from the branches of trees, as a supposed deterrent to other crop eating birds.

I lay in ecstasy as the dappled sunlight played on the leaves above:

> He cam also stille
> Ther his mother lay,
> As dew in Aprille
> That falleth on the spray.
> *The Incarnation*

David Munrow's last recording with James Bowman was Monteverdi's Contemporaries, recorded 6th-7th November, 1975. It includes a magnificent, doleful piece by Alessandro Grandi, (1515-1630): '*O vos omnes*', a type of lament based on the liturgy of Good Friday:

> O all you who pass by the way, behold and see
> If there is any sorrow like my sorrow.
> Heavens be amazed at this,
> And their gates forcibly forsaken.

This final recording has a front-cover image of a beautiful Bronzino (1503-1572) painting, 'Eleanora of Toledo and her son Giovanni'. It is in the *Galleria degli Uffizi*, Florence.

Despite David Munrow's beguiling, hyperactive and academic personality, according to James, he often worked his artists to exhaustion, and he could be deeply morose in private.

James admired David Munrow's ability to communicate, and enjoyed his sense of fun in performance, but said that 'a figure like David cannot exist any more, an image based on evangelism, sounds and stars, not repertoire and composers.'

Rumours and speculation surround the reasons for Munrow's suicide at his home in Chesham Bois, Buckinghamshire, on 15th May, 1976. He was said to have been suffering from depression, intensified by an inhuman work load, an unhappy marriage, and the recent death of his adored father, a Birmingham University lecturer, followed shortly afterwards by that of his father-in-law, to whom he was also very close. Although these events appear to be the key to his suicide, there were also reports, even at the time of him being confused as to his sexuality. My mother, who was a keen fan of David Munrow, and always listened to his 'pied-piper' programmes, has told me that Munrow's death was always seen as 'mysterious'. When his demise was first announced, it was difficult even to learn that he had taken his own life, and my mother thought it very odd that no subsequent biography appeared. A few years ago, my mother, waking from an afternoon doze, heard Humphrey Carpenter (Benjamin Britten's biographer) asking on Radio 4 for anyone to come forward who had information on David Munrow. Carpenter said that he was thinking of writing about him. As far as I know, nobody came forward and then of course, Carpenter himself died of cancer and heart failure. My mother has always believed that things were concealed at the time to protect reputations and careers. Certainly, the remains of David Munrow's circle appear to be staying silent.

On the day of David Munrow's death, he and his wife, Gillian Reid, were intending to go to Venice. She has remained a rather shadowy figure and from the little I've heard, not popular with members of David's all-male consort, who were always touring the world without her. James has claimed that women were excluded 'simply for practical purposes ... it was just easier with blokes'.

The musicologist and current early music performer, Douglas Kirk, gives prominence to Munrow's unresolved sexual identity in his decision to end his life by suicide: 'He hung himself one night in the doorway of his barn/garage, facing the kitchen windows, so that the first thing his wife would see when she came down for breakfast the next morning was his body swinging there...'

'I turned my home into my hanging place.'

Like Dante's anonymous Florentine suicide in 'The Wood of the Grieving Suicides', David Munrow had hanged himself in his own home.

James had in effect lost his voice after Munrow's death, the voice with which I had fallen in love in 1972, and I reflected on the meaning of this for such an artist and man. In his Radio 4 programme *Lost Voices*, David Rayvern Allen uncovered the physical and psychological scars that are left behind when a professional singer's once wonderful voice disappears: 'Singing is an unnatural act ... Singers are terrified that something will go wrong with their voices... The Singing Voice, particularly that of a professional singer, is never taken for granted, for that is part of who they are, precious, personal, a kind of second face, their very identity. To lose it is nothing short of a catastrophe, they become a non-person.'

James always described his voice to me as 'Something unnatural perfected until it sounds natural.' Occasionally, he brooded on the terrible prospect of retirement, but usually reassured himself that as long as he took great care of his voice he'd probably be able to continue singing well into old age. Peter Pears had remained working until he was seventy, and still looked beautiful even when he was old. Alfred Deller continued to sing until the age of 67, the year of his death. 'I can't conceive of life without music, and I believe that if it did stop, I would be unable to do anything else. It's the one thing that gives meaning to my existence – my work, my music. Everything stems from it. Everything.' Alfred Deller, quoted in his biography, *A Singularity of Voice*, by Michael and Mollie Hardwicke.

In winding down his international career, James is definitively shedding one life for another, a sort of withdrawal without any final farewell. He had said to me long ago that he had no intention of becoming 'a lonely Phantom of the Concert Hall or Opera House'.

Having retired from opera some years ago, and cut back on his schedule, James at 65 is still giving solo recitals –

Burning in Blueness

especially of the 'quieter' lute song repertoire – and has joined the choir of the Chapel Royal, where he now sings the services as part of a team, just as he did as a boy in the Choir of Ely Cathedral. A lovely thought. According to *Times* Music Critic, Hilary Finch, 'No one should underestimate the isolation of an opera singer on the concert platform', but James has always thrived on, and always coped brilliantly with this transition. 'My nearest and dearest will tell me when the time has come to go. One day I will have to disappear and become a mystic memory – but not yet', said James.

> When the day came, as come it had to, that his friend confessed to him her fear of a deep disorder in her blood, he felt somehow the shadow of a change and the chill of a shock.
> Henry James, *The Beast in the Jungle*

In a passionate outburst beneath the cold winter moonlight in Ilkley, on Wednesday 11th February, 1998, James said 'My work is the most important thing in my life, Maxine – it comes before everything. I cannot return others' feelings for me…'

Semper gratus desiderabilis,	For ever welcome, for ever
semper eris in me.	longed for, you will always
Veni, O care, totus amabilis,	burn within me. Come,
In aeternum diligam te.	beloved, O wholly exquisite,
	I shall love you evermore.

Alessandro Scarlatti, Cantata *Infirmata Vulnerata*
sung by James Bowman, countertenor

▲   ▲   ▲

PART THREE

The Memory

Soliloquy

Tune thy music to thy heart;
Sing thy joy with thanks and so thy sorrow.

Though devotion needs not art,
Some-time of the poor the rich may borrow.

Strive not yet for curious ways;
Concord pleaseth more the less 'tis strained.
Zeal affects not outward praise,

Only strives to show a love un-feigned.
Love can wondrous things affect.

Sweetest sacrifice all wrath appealing.
Love the highest doth respect;
Love alone to him is ever pleasing.

>*Soliloquy* for Countertenor, Treble Recorder, optional Lute, Cello and Harpsichord.
>Alan Ridout AR (Canterbury)
>Words by Thomas Campion 24.1.85

The history of the music manuscript for Alan Ridout's *Soliloquy* is a most interesting one. From Peter Giles I learned that Alan Ridout hardly ever published his scores. He wrote them as gifts for friends to perform, and was always writing and offering wonderful 'miniatures' to James, who never had to commission anything from him. And having converted to Catholicism shortly before his death he left almost everything to the Benedictine Monastery Library at Ampleforth Abbey in Yorkshire. With great patience and perseverance I traced it to Father Anselm's care and persuaded him to send me a photocopy of the score, which I treasure. He also gave me permission to photocopy it for Alan Ridout's literary/works executor Robert Scott. Robert was absolutely delighted by my success; for years he had been trying to extract a copy from my Benedictine monk, but he had refused. And Robert declined to ask James Bowman for a copy of his score of the piece saying 'I'm certainly not approaching him, he's so rude that he never bothers to respond and if one telephones it is always "inconvenient".' On receipt of the manuscript Robert most kindly wrote a piano arrangement of the score and at once sent it to me.

I'm fascinated by soliloquy – we glimpse inward action, which is often frenetic, and we come close to the centre of things when a character speaks in conversation with himself, or with his audience. Episodes of the utmost privacy and introversion are presented to an audience in public performance – an individual voice contains infinite possibility. Soliloquy is a 'window' on the innermost individual psyche. Never have I experienced a greater sense of plangency and mystery – never again did we enjoy such a pitch of communication and empathy as in this piece. James was without his glasses, and his dark blue eyes looked deeply into mine with all the divine beauty of Leonardo's painting, come to life. 'A mirarvi io son intento, occhi cari del mio ben.' I wondered if they were his mother's eyes, which had been handed down to him like ancestral jewels.

> Like the very gods in my sight
> is he who
> Sits where he can look in your
> eyes, who listens
> close to you...

Alan Ridout's *Soliloquy*, (although originally written in memory of Alfred Deller, and re-dedicated to David Munrow) which James sat down to sing in Hinckley Church, conveyed his innermost thoughts and Munrow's melancholy. 'The man closest to my heart has gone mad.' It reminded me of William Blake's painting of Isaac Newton, as a self-absorbed, mad Genius, seated naked on a rock under the water, obsessively drawing triangles. I once likened James to a holy triangle and he said, 'I love your idea of me as a triangle, Maxine, equilateral of course! I'd like to incorporate it into some of my work, one day...' He responded to my symbolism with a beautiful monochrome photograph of the Louvre's glass pyramid in the light-sensitive darkness. The transparent pyramid is viewed from the shadowed geometric floor, and soaring vaulted ceiling of the Louvre's Grand Gallery, which contains the Leonardos, including the other version of the *Virgin of the Rocks*.

Orlando

> Repetition of theme a reaffirming,
> like figures in harmony with their right consorts,
> with the world also, broadly understood;
> each of itself a treatise of civil power,
> every phrase instinct with deliberation
> both upon power and towards civility.
>
> Geoffrey Hill, 'G. F. Handel, Opus 6' from *A Treatise of Civil Power*

Orlando, wrote Percy Young, offers 'The most penetrating and awe-inspiring examples of Handel's capacity for uncovering the raw nerve centres of mental agony ... Mental affliction crosses recitative and aria, ebbs to exhaustion through the healing influence of the "vaghe pupille" gavotte and finally reposes Orlando in troubled sleep.'

My favourite operatic roles for James were those written by his own dear Handel for the contralto castrato, Senesino. Senesino's voice was famously described as 'a powerful, clear, equal and sweet contralto, with perfect intonation and an excellent shake [trill]'. Senesino was the stage name of the alto castrato Francesco Bernardi, and is remembered today primarily for his association with Handel as Primo Uomo (first man) of London's first great opera company, The Royal Academy of Music, from 1720 to 1733. Handel wrote seventeen operatic roles for him, including the title roles of *Radamisto, Guilio Cesare, Orlando*, and Bertarido in *Rodelinda*. Senesino was Handel's star castrato. I often put a Miltonic quote, which James adored, at the head of a letter to him, which I thought perfectly described James' symbiotic relationship with Handel:

For James and Handel

That in the colours of the rainbow live
And play i'th' plighted clouds.
Milton, *Comus*, 1634

Theirs was a musical love affair made in heaven; James had almost single-handedly revived Handel's castrato roles and made them central to his specialist repertoire. On one memorable occasion following a temporary conflict between us he sent me an exquisite 'rainbow card' of the desolate Ardnamurchan peninsula. Not only did this express our covenant, but it also referred to words from Geoffrey Hill's poem 'To John Constable In Absentia', which I had sent him previously: 'a perceptible radiance – arched and spectral – the abrupt rainbow's errant visitation'. During one of his periods of low spirits, I sent James a multicoloured bouquet to overcome his melancholy.

In the seventies and eighties, James Bowman was *the*

Handelian countertenor, and has influenced all singers of his repertoire around today. With exquisite taste and good judgement he prefers to do his own ornamentation in the *da capos* which, like use of vibrato, he keeps to a minimum. James likes to be seen as a specialist in high-Baroque music, such as Vivaldi, Bach and Handel.

In baroque *opera seria* the recitative advances or describes the action, whilst the *da capo* aria explores and develops character and psychological motivation. The *da capo* arias are Handel's essence in the safe hands of a great and thrilling singer like James Bowman. The repetition with minimal ornamentation combines to rise to a climax.

Modern opera producers are often embarrassed by this tradition in baroque opera, but the 'stand and deliver' approach exactly suits James. The singer is physically static and sings alone; all the drama must come from within his voice. The restrictions on the body increase the power and complexity of the purely vocal drama. Britten used this device in his *A Midsummer Night's Dream*; Oberon is barely expected to move. James once described to me the horror of being in a production of the *Dream*, in which, as Oberon he was expected to ascend and descend a narrow, moving spiral staircase whilst *singing*...

According to Ellen T. Harris, Handel's Orlando has to master the woman's voice within himself, to learn to control this feminized expression of innermost feeling through concealment. 'Handel found the breadth and depth of his own expressive voice by trying on the voices of abandoned women.'

James' falsetto is strikingly effective for many of the heroic Castrato roles in Baroque opera: 'The true high male solo voice in the 18th century was the hautre-contre...and now we have a type of high male voice which fits the bill for singing alto/castrato roles...' James said. 'If a singer has got the technique, the staying power, the vocal beauty and the acting ability required for a role, then they can do whatever they like, surely? The point about the countertenor voice is that it is an invention of the 20th century. We're not trying to be castrati or to sing like women. It's a voice in its own right and of its own time... It has been around as a choral voice for centuries, but it's only recently that its solo possibilities have been explored.' It was the countertenor Alfred Deller, seen as a lone voice crying in the wilderness, (which he is said to have secretly enjoyed), who was the only singer acknowledged by Janet Baker to have inspired or influenced her work. Some critics have likened her voice to that of James Bowman, and regarded them as rivals for Baroque 'trouser' roles, like Handel's *Guilio Cesare* and *Ariodante*, (1735), which contains *Scherza infida*, one of James' favourite arias for a character in soliloquy; he sings it on his *Heroic Arias* disc of 1990:

> Sport, faithless one, in your lover's embrace.
> Because of your betrayal I now go forth into the arms of death.
> But to break this vile bond
> I will return to haunt you
> As a gloomy shade, a mere wraith.

Ariodante is in deepest despair, imagining himself to have been betrayed by Princess Ginevra, to whom he is betrothed.

Working with James in 1972 on Cavalli's *La Calisto*, realised by Raymond Leppard, with Janet Baker as the goddess Diana and James Bowman as Endimione, a shepherd in love with Diana, Janet Baker commented on his youthful genius and lack of concentration. During a six-part Radio 3 series in tribute to her, she spoke of the extended scene in *La Calisto*, which includes the duet '*Dolcissimi baci un nettare siete*, Oh sweetest of

Kisses with tenderness burning'. Diana and Endimione vow eternal, chaste love. Rehearsing this tender duet, Janet Baker described herself as 'like a laser beam', whereas James was 'like a floppy Labrador puppy, all over the place. You wanted to gather him up, hug and then slap him!' She said that although 'brilliant', he was not sufficiently focussed in his early career. In 1977, also with James Bowman, she recorded Handel's *Ariodante*. Janet Baker took the title role of the Prince, written for the castrato Carestini, and James Bowman had the subordinate castrato, or contralto, role of the villain Polinesso, Duke of Albany.

Although gender reversal, as a most effective dramatic device, occurs so frequently in Handel's operas, not even the great Janet Baker can reproduce the masculine resonance and force of the male high voice. James has reclaimed repertoire from basses, tenors and women. In conversation with Michael Church, he described his reaction to recording the title role in Handel's *Guilio Cesare* shortly after Janet Baker had sung it: 'She was wonderful in the role, but she was also – shall we say? – handicapped. Whatever my faults, people generally agree that I sound like a man.' Early German recordings of Handel used basses for the male high voice roles, so incorrectly assigned they sound absurd.

The pioneering work of James Bowman and the Handelian conductors, Sir Charles Mackerras (who produced the 1972 *Saul*), and Sir David Willcocks in the 1970s, has benefited singers like David Daniels. Daniels especially relishes baroque full-blooded heroic repertoire for the male high voice, finding much contemporary writing lacking in virility; he says that there is a great need for satisfying new masculine operatic roles; only then will the countertenor evolution be complete: 'From Britten right through to Philip Glass, it has been extraterrestrials and fairies all the way.'

Modern mezzos and contraltos are now attempting to sound like men or boys, in order to sing castrato roles, but this too is unsatisfactory. Imagine the horror of Handel's Italian duets for alto and soprano sung by two women; all the eroticism would be lost.

In his magnum opus *The History and Technique of the Countertenor*, Peter Giles expresses disagreement with James' views on the history of the voice as a solo instrument and his use of the word 'falsetto' to describe it. For Peter it is a wholly 'natural' voice, an extension upwards of the normal male range, and a use of both chest and head register.

James is largely in agreement with the musician and academic Peter Holman, who has pointed out that 'countertenor to Purcell didn't mean a voice; it meant a range'. Also, in opposition to Peter Giles, James acknowledges that the countertenor voice could be described as fake: 'It's an acquired technique. Nobody speaks in that register.' This is not strictly true, as the artist Francis Bacon frequently spoke in falsetto when amongst friends in his Soho haunts.

On June 15th, 1995, just a few months before the publication of his book, Peter Giles had written to the editor of the *Daily Telegraph* attacking their article on the countertenor voice. He sent me a copy of his letter:

> Dear Sir,
> It is often repeated that all publicity is good publicity, but I am not totally convinced. Your recent feature on the countertenor, 'Tenors Aim Ever Higher', was interesting, and I suppose, generally useful to the countertenor cause. Unfortunately, the reader was left with the impression, yet again, that this type of male high voice has always been uniquely English. This is not so. It was, at the least, a European phenomenon which merely *survived* successfully here – just! – hence its revival has sprung from England. ...

Another misguided idea was given a further boost by Brian Hunt's article that the male high voice is 'acquired', artificial, and by implication, is unnatural and freakish. Growing a beard or moustache is a natural male capability. Merely because the majority of men, in the west, choose not to take advantage of this capability does not make beards and moustaches artificial or unnatural. Similarly, how a vocal capability – which happened to use the misleadingly named 'falsetto' register – possessed by and (to some extent at least) developable by almost every adult male on this planet – can be called artificial, is difficult to understand. In any case, it is arguable that all expert, sophisticated singing is done using an 'acquired' voice. This is partly what vocal pedagogy is all about! All this, and much more, is dealt with fully in my book, *The History and Technique of the Countertenor,* Scolar Press, due out this August.

Yours faithfully,
Peter Giles

As I read Peter's letter, all I could think of was James' disparaging remark on 'small men with beards', (like Peter Giles), and his horror when I told him that Peter was writing two more volumes on the countertenor: 'Oh, God, no! We don't need any more,' said James.

I never loved James more completely than in his performance of Handel's *Orlando*, described by James as 'like being inside a melancholy cocoon – I love that'. Like *Alcina* and *Ariodante*, it is inspired by Ariosto and has a reflective, pastoral libretto. The character of Orlando is based on the tragic Roland of French mediaeval history. It vividly displays James Bowman's absolute grasp of an extremely complex role. Orlando is torn between love and honour, and maddened by fate and women, 'a shade divided' from himself, suffering a series of visions of the underworld. In Act Three comes the hauntingly memorable *'Già l'ebro mio ciglo'* for Orlando, sung as he falls into the healing sleep induced by Zoroastro, accompanied by two violas with sympathetic strings giving additional plangency to the characteristic veiled tone of the instruments. In the anguish of unrequited love he furiously throws the compassionate Angelica into 'a gloomy Cave', and determines on suicide. As he descends into madness, the direct effect of his jealous obsession, he is given repose under the influence of a narcotic, and 'sleeps on a stone':

> *Già l'ebro mio ciglo*
> *Quel dolce liquore*
> *Invita a posar.*

James described to me one summer performance years before at Glyndebourne; singing *Già l'ebro* whilst lying on his back on stage, he had undergone an ecstatic epiphany, moments which haunted him all evening as he drove home in his car.

James' sensuous intelligence enters into this ambiguous, tragic, comic, childlike, and heroic character, with a sense of disturbance throughout. My booklet of the recording is 'suitably inscribed' by James:

> For Maxine
>   In her Cave
>   James Bowman

Suicide Notes

> From my very soul I pity him, and
> think myself ungrateful in that
> I never did return his love.
>   Angelica, in Handel's *Orlando*

During the interval at the Marjorie King Memorial Concert in Hinckley, in September 1997, I suggested to James that he explore the *Voices of Death* in the literature of suicide, and commission a piece constructed from suicide notes. Edwin Shneidman's book *Voices of Death* details a number of compelling case histories, and movingly illuminates a dark subject. Taints of blood – (Death – Blood) elucidates the biology of suicide. In the now famous meeting of Freud and others in Vienna in 1910 – the only meeting of the psychoanalytic group specifically on the topic of suicide – Wilhelm Stekel enunciated what was to become the orthodox psychoanalytic view – 'No one kills himself except as he wishes the death of another'.

In a state of anguish and low-spirits outside the King's Hall at Ilkley, on Wednesday February 11th, 1998, James confided to me that someone in France was threatening to commit suicide over him. He was being disturbed by nightly phone calls from this person, making it increasingly difficult for him to have adequate rest and concentrate on his work: James loved to receive but was less capable of giving: 'My work is much more important to me than people – although I'd probably go mad without my friends – but I can't respond to others' feelings for me,' James repeated.

> Night falls fast.
> Today is in the past.
>
> Blown from the dark hill hither
> to my door
>
> Three flakes, then four
> Arrive, then many more.

James was especially sensitive to stressful relationships which followed him into the privacy and sanctuary of his home. He was fearful that crises in his personal life might provoke a vocal crisis such as he suffered after the tragic death of David Munrow, which would change his singing voice for ever. James preferred to withdraw rather than confront a situation directly, so a friendship might come to an abrupt end whenever some inner conflict or tensions arose. An innocent remark might be misinterpreted and any relationship that in his opinion was becoming too intense or demanding, he disliked and severed. Hence his earlier remark that he was always having 'to get rid of people.' He was vulnerable to brooding melancholy and grateful to me for having brightened his darkness with my yellow Roses – 'They're just beginning to open to me':

> As yellow is always accompanied with light, so it may be said that blue still brings a principle of darkness with it. This colour has a peculiar and almost indescribable effect on the eye. As a hue it is powerful, but it is on the negative side, and in its highest purity is, as it were, a stimulating negation. Its appearance, then, is a kind of contradiction between excitement and repose.
> Goethe, *Theory of Colours*

James was a founder member of David Munrow's *Early Music Consort of London*, and his death affected him deeply. 'It was total meltdown,' said James.

> I can feel that I have been changed, I feel that death has come near me.
> Sappho of Mytiléne, 620-550 BC

James, having suffered a throat infection, sang on through it and seemed to have done irrevocable damage to his voice. He turned to a singing teacher, Barbara Aldene, who helped him to rebuild his voice over a period of two years. Whilst having his voice retrained, he also studied the Alexander Technique in order to improve his body awareness and help him to relax.

On Radio 3, James has spoken bravely of his problems, the result of shock and grief: 'David Munrow was a Svengali figure for me. When he died, there was a terrible void and I felt completely directionless. I had to be very careful what I did at that time. I just had to take the voice to pieces and start all over again. But I came out of it and Hall's *Dream* restored my self-confidence'. All this is in the public domain, but James also referred to this period when in private conversation with me, saying, 'You are too emotional, Maxine, like David Munrow... It seems a long time ago, now, Maxine, such a long time ago since David died. I'm always thinking of him.'

Whilst staying in my London flat I received a call from a friend who had already arrived at the Wigmore Hall and was waiting for me to join him there. James had entered the foyer after rehearsal, and overhearing him in conversation with me, he snatched the phone from my friend (without his permission) saying 'Where is she? Where is Maxine? She wants to speak to me.' Once on the telephone to me he expressed great hurt that I had seemingly not been longing to talk to him. He told me that my friend (who had just put several pound coins in the box), refused to give him the phone, and had outrageously suggested that I had not wanted to speak to him. James resolved the situation by glaring at my friend and telling him to go. A few days later on the telephone at home, James obliquely referred to this incident by asking me 'Is he a *friend* of yours? Has he been to university?' When I replied that my friend had read Health Physics at the University of Salford, James uttered a derisive expletive. The episode at the Wigmore Hall was a very typical example of James' resemblance to Oberon, especially when he is listening in on the lovers' quarrel between Demetrius and

Helena. It is Oberon's interference that has caused the dispute: 'I am invisible;/I will overhear their conference.'

The fear that lived within his reverence for me gave rise to occasional aggression, and an assertion of his power over me.

In addition to restoring James' self-confidence, the Glyndebourne *Dream* also assisted his acting abilities. James generally regards theatre directors as a 'menace'; he is primarily engaged 'to sing – not to act'. But despite disparaging remarks about Peter Hall, he felt that he had learnt an awful lot from him. 'He taught me to think about the motivation of a character.' James was honest enough to admit that his limited acting abilities required improvement. 'Somebody once said to me – you've come on the stage – you look as if you are reading the departure board at Paddington Station.' One almost expected James' battered, leather music case to bear the words 'Please look after this countertenor!'

In the beautiful *Galuppi* Commission card that James gave me he is shown in profile, seated in front of his model theatre, and holding a miniature Oberon, like a talisman. Peter Hall's 1981 Glyndebourne production of *The Dream* marked a turning point for James in recovering from a five-year breakdown: 'the main thing I learned from him was that, when in doubt, do nothing. Oberon is essentially the still centre, the incredibly calm core of the piece'. When I asked James, why in his portrait, he chose to hold the Glyndebourne Oberon, he said rather dismissively, 'O, that was *her* idea', meaning June Mendoza, the artist.

David Munrow and James

> The glory of the Arcadian groves
> Is gone and here ne'er to return.
> > Jeremiah Clarke, performed by David
> > Munrow and Alfred Deller, 1969

To mark James' 60th birthday in November 2001, and the 25th Anniversary of the death of David Munrow and Benjamin Britten, I suggested much earlier in a letter, that he record a CD of Hinckley Music Club Commissions, including Alan Ridout's *Soliloquy*, Gordon Crosse's *Verses in Memoriam David Munrow*, and my own private Commission, Arthur Wills' *A Toccata of Galuppi's*, complemented by Benjamin Britten's *String Quartet no 3 opus 94*. But by then, like Henry James, 'James had arranged many of the presences that meant most to him, as absences':

On New Year's Eve in 2001 there was a 60th birthday celebration concert for James at the Wigmore Hall, Handel Arias from Operas and Oratorios. By this time James Bowman did little with the King's Consort. He had chosen to be almost totally replaced by his former pupil, Robin Blaze. I had attended nearly every New Year's Eve concert at the Wigmore for a decade, including one very rare occasion at which James had looked really dishevelled. My mother had been shocked at his appearance. In fact, the entire consort looked drunk. *The Times* critic later commented 'Was it really necessary for James Bowman to wink at the soprano; did he think he was busking?'

I bought tickets for James' 60th, but did not attend ... an elegiac gesture:

Burning in Blueness

'Solitude' – 29th January 1998

Dear James,

I hope you will record *Soliloquy* in memory of David Munrow; I'll always remember your 1997 performance at Hinckley. Have you read the poignant *Dissertation on Castrati* by Oskar Herzberg? – it formed part of the *Beyond Reason – Art and Psychosis* – works from the Prinzhorn Collection exhibition at the Hayward Gallery.

Take great care of your shadow; I hope the February flowers are exquisite and give you Joy.

Maxine

Gordon Crosse's Memorial piece was broadcast from Christchurch, Spitalfields by Radio 3 in June 1996 to mark the 20th Anniversary of the death, in May 1976, of David Munrow, 'the pied-piper', using the tenor Martyn Hill instead of James. I have a different recording of this piece, from BBC archives and sung by James. He first performed it at Hinckley on 24th January 1985. It sets a plaintive, deeply felt English text, and the Radio 3 tribute opened with the closing words of *'Anglia planctus itera'*, a plaint on the death of Geoffrey, Count of Brittany (anon):

> O day, daughter of light.
> O day, with nothing to redeem it.
> O day, full of darkness.
>
> Death hath deprived me of my dearest friend.
> My dearest friend is dead and laid in grave.
> In grave he lies until the world shall end.
> The world shall end as end all things must have.
> All things must have an end that nature wrought.
> That nature wrought shall unto dust be brought.
>
> Death hath deprived me...
> My dearest friend...
> In grave he lies...

> The world must end…
> All things…nature…Dust.

The Middle section has an eerie insanity, with its withdrawn, broken language. The Third section returns to the first stanza and conveys the haunting resonance of his solitude. David Munrow's spirit is felt in John Turner's anguished and ghostly recorder playing which accompanies James' voice until it slowly darkens and fades, and the recorder is alone. Gordon Crosses's heartfelt songs were inspired and influenced by the instruments of David Munrow's Early Music Consort. The piece is very much a personal response to David's death, with a 'pied-piper' feeling at the end. 'It's very austere music,' James said. 'I remember the bells being quite haunting at the end. He was clever, Gordon, in the way he summoned up the spirit of David in a rather melancholy way.'

I noticed that as James spoke these words his voice was breaking up with emotion. 'And thou in this shalt find thy monument.' (Shakespeare, *Sonnet 107*.)

The Most Beautiful View in the World

> Let the Moths flutter round your gabardine – until like snowflakes they form a silent storm around the light.
> Peter Ackroyd, *Hawksmoor*

Henry James' letters from his Florentine hilltop breathe an air of calm and release, a sense of enchantment. He had discovered a Paradise, 'The most beautiful view in the world.' When I saw James Bowman at concerts I would refer to him in these words, and he'd smile at me with delight and amusement, followed by a mischievous, 'Yes, I am!'

Henry James adored living on Bellosguardo, where 'the bells of Florence talk to you, at a distance, all day long'. Every time he raised his head from his writing desk at his 'supercelestial' Villa Brichieri, 'the most beautiful view on earth' filled his eyes and his spirit. One of James Bowman's loveliest cards to me, mentioned earlier, was of the snow-covered rooftops of Florence and the great Duomo – 'A Geometric Joy.' Henry James' *The Aspern Papers*, which I gave to Arthur Wills, was begun and all but completed at the Villa Brichieri, and is Henry James' attempt to recapture the visitable past. 'I delight in a palpable imaginable visitable past…the poetry of the thing outlived and lost and gone.'

He and his friend Miss Constance Fenimore Woolson had neighbouring apartments in the Villa, she upstairs with a rose terrace and he below with a garden. Henry's lower-floor quarters looked through a single door and three arches to the Duomo and towers of the city. Guarding the Casa Brichieri-Colombi were two great pine trees. Miss Woolson enjoyed a sense of communion with Bellosguardo's Jamesian past, and Henry knew that he and Fenimore would be alone on their hilltop. 'There had been between him and Fenimore a strange matching of personalities and strange distortions of their mutual vision of one another.' (Leon Edel). She adored Henry and he was very fond of her and kind to her, within the limits of his deep egotism. His time with her at the Villa Brichieri was probably the closest he ever came to any sort of intimacy, domestic or otherwise, with a woman. In Emma Tennant's *Felony: The Private History of the Aspern Papers*, she imagines him saying the following: 'Constance,' he whispered, 'I have come as close as I could, as near as I dared'. Lyndall Gordon's *A Private Life of Henry James: Two Women and His Art*, has wonderful lyrical insights into the relationship between Henry James and

Fenimore. Although it is a biography, it reads like a novel. Her description of their friendship resonates for me with thoughts about mine with James Bowman.

> Passion is indifferent to reciprocal emotion, it needs to express itself to the full, live itself to the very end, no matter if all it receives in return is kind feelings, courtesy, friendship, or mere patience.
>
> Henry James,
> 'The Altar of the Dead', a short story

The poignant and tenuous relationship between the lonely friends ended with her suicide in Venice and burial in the non-Catholic cemetery in Rome. Fenimore loved high places like sky-rooms, promontories, cliffs and ledges; she chose her death-leap from a high window of her Venetian *Casa-Semitecolo*. 'Couldn't he see that in relation to her private need the rites he had established were practically an elaborate exclusion?' said James Bowman, quoting Henry James' 'The Altar of the Dead', which I had given him.

Henry James was horrified and descended into an abyss and a dark chapter in his life.

Living for five weeks in her sealed death-room at the Villa from which she had planned her jump, he retrieved his letters to her and destroyed them. Leon Edel writes, 'In the tale, all the Aspern papers are burned – sadistically almost – "one by one" – nothing is left to posterity.' It is a defense of privacy by a writer endlessly curious and observant, but also intensely private and secretive. In destroying Fenimore's possessions, including her clothes in the Venetian lagoon, 'He seemed engulfed by these dark simulacra, by the nightmarish representations of Fenimore that rose one after another irrepressibly, making their claim of attachment, as if they belonged to him forever.'

Henry James was to remember the Bellosguardo days as 'probably, on the whole, the most charmed and appeased, the most gratified and rewarded and beguiled days that ... ever passed.' After the death of all the friends who once inhabited the enchanted, but now deserted, hill overlooking Florence, Henry James described Bellosguardo as 'ghosts and glorious views'.

His friendship with 'Fenimore' as he called her, was concealed from all but his closest family members and friends. Fellow Americans in Florence included the art collector and amateur musician Francis Boott and his daughter Lizzie; Henry James introduced Fenimore to the Bootts, of whom she became very fond. Constance Fenimore Woolson's novella *Dorothy* (1896), is an elegy to Bellosguardo, and is haunted by a cradle song of grief, 'Through the Long Days'. The words were by John Hay, and set to music by Henry James' friend, Francis Boott. Fenimore used to play and hum this favourite song while she lived on Bellosguardo, and spent evenings in her lonely, elevated terrace. The heroine of *Dorothy* mysteriously fades with the refrain of 'Through the Long Days' on her lips. Dorothy becomes a shade divided from herself, and the mystery of her death is impenetrable to the medical profession. She dies attached to a posthumous bond; her death determined by the power of a hidden trauma.

Through the Long Days

Through the long days and years
What will my loved one be.
Parted from me?
        Words by John Hay, music by Francis Boott.

Several years later Henry James was at last able to bear a first visit to Fenimore's grave, near the pyramid of Cestius and Keats' grave, in the old walled Protestant cemetery in Rome:

> The most beautiful thing in Italy.

Ten Blake Songs

> He who binds to himself a Joy
> Doth the winged life destroy;
> But he who kisses the Joy as it flies
> Lives in Eternity's sunrise.
>> William Blake,: from *Ten Blake Songs*, set by Vaughan Williams in 1957, for viola and oboe recorded by James Bowman, countertenor, and Paul Goodwin, oboe d'amore, 1988

James' contemporary English repertoire was probably dearer to me than all else, and warmly acknowledged by the critics: 'James Bowman has virtually created a new repertoire for the countertenor and given that most delicate and ethereal of male voices new prominence and importance.' James Bowman, *Artist of the Week*, Radio 3, 6th-9th July, 1993.

I trusted that one day he would again sit godlike at my side – holding separation away. As we stood together on the pavement outside the King's Hall in Ilkley, he touched my arm and expressed his wish that I see his concert *Dream* and forthcoming *Blake Songs* – 'Come to my *Dream*, Maxine, and the *Blake Songs* at Snape on Easter Monday'. James asked if I had a ticket for his *Dream* and offered to send me one. Having in anger told me 'go home to your children; they're the ones you adore', he then relented and withdrew his possessive, jealous reproach, saying that I had 'exquisitely good manners'. Of course, I forgave him, because he'd also told me that his mother was dying, 'I'm wounded and bleeding, Maxine, bleeding.'

> And now snow falls…
> In the twilight the wound gapes open, vermillion.'
> Hans Werner Henze, *Six Songs from the Arabian,* v 'Fatima's Lament'

I arose at dawn on Easter Monday as the recital was to begin in the Maltings at 11:30am. James was to perform Lute Songs and Vaughan Williams' *Ten Blake Songs*. He looked for me in the audience and having immediately found me, he had sung to me in my aloneness. James was always fascinated by the aura which my hours alone gave to me. Afterwards, I saw him sitting at a table in the sunlit foyer, his head resembling the Farnese Antinous. 'You didn't come to my *Dream*, did you?' he said. 'I missed you there.' I explained that I had been ill, but it was to no avail. He resented my absence and said that it had been 'a magical occasion – but of course you didn't come…' He never forgave me for that omission. I had sent him yellow Roses in Blue, but he could barely bring himself to thank me, and even reproached me for having failed to attend his Chester Cathedral concert years before. At the time he had indicated that it would be an unsatisfactory, melancholy occasion because he loathed singing 'in the acoustic of red sandstone'; the mere sight of it made him melancholy. A card to me from his Lichfield recital deliberately refuted that view and was intended to be disconcerting. 'Lichfield Cathedral turned out to be rather charming, even though I dislike red sandstone'. But also, knowing how concerned for him I was, 'I expect you to protect me, Maxine' – he would have wanted to reassure me that he'd been alright in a potentially upsetting situation. When I told him that I'd risen at first light to come to see him, he simply said that he'd got up even earlier to get to Snape. He was determined to be as frigid as possible.

Sitting alone in his white gabardine coat and wearing glasses, he looked unbearably solitary and morose – 'mantled in mist, remote from the happy.' I said goodbye and turned to go when he said 'Maxine, give me a kiss before you go.' – I embraced him with a kiss, and held him in my arms, tenderly pressing my face against his cheek. He was as unresponsive as stone.

I wrapped my soft burgundy scarf round me (it had belonged to my father) and stepped outside into the solace of gently falling snow.

> ...it was only later that its meaning dawned on me: that it had been your farewell. One rarely knows when a word or an act will trigger some final irreversible alteration in any relationship.
>
> Sándor Márai, *Embers*

Afterwards, I walked briefly on forlorn Dunwich beach and thought of Henry James having visited it. A childhood memory of my mother ('a lovely mum' as James so often called her), also returned to me, and a description of the incident that I'd written for him in response to hearing him sing *Almost Peace*. He told me that he loved its beauty and that in mythologizing my mother it expressed our empathy.

'At six years of age, during deep January snow in Birchanger Lane, I was warmly wrapped inside my mother's old musquash fur coat, with only my face and hands gently caressed by the beautiful falling snow. Ecstatic melancholy enclosed me until I noticed that the coat was torn: overwhelmed by love for my mother and distress at her damaged coat, which she was too poor to replace, I began to cry…

A few years later in that same village lane, our white miniature poodle, Gina, was killed by a lorry. She died instantly. It was not the driver's fault; the dog had run out in front of him. His visibility was obscured by heavy snowfall. I remember my mother carrying Gina back to the house, and a neighbour burying her at the bottom of our garden before my Father returned home in the evening from London. My brother and I were devastated and terribly upset when we saw our mother's white trench coat, covered with blood where she had held Gina in her arms after the accident. She felt that she was to blame for failing to put the dog on a lead. My mother felt guilty and responsible for her death, but that night everything was peaceful in the moonlit snow-covered garden.

When I grew up and left home for University the adored old fur coat was given to me and was sometimes worn inside out to light the 'changeable taffeta' and reveal a mysterious red mark within the lining. As a child this strange stain had always intrigued me, and became my favourite feature of the coat…'

> It ceased to hurt me, though so slow
> I could not feel the Anguish go –
> But only knew by looking back –
> That something – had benumbed the track –
>
> Nor when it altered, I could say,
> For I had worn it, every day,
> As constant as the childish frock –
> I hung upon the Peg, at night.

> But not the Grief – that nestled close
> As needles – ladies softly press
> To Cushions Cheeks –
> To keep their place –
>> *Almost Peace*, a setting of poems by Emily Dickinson, composed by Geoffrey Burgon for the voice of James Bowman

Whenever I heard James sing the Burgon setting of *Almost Peace*, it reconnected me with those intense memories and the contact I had enjoyed with James. Together, in imagination, we had revisited the classical world and childhood, travelling in time, elegizing friends.

The *Almost Peace* songs are not commercially available, but I heard James perform them in a live broadcast on Radio 3 on the 1st October, 1995, and recorded them. The *Almost Peace* settings were commissioned by BBC Radio 3 for the programme *The Fairest Isle Songbook*; the idea behind the programme was to celebrate current English music and song in the tradition of Purcell/Britten. James often referred to Geoffrey Burgon as 'Britten's heir'.

The Orante

> Awake, sweet love, thou art return'd,
> My heart, which long in absence mourn'd,
> Lives now in perfect joy.
>> Dowland's lute song, 'Awake, sweet love', recorded by James Bowman, February 1990

James' *Awake Sweet Love* recital at Snape Maltings on Easter Monday, 13th April 1998, was to be the last time that I was left 'in suspended ecstasy'. All my intensities were to end in the

King's Hall of the Armstrong Building at Newcastle University, close to leafy Jesmond, where James had spent his formative years. I suspect that this place has a malevolence inherited from James' childhood in constant exile. Peter Ackroyd's words from his book *London, A Biography*, published in 2000, describing 'The Tree in the Corner' are equally applicable to my impressions of Newcastle: 'It is possible, too, that an unpleasant or unhappy atmosphere may persist like some noisome scent in the air... The act of building may itself determine the character of an area for ever, in other words, it is as if the stones themselves carried the burden of their own destiny.'

James Bowman has an honorary degree from the University of Newcastle, and is viewed as 'a local hero'. He received the Honorary Degree of Doctor of Music in May, 1996. It was a tenebrous cessation of contact, at the King's Hall, on Saturday, 27th February, 1999, 'leaving me alone like a man new fallen from fairyland in the black darkness of night', although the letters continued for a few more weeks. During Tenebrae in Holy Week fifteen candles, fitted on a triangular frame, are extinguished one by one until the service ends in darkness. James had sometimes presided at this ritual in his local church, St Mary's.

> If thou be near me I go joyfully to death, which is my rest. Ah, how blissful will be my end, if thy beautiful hands will close my faithful eyes.
> J S Bach *'Bist du bei mir'*, written for Bach's second wife, Anna Magdalena.

In his notes on this piece as performed by the countertenor Alfred Deller, S. W. Bennett wrote: 'It is one of the most tender, lovely, simple and perfect songs in all music literature.'

When my father lay dying on the day before Christmas Eve, he had lost so much weight that his buttocks and scrotum were indistinguishable, but his upper body remained strong, and his eyes and hands as beautiful as they had always been. He was attended by his doctor son, Mark and dear Dr R. O. Chapman, my own family GP who administered the morphine. I still keep my father's last shirt in a drawer on the landing. During the days preceding his death my mother never left his side.

For his funeral service my father had the same readings as Sir Laurence Olivier: Donne's Holy Sonnet no 6 (1609) 'Death be not Proud', and Shakespeare's Sonnet 116, 'Let me not to the Marriage of true Minds Admit Impediments'.

I thought of my father's final moments when, some few years later, at the Archaeological Museum of Rhodes, I was standing with my mother and young children, in front of a wonderful life-size Greek bas-relief of the 5th Century BC. This six-foot long grave slab from Kamiros depicts Krito bidding farewell to her dead mother, Timarista. It had been left outside in a covered stone courtyard and as we looked at it a shaft of sunlight fell upon it, making it special:

> I know
> you touch so blissfully because the
> caress preserves,
> because the place you so tenderly cover
> does not vanish; because underneath it
> you feel pure duration. So you promise
> eternity, almost,
> from the embrace.
>
> Rainer Maria Rilke, *Duino elegies*

'My face is all covered with shaving foam, Maxine'

As James gave me a brief list of his 1998 engagements which he felt would interest me, he said, 'My face is all covered with shaving foam, Maxine.' It was a shared intimate moment on the telephone. He also told me that in the privacy of his own home, he often talked to himself, whistled and hummed. I'd once heard his falsetto hum on stage, and for one performance, his usually immaculate appearance and perfect skin was disfigured by savage razor marks and an alarming red rash on his face.

At the age of three, whilst walking with my father on the frozen marshes of northern Kent, I cut my fingers on the razor-sharp reeds, as I foolishly attempted to pick one. They bled profusely so my Father bound my hand with his white handkerchief, played a game to distract me from the pain, and carried me home on his back, where I often clung to watch him shaving, loving the swishing water and male scents. After the trauma of James' suspicious and hostile words at Ilkley, I'd suffered from continual uterine bleeding which my Consultant told me had been brought on by a terrible shock. 'If you ever want anything back, Maxine,' James said, 'you have only to ask – but as all these things are in my house it is the same thing as being in yours, and there will never be any need to return them.' This was the fate of three of my CD booklets, which he had claimed to have 'lost', including that of Britten's *Rejoice in the Lamb*, recorded with King's College Choir, Cambridge. I knew that he had deliberately withheld them from me, but carefully concealed the lesions.

> privatize to the dead
> her memory:
> let her wounds weep
> into the lens of oblivion   Geoffrey Hill, *Canaan*

Even at Ilkley, on Wednesday 11th February 1998, I had anticipated the obliteration of an exclusive empathy such as that described by James himself when talking of Benjamin Britten and Peter Pears. 'Ben obviously loved Peter's voice,' James told me. 'He never wrote for any other tenor voice at all, wouldn't even consider it – and this I found extraordinary. And when they performed together it was a sort of symbiotic relationship, musically; it was quite uncanny to watch them. When Peter breathed Ben's fingers moved; I mean it was just amazing.' The singer John Shirley-Quirk has also commented on what he called 'the miracle of their joint musicality', saying in discussion with John Evans on Radio 3: 'Ben knew exactly how to write for Peter, and Peter knew exactly how to sing for Ben.'

Britten's realisation of Purcell's *Sweeter than Roses*, was originally made as a love offering for Pears, but on the CD recording it was transposed specifically for James, and added as a filler to the *Journey of the Magi* recording. 'It transcends all pious principles about authenticity, so profound was Britten's love for Purcell.' (George Pratt – music critic.)

The Britten connection was immensely important to James and to the beginnings of our friendship and empathy, and not just because of the National Gallery concert performance of Britten's 'Sweeter than Roses' and *Abraham and Isaac*, which had been a pivotal occasion for us both, for different reasons, and one we would always remember.

His debut in the *Dream* in 1967 at the age of 26 had launched his professional career, and Britten said that it was Bowman who had finally vindicated his choice of the countertenor voice for the role of Oberon. On *Desert Island Discs*, Sue Lawley introduced James Bowman as a man whose 'career started in March, 1967, and who's never been out of work since!'

In creating the role of Oberon for Britten's *A Midsummer Night's Dream*, James awakened a new enthusiasm for the countertenor voice. 'I was jolly lucky,' James said, 'to have been around in the right place at the right time and to be able to sing that particular opera immediately gave me a very high profile.'

And when he worked with Peter Pears on Britten's Canticle 1V, *The Journey of the Magi*, he said that he had been 'terrified'. He remembered how wonderfully supportive Peter Pears had been, holding James' hand as they ran across the lawns at Red House on their way to rehearsal, Peter Pears saying encouragingly to the young and nervous James, 'Yes, you can do it, you can...'

James said that the very first time he heard Britten's *Sinfonia da Requiem*, he 'knew then that Britten was a genius'. Shortly before Britten's death in 1976, he was planning to write a Song Cycle for Countertenor and Julian Bream on lute, dedicated to James Bowman. Britten wrote music which challenged the virtuosity of his friends without losing intimacy and dialogue.

> '...The greatest secret and the greatest gift any of us can be offered is the chance for two *similar* people to meet. It happens so rarely – He did not stand on the far bank beyond my reach.'

On that September evening in Hinckley, sitting close beside me, James had said 'Who else do you love, Maxine?' When I answered 'Only Peter Pears,' he said, 'How strange! Well that's alright then – he's dead. I adored him! Maxine, he was still beautiful, even when he was quite old. He came from somewhere else, he did. Unfortunately he became overly fond.

You mustn't become too obsessed, Maxine, there are other singers in the world – but I can't think of any at the moment! But you must admire Andreas Scholl and Robin Blaze?' James then acknowledged that my love for his own voice was a 'beautiful and personal thing, as beautiful and personal as Britten's realisation of Purcell's "Sweeter Than Roses".'

On this particular occasion, my obsession seemingly brought out a strange fear in him; he was not afraid *of* me but *for* me. Shortly after the Hinckley concert, I wrote to him a postcard of St Alban's Abbey, ending with an ominous quotation from Edna O'Brien's *The Girl with the Green Eyes*: 'I watched him go. I saw him as a dark-faced god turning his back on me. I put out my hand to recall him and caught only the rain. I felt that it would rain for ever, noiselessly.'

Since the new millennium, Blaze has been James Bowman's successor in the King's Consort, and the German countertenor Andreas Scholl has been hailed by the critics as the new Alfred Deller. In 1998, Scholl made an outstanding operatic stage debut with the Glyndebourne Festival Opera as Bertarido in Handel's *Rodelinda*. *The Sunday Times* said of his performance: 'Scholl rightly stops the show with the grave beauty of his alto voice and rapt musicality.'

Scholl's status as the top European performer of the new generation was confirmed in the review of Prom 55 at the Royal Albert Hall in 2001, in *The Independent*: 'The last time male altos attracted the popular following enjoyed today by Andreas Scholl was surely at the height of the Victorian Music Hall craze. Even countertenor revivalists Alfred Deller and James Bowman at their finest could not have hoped to fill the Royal Albert Hall for a late night concert. Scholl's wide appeal rests securely on one of the finest voices of recent times, an instrument capable of extraordinary technical precision and tonal riches beyond the scope of other falsettists.'

This critic has clearly forgotten that more than *three* decades earlier, David Munrow, performing with James Bowman, often enjoyed capacity audiences in the Albert Hall. Conversely, when I attended Andreas Scholl's Handel recital in Manchester's Bridgewater Hall, there were many empty seats. As Michael Church has said of James Bowman, 'No countertenor before or since has managed to match his brilliant, clarion sound'.

I have seen Andreas Scholl on a number of occasions and been captivated by his brilliance, but even he has been involved in 'crossover' music and 'populist' recordings like his 2001 recording of folk songs, *Wayfaring Stranger*, in which for one song, 'The Wraggle-Taggle Gypsies, O', he unsuccessfully sings as a baritone and an alto. A further folly is his other life as a 'pop' singer, creating recordings in his private studio in Germany. Decca may release such a record, which Scholl terms 'soul-funk for grown-ups'. I've heard some of these compositions on the radio and they are embarrassingly dreadful, rather like the lapse in taste when Scholl performed duets with his sister, Elizabeth, (a very ordinary singer) at the Albert Hall.

Generally speaking the new wave of countertenors is now over-evident; James Bowman himself is in agreement with this view, having given defamatory verdicts on many of the countertenors in this over-subscribed field. He feels that there are now too many diverse forms of the male high voice, a multiplicity of 'mediocre' sounds.

In Alfred Deller's time, countertenors were very thin on the ground, so one of Alfred's sons, Mark Deller, joined his father's Consort as a countertenor. Mark's voice does indeed sound like the authentic 'cat that has had its tail trodden on'. I observed Mark Deller at one of James' performances of the *Dream* at Sadler's Wells. Mark has the dramatic, dark, gypsy good looks of his famous father.

James said to me, 'I *like* Mark Deller, he's always admitted that he cannot sing... he's not one of mine but at least he's honest about his limitations.'

I gave James a wonderful 1976 postcard of Benjamin Britten in a wheelchair, holding a posy of pink roses. 'That's just how I remember him,' he said, and promised to treasure it all his life. James told me that Ben had died in Peter's arms. Peter had never really recovered from the devastating loss of Ben; he slowly disintegrated. James told me Peter, in a phone call, said: '"I feel fucking terrible," and two days later he was dead.'

James had also promised me that he would never forget my story about the solace of falling snow. 'I promise to remember that always, Maxine, did it help?...my mother's funeral is arranged down to the last detail – her coffin is to be completely covered in snowdrops.' He discussed all this with me long before his mother's death. When I told my own mother about the intended snowdrops, she said 'What will he do if his mother dies at the wrong time of year for those particular flowers? Too bad, I suppose...' adding that probably it would be all right because James could afford the necessarily large number of snowdrops – even when out of season.

I often wonder if the day will come when the snow and he are intimate, like Gabriel in James Joyce's short story 'The Dead'. I gave James an inscribed copy of Joyce's quiet and intimate masterpiece, which contains images of musical angels and lots of references to singing. The action is set on the Feast of Epiphany, January 6th, 1904, in Dublin and the protagonist Gabriel's experience is epiphanic. Gretta, the wife of Gabriel, is set apart by a secret sadness, reflected in the chiaroscuro of the house with its dark, unknown spaces. Wearing a blue headscarf and framed by the stained glass window behind her, Gretta resembles a Marian icon, but cut deep by love. She discloses that she is thinking of a lost boy from long ago, who used to sing to her. Gabriel stands at the window to watch the falling snow, and meditates on the relationship of death and love. The snow which he watches mesmerically falling and dissolving, provides an image of resolution. Gabriel accepts his transience as snow falls 'on all the living and the dead'.

The Sepulchre

> the gifts
> set down to derision
> rejoice in them
> as things that are mourned.
>   Geoffrey Hill, *Canaan* collection

It is painful to trace the irreversible and inevitable descent into anti-climax, and difficult to acknowledge it even privately. Unfortunately, events cannot be reversed by the writer's pen; they can only be chronicled and remembered. And a memoir can become a work of art. I've sometimes wondered if James has felt any remorse of the heart over his cruel, never explained return of seven unopened letters. Britten did exactly that to W. H. Auden, but later regretted it.

    Long before my gifts were foreclosed on and the twilight magic of his presence disappeared from me forever, I had sometimes felt, like Henry James' Strether, that I was an experiment and a verdict would be passed on me. After a recital of German Baroque music at the Wigmore Hall, on Tuesday,

29th December, 1992, I was in the restaurant with a friend when we saw James at the adjacent table having a drink with Gustav Leonhardt, the great harpsichord player, his wife, Maria, the Baroque violinist, and a Frenchwoman, 'an admirer' described by James as 'a bore and a bit of a strain' because her English was poor. James kept glancing across at me and duly introduced me, whilst saying to my companion 'Get yourself a drink,' and then ignoring her. 'Are they Hebrew?' said Leonhardt, and James replied, 'Maxine is! – anyway she'll do,' and put his arm round me. He later told me that 'It was like the film of *Separate Tables*', which James loved, and I agreed that, on that emotional evening, we shared the loneliness of Terence Rattigan's eccentric misfits who 'bare their innermost secrets ... and change each other's lives for ever.'

Gustav Leonhardt gave me a charming smile and bowed, before James initiated an hilarious Nazi-style pastiche of J.C. Bach's lament: '*Ach, dass ich wassers gnug hätte*' which he had just sung that evening. Of course, James is a perfect mimic. In conversation with me a month before his CBE ceremony at the Palace, he had perfectly imitated the Queen's voice, speculating on her probable words to him; 'You must have been singing for a long time...' he said, in Queenly falsetto.

'Strether was left musing on many things. One of them was the question of whether, since he had been tested, he had passed. Did the artist drop him from having made out that he wouldn't do?' Or perhaps, like Peter Pears, who 'came from somewhere else', I had become 'overly fond'. My friend Peter Giles had once said 'You'll be all right, Max, until he gets a new companion,' and also suggested James feared that one day I'd ask for all my letters back. By then he had all he needed from me and didn't want any more, but would never part with those that still seemed to serve a useful purpose.

> The copyright in unpublished letters is the property of the writer of the letters. The physical letters themselves are the property of the recipient. Unless ... he returns the letters to her possession.
>
> A. S. Byatt, *Possession*

At first, James missed the frequent flowers, but eventually they too were concluded. Sadly, at the last, even my exquisite flowers, once so loved, became an irritant because he had to respond to them; henceforth they were confined solely to Easter:

> And her flowers be upon him
> Leviticus, 16

One of the things James so respected about me was that I never burdened him with my personal problems. When I entered the enchantment of his presence, such things were always left behind. 'Unlike almost all people, Maxine,' he said, 'you have never sought to take advantage of me.'

> I hide myself within my flower
> That fading from your Vase,
> You, unsuspecting feel for me –
> Almost a loneliness.
> Emily Dickinson

In my last letters from James I received both a warning and a telling off. He reprimanded me for indiscreetly writing on the envelope: 'Unless concealed inside an envelope – such things are in the public domain – and open to speculation... If you wish to convey your innermost thoughts to me I suggest you find a more private means of doing so.' He reassured me that my correspondence to him was perfectly safe from intrusion. 'It is all placed in a large box in the privacy of my study.' His last letter written and dated on green paper gave me my ambiguous dismissal, in the words of the poet Geoffrey Hill, 'Overnight the inmost self made outcast.'

6th October 1999

Dear Maxine,
  I think the time has come for your correspondence to cease. It started out as a charming gesture, but now seems to be serving no useful purpose.
Yours sincerely,
James

King's Hall, Newcastle

To wound a soul is as great a criminal act as killing a body.
The words of a Jewish survivor of Auschwitz.

The concert which preceded this final letter from James in October, 1999 was his performance of David in Handel's English oratorio *Saul*, where formalities preserved us: 'Hello, Maxine, thank you for coming,' he said. I shall not describe the occasion but instead, include my mother's reaction and transcribe the letters I wrote to her and to James, after the act of destruction had taken place.

My mother said that the effect on me of this final letter from James Bowman reminded her of Henry James' description of the effect on *him* of the outbreak of the First World War. Henry James believed that 'this crash of our civilisation' and possible destruction of 'exquisite England' had turned his life and work into a gross lie: 'It seems to me to undo everything, everything that was ours, in the most horrible retroactive way –

but I avert my face from the monstrous scene.' It was to his friend Rhoda Broughton that Henry James poured out his deepest anguish in a letter, and these letters which he wrote in August 1914 are among the most eloquent of his life.

I had of course given these very letters to James Bowman, in a magnificent collection edited by Leon Edel. James told me that Henry James' letters were his 'absolute favourites'.

I wrote to my mother:

> Dearest Mum,
> I enclose a copy of my brief and final letter to James Bowman; I had to conclude ... in writing. All the quotes are from his performance of Handel's *Saul* and thus are David's own words. I hope you agree that it perfectly expresses both our former 'closeness' and the plangent fact that we also have nothing in common...

The 'wound' was intensified by my memory of first hearing James sing the role of David, a recording he had made in Leeds Town Hall in May, 1972, in the place and year of my apotheosis in the Meanwood Cottage:

> For thee, my brother Jonathan,
> How great is my distress!
> What language can my grief express?
> Great was the pleasure I enjoy'd in thee.'
> > David's solo lament for Jonathan, from Handel's oratorio *Saul*, performed and recorded in Leeds Town Hall, May 1972, sung by James Bowman

It also seems significant and ironic that when Handel wrote *Saul* at the age of 53, he had just recovered from a mental breakdown. It is David's singing and playing on the harp, and the evocation of a green, pastoral landscape, that charms away Saul's madness.

A review in *The Gramophone* in November 1973, when the

countertenor revival was still in its infancy, and critics preferred women, described James' brilliant performance thus: 'The part of David was intended for a countertenor by Handel, and it is here sung by James Bowman who brings a vigour to the more dramatic arias that could not be surpassed by any other singer of his kind today. His runs are true, and he has one marvellous high F.'

In the early 1990s, I had bought a *boxed* set from the 1973 production of *Saul*, and the reissue on CD by Archiv Produktion. James in conversation emphasised the fact that the German company is spelled without 'e': 'It's Archi*v*, Maxine, it's on Archi*v*!'

The original LPs are accompanied by a photograph of the youthful 31-year-old James, in sports jacket and striped tie, his shoulder-length 'beautiful curling hair' resembling that of Leonardo da Vinci, in the Anonimo Gaddiano description. I like to think that *Burning in Blueness* is a fine-art 'memorial' to James:

> A picture lives by companionship, expanding and quickening in the eyes of a sensitive observer. It dies by the same token. It is therefore a risky and unfeeling act to send it into the world.
>
> Mark Rothko, *Tiger's Eye*

Peter Giles once said that I should be the one to write a biography of James: 'Someone must write about him, and you, Max, are the one to do it.' He added that I would have to wait until after his death, or certainly that of his mother.

Whatever the difficulties between James and his mother, theirs had obviously been an unbroken relationship enduring until her death in a hospice. James told me that when his mother had met Benjamin Britten, 'Ben was perfectly horrid at first, until he got to know her, and then he was rather sweet.' Given that

James was twenty-six years old at this time, one wonders why his mother was there at all.

    Like the relationship between Henry James and Minny Temple, mine with James Bowman was full of contrasting light and shadow. On reading this memoir my mother said 'You write about James Bowman as though he is dead. I'm reminded of Henry James' description of his beloved cousin, Minny Temple, as "an immortal absence".'

The Opened Mouth

> The erotogenic zone of the mouth was given an emphasis which it never afterwards surrendered.
>   Sigmund Freud, on Leonardo's
>   *St Anne With Two Others*

The prominence of the mouth zone in Leonardo's art is explained by Freud as compounded from the memory of being suckled and being kissed by his mother.

    One of James' favourite cards from me, which delighted and amused him, was 'The Opening of the Mouth Ceremony', in celebration of his performance at the QEH on March 26th 1996 of the title role in Handel's oratorio *Joseph and his Brethren*. I think it appealed to his Irish fascination with and fear of death, but it also reflected his dual preoccupation with singing and eating. 'The Opening of the Mouth Ceremony' is from the *Book of the Dead* of Hunefer, Nineteenth Dynasty, c1300 BC. This ritual restored to the mummy all his faculties so that he might enjoy the afterlife to the full. '…you have gone away, but you have returned; you were asleep, but you have been wakened. You died, but you live again.' It is the ancient Egyptian equivalent of the resurrection, or Christ's raising of Lazarus as described in

Donne's Sermon Number 7 'Jesus Wept', preached at Whitehall the first Friday in Lent 1622/3.

James responded to this image and the beautiful roses, by sending me three wonderful 'Singing Photographs' of himself at work, with opened mouth – at the Paris Opera in concert performance with Jean-Claude Malgoire's La Grande Écurie et la Chambre du Roy, in Handel's *Ariodante* at Geneva, and as Oberon in a famous production of Britten's *Dream* at Covent Garden. In all three photographs, chiaroscuro is effected with the use of 'Rembrandt lighting.'

> To James:
> Your beautiful portrait at the Paris Opera ... is gloriously laurelled in black and dove, Ariodante is similarly honoured in black and cloud! – Oberon dazzles!!
> Best wishes, always,
> Maxine

In The Opening of the Mouth Ceremony, those making obeisance are offering food and wine to the Mummy; James was always very fond of his food! And vocal restoratives included garlic, orange juice, mineral water and 'a cup of tea in the interval'. 'James heads straight for rich, red Borscht, thick with beetroot and onions, when he wants to restore vocal cords after a gruelling performance,' as noted in *The Singer*, described by James as 'a silly little magazine'. I once caught a glimpse of James in the wings at Sadler's Wells, cup of tea in hand, during his *Dream*; I was seated to the far left, next to Paddy Ashdown and his wife. Paddy invited me to join them in the interval for a gin and tonic, but I politely declined.

James was anxious about getting fat, but when I asked him if, like so many singers of the younger generation, he worked out at the gym, went swimming and took regular exercise, he said, 'Not if I can help it.' On his 60th birthday, in conversation on Radio 3, he said that he would be 'celebrating with a salad rather than a cake'. My mother thought that James looked as though the only exercise he ever took was 'in the bedroom'.

An article in the Winter 2006 edition of the Canadian music journal *The Music Scene*, throws light on 'Why Singing Makes You Fat': 'Research carried out by Dr Peter Osin, consultant at London's royal Marsden Hospital, suggests that a singers constant use of their lungs triggers an overdose in the excretion of leptin, causing the brain to build up a resistance to the protein. Leptin is a hormone, a protein made in fat cells that helps the brain assess how much fat the body is storing. The resistance to leptin suggests that the physical action of singing can actually make you gain weight.' Wah Keung Chan.

James has likened his own love of food to that of Handel. Having been left permanently hungry at school in Ely, I think James had been making up for it ever since. When he apologized to me for breathing garlic all over me, I reassured him that I loved the smell, especially as it reminded me of my early infatuation with a French teaching assistant named Joseph René, from whom garlic constantly emanated.

James always had a good meal before performing. According to Peter Giles, eating before a concert was a cardinal sin for a singer. 'Alfred Deller always ate after performances,' he emphasized. But as usual, James broke all the rules, sublimely.

He also had a strange obsession with toilets, and during long performances, sometimes lasting over three hours, would ask me 'Will you be all right for the toilet, Maxine, there is only the one!' I assured him that I was absolutely fine, as I had no problem at all in that area. I think his preoccupation went back to the days when his mother attended his concerts, often in ecclesiastical buildings, and always sat in the front row, afterwards saying in a peremptory tone 'Come along, James.' He told me that his mother had always been supportive, but his father was absent and uninterested. Like Benjamin Britten he had a 'thing' about absent fathers and utterly disapproved of them. When I told him that Tamsin and Leon's father worked in London, and rarely returned home, even at weekends, James expressed his disgust and anger. Nevertheless, he regarded divorce as 'terrible and traumatic', because his mother had a 'very difficult time when she was going through this process'. James mentioned his Mozart-loving stepfather, a brother who 'escaped' by joining the Navy, and his mother's insensitive comment when she heard him singing in falsetto at home during the summer holidays, 'Hasn't your voice broken yet?!'

After his time at Oxford, where he was a choral scholar with New College Choir, he underwent a period of semi-estrangement from his family. 'I'd graduated from Oxford with a fourth class degree in History, so it was pretty obvious that my future didn't lie in academia.' He'd been 'vivaed up from a fail' and had become a prep school master, a fate from which he had been rescued by Britten. 'Music – It was like a secret hideout, where the world could not reach him.' Peter Giles said to me that 'Britten and Pears saw something in Bowman that others had never seen'. David Willcocks had turned him down when he auditioned for a choral scholarship at King's College, Cambridge. He described this failure as 'The biggest disappointment of my life, I suppose'.

James' relationship with the Chapel Choirs of Cambridge remained slightly ambivalent and defensive. 'You ask me, Maxine, if I ever sing in Cambridge – well I'm simply never asked.' This was said to me before a wonderful recital at the Sheldonian theatre in Oxford on Saturday, July 3rd, 1993. The title of the concert was Handel Love Songs. At the conclusion of *Ombra mai fu*, James attentively bowed to me alone. We had chatted beforehand about Henry James' letters and my hope that James would soon sing in Cambridge.

Of course, he was subsequently 'asked' on many occasions, and years before had in fact made the greatest ever recording of Handel's *Messiah*, with David Willcocks and King's College Choir. He told me that he much preferred Cambridge to Oxford, as it was so much greener and prettier, and it gave him special pleasure to sing there. Like me, he loved 'the Cambridge smell of river, mist and loamy soil'. James seemed to believe that Oxford and Cambridge were somehow in opposition to one another, but in his later life they appear to be reconciled in his mind. A brief glance at his UK list of engagements for 2007 reveals that in March and April he gave performances at three Cambridge colleges: St John's, Trinity and King's.

Henry James described King's College Chapel as 'the most beautiful Chapel in England':

> In the choir behind the great screen which divides the chapel in half the young choristers were rehearsing for the afternoon. The beautiful boy-voices rose together and touched the splendid vault; they hung there, expanding and resounding, and then, like a rocket that spends itself, they faded and melted toward the end of the building. It was positively a choir of angels.
> Henry James, *English Hours*

Like my Jane Austen tutor at Leeds, Dr Alexander Edward Henry Scrope Viner, I think James was 'a different kind of man' and sometimes felt oppressed by his family background, and their expectations of him. 'Sandy' Viner's mother lived at Fountains Hall, near Ripon in Yorkshire; his academic life at the University allowed him to escape his oppressive aristocratic ancestors and pursue his twin loves of literature and fine art. He was a friend of the great painter and Leeds University academic Professor Lawrence Gowing. Sometimes he visited his mother at weekends and returned to his City apartment near adored St George's Square, with an 'old master' from Fountains Hall. The Georgian Water Garden, and 'surprise view' of the twelfth century Cistercian Abbey, had featured in my postgraduate essay on the picturesque.

James' background was ecclesiastical northern Irish on his mother's side – his great-grandfather was a bishop of Ireland – but always put me in mind of Henry James' *Owen Wingrave* (a short story made into the opera of that name by Benjamin Britten). It focuses on a young man facing the realisation that he cannot continue his family's military tradition, and who, like Virginia's Woolf's *Orlando* just wants to be literary and creative.

> I was surrounded with love, nursed in hope.
> Spoiled with admiration,
> But all for the image they made of me,
> For the man they planned to make of me.
>
> In peace I have found my image,
> I have found myself.
> In peace I rejoice amongst men
> And yet walk alone.
>
> Benjamin Britten, *Owen Wingrave*

On the radio James spoke affectionately of childhood visits to his grandmother in Armagh, dangerously close to the border, and idyllic holidays in Donegal, where he could express his passion for the sea. James' superstitious nature comes from the Irish side of his family. James sees the English Cathedral Choir as the most secure place to develop a countertenor voice, and he still loves to be part of a team, but his time as an Ely Chorister had undoubtedly given rise to tensions and conflict within himself. He described Ely as a 'monastic environment' devoid of women. The all-male authoritarian environment permanently damaged James.

> For this is not one life; nor do I always know if am man or woman ... so strange is the contact of one with another.
> Rilke

Some years earlier I'd written to the countertenor Michael Chance: 'Looking on from the outside it would appear that a so-called "world famous" countertenor can yet pass almost unnoticed by most. I wonder if there is still an indifference to this voice as a great solo instrument...you mention a peculiar attitude towards the male alto voice, by some for whom it is "unnatural" and who relate it to the castrato...wherever a countertenor is featured...it is always the "sexuality" of his voice which receives attention'.

Even ten years ago this was true of an internationally renowned countertenor such as James. Neither he nor I ever expressed any interest in the 'sexuality' of the countertenor voice; we did not think about it. James told me that it was another thing that made us 'alike'.

For more than thirty-five years, James Bowman has led the field with a voice that is pure and powerful, sexless yet seductive, ethereal but also deeply sensual. For more than a decade James has been privileged to receive my letters.

'It's almost as if she had passed away from having served her purpose...that of inviting ... me onward by all the bright intensity of her example.' Henry James' description of his dead, consumptive cousin Minnie Temple, immortalised by him in *The Wings of the Dove*: 'Her memory's your love – you need no other...' As Lyndall Gordon says, 'Milly's wings bear her beyond her lifetime'. Henry James also included a memoir of Minny, his 'dancing flame of thought' as the last chapter of his autobiographical *Notes of a Son and Brother*. His portrait of Minny is based on letters and is not accurate in every detail, but it does, as he claimed, bring her back from the dead. In the Memoir, although his part in her story is omitted – he only quotes her side of the correspondence, never his own – he nevertheless creates a plangent portrait of the cousin who loved him deeply, 'wrapping her', as he says, in the 'dignity of art'.

'We shall never be again as we were'

> All this was a long time ago.
> I remember.
> And I would do it again,
> but set down.
> This set down
> This: were we led all that way for
> Birth or Death?
>> T.S. Eliot, 'The Journey of the Magi' set to music by Benjamin Britten: Canticle IV, conceived by Britten with the particular gifts in mind of James Bowman, dedicatee

With a triumphant career that has spanned opera, oratorio, contemporary music and solo recitals, and almost 200 records to his name, James Bowman now describes himself as having a 'gentle retirement' and as being in his 'twilight years'. When questioned on 'the future', he replied: 'There are certain things that I can't sing anymore and I'm purposely not working as much as I used to.'

Burning in Blueness

James' verdict on himself is difficult to approach. The 'vanity' and modesty in his character would doubtless combine in any self-portrait. His inconsistent remarks on Michael Nyman's *Self-laudatory Hymn of Inanna and her omnipotence* (a BBC Spitalfields Commission) are very typical of James. On Radio 3 he praised it as 'a wonderful piece', but inscribed my CD booklet 'A pretentious piece, nonetheless!' Interestingly, James believes that when Nyman wrote *Inanna* for him he had an image of James as: 'I think a supremely arrogant, self-confident goddess whose word was law and was able to override all musical problems placed in his/her path'. At the first performance of this piece, which I attended on 11th June, 1992, two incidents occurred to give an insight into his contradictory personality. During the interval, James ran down some temporary wooden steps erected alongside Hawksmoor's great Christ Church of 1725, and which led directly to a grassed area with refreshments. Some members of the public assumed he had come to 'mingle' with them, but he immediately grabbed several fairy cakes and opening his mouth very wide, popped them in whole, one after another, then glaring at the people outside, he ran back up the steps and straight into the church. In the second half, James changed the order of the programme so that the Nyman piece concluded the concert. This proved to be an excellent decision, given the demands of the piece, but it did not please everyone. 'If I might just be allowed to get on with it,' he exclaimed in a peremptory tone of irritation to a woman in the audience who interrupted him to ask why he had changed the order of the pieces. The tension increased in Hawksmoor's magical and sombre masterpiece, but was dispelled by James 'awe-inspiring, insane' performance, made more insane by the presence of a green Bic biro, which James placed behind his ear when he was not conducting with it. Generally speaking, James disliked combining Elizabethan or

Renaissance repertoire with the contemporary, but he sometimes made exceptions to this rule, and his remarkable singing of Byrd on this occasion was just such an example.

Later I reflected on the words of one critic on a previous lute song recital there: 'James is no stranger to Spitalfields and the Church's extraordinary acoustics suit his ethereal voice to perfection.' The luminous, if dilapidated, Church has a primitive, sinister atmosphere, brilliantly conveyed by Peter Ackroyd in his novel *Hawksmoor*, and ideally suited to the Nyman 'Hymn of Inanna' in James' unforgettable interpretation.

> I build in Hieroglyph and in shadow, like my Ancients ... I wish my buildings to be filled with Secresy ...
> Peter Ackroyd, *Hawksmoor*

In Peter Maxwell Davies' 1983 opera, *Taverner*, James took on the soprano countertenor role of an 'hysterical, nervous, twitchy, slightly mad, dissolute priest in the pre-reformation Church', stretching his voice to its limits. James is often uncomplimentary about modern repertoire, some of which he finds very unsingable. In October, 2002, he said: 'One composer presented me with the score of a piece which I thought to be vocally destructive. No matter how clever it was, I just couldn't sing it. It was far too difficult, and apart from Nick Clapton, I can't think of anyone who can do that sort of material properly. A lot of the time the range is too high and, in my opinion, a lot of it is scored badly. Singers are consulted rarely over such music; instead it is presented to them as a *fait accompli*, and much is written without any consideration of the artist the composer has in mind.' (Internationally acclaimed countertenor, James Bowman, looks back over a lifetime devoted to music.)

Although he has of late made many solo discs, in most of his over 180 recordings he is one character in an Opera or Oratorio, or part of a vocal ensemble just as he was at Ely, New College and Christ Church. James once said to me that he could not imagine who would want to come and visit him at home, although at the same time he asked me tentatively, 'Do you play bridge? If so, perhaps we could combine?' He said that I had great charm and he had none. He definitely bears grudges and can be paranoid in his belief that people take advantage of him: 'Unfortunately for me, Maxine, most of my friends are neurotics,' he said.

Peter's description of Sir Francis Drake, thought to have sung countertenor, could equally describe the persona that James liked to project, even though he was frequently morose, introspective and vulnerable, resembling Giorgione's *Blue man in a pink hat*, a postcard of which he sent me. The original Giorgione painting is in Glasgow Museum and Art Galleries, where it is known as 'Head of a Man'. 'He [Sir Francis Drake] seems to have had many qualities which might have encouraged countertenor singing. He was extrovert, daring, dashing, mercurial, self-confident, artistic and humorous, with a touch of flourish and eccentricity.' On August 22nd, 1997, Peter Giles sent me a beautiful postcard of 'The Falconer', 1647, by Ferdinand Bol, inscribed with the following words: 'This man must be a countertenor: the young JB I feel! He looked like this when first I knew him!' This striking painting can be seen in the Suffolk Collection G.L.C. Ranger's House, Blackheath.

Certainly James' success, tactlessness, ingratitude, and outspokenness have made him unpopular with some people, but as a musician, James is 'an inborn aristocrat'. Endearingly, he is notorious for fidgeting and pulling faces, especially during his rare televised performances. All other soloists seem to remain perfectly still whilst waiting to sing. In 1994, I watched a live broadcast on BBC 2 of *Carmina Burana*, by Carl Orff. It was part of the Proms season from the Albert Hall. James couldn't stand this piece, which found great favour with the German Third Reich. He has only one solo, 'The roasted swan'; it is both chilling and unintentionally hilarious. James said that he was 'much too comfortable' to sing the role of a dying swan, beginning 'Once I lived on lakes', but did record the work in 1984 with the Radio Symphony Orchestra Berlin and choir. At the end of the Prom performance, he glared at the embarrassing baritone, Donald Maxwell, who was unwisely attempting to 'act' as well as sing his part. James pulled a face of disgust, and continued to fidget. I lip-read him exactly, saying to himself, 'Thank God that's over!'

It is perhaps not surprising that James loved to be seen through my eyes: 'A unique point of view that is a nightmare, a treasure, and a life-long possession…equal in its rapture and chilling exposure.' Janet Frame. At that period, although he admitted to being 'a slow reader', he was keen to impress me with his literary enthusiasm and attention to the details of my correspondence.

> Dear Maxine,
> I fear you are misled over Ely on 20 December. That concert was cancelled, for me at least, some weeks ago. The Dean and Philistine Chapter decided that they wanted a more 'Popular' programme. I declined to sing in 'Christmas with JB and the Spice Girls.
> (More Peter Giles than me!)
> Best wishes,
> James

As he had made clear after the Ilkley recital, James did not want any 'outsiders' or negative influences to spoil the beauty of the thing we shared. 'Their bond of friendship, fragile and complex in the way of all significant relationships between people, must be protected for a lifetime.' At moments of openness he would admit a resemblance to Oberon in his occasional sadism, spitefulness, and selfishness, and capacity to inflict damage and then disappear. To do something irredeemable, that should never have happened, but which has altered everything and left a petrified heart. 'I do not like myself,' said Sviatislav Richter, one of the greatest pianists of the twentieth century; I think that only self-censorship prevented James from voicing the same verdict. 'I was going to write you a letter with my thoughts on *all this...*' James to Maxine on the telephone after returning from a recital in Portugal, to be greeted by my card and flowers in his porch.

Finale

My final letter to James, written shortly after the Newcastle concert, read:

> Dear James – Burning in Blueness
> Thank you for your wonderful live performance of the 'God-like David' in Newcastle last Saturday evening. 'Great was the pleasure I enjoyed in thee', before you turned your elegiac back on me to disappear with your friends through the revolving door of the Armstrong Building, and I returned home to my children:
>
> > O Lord whose mercies numberless
> > O'er all thy works prevail;
> > Though daily Man thy law transgress,
> > Thy patience cannot fail

> If yet his sin be not too great,
> The busy fiend control;
> Yet longer for repentance wait,
> And heal his wounded soul.

Maxine

'All the reading, all the dreaming had been one long preparation for his arrival…How wonderful this is to think that he looks at me and sings to me…'She had felt his attention around her even when he wasn't there. She had felt herself a part of his quest…part of the creation…How could he disappear, go from her like this? They had talked…never really touched, but she had known the focus of his mind. And now this was gone; the complex symbolism that had described the meaning. This absence was something taken from her…a sense of loss so brutal it stunned and confused her.'

I felt like Bertarido in Handel's *Rodelinda*. By his own Cenotaph, Bertarido, in disguise, reads the epitaph: 'Bertarido was king, conquered by Grimoaldo he fled; he lies in the lands of the Hun. May his soul have rest and his ashes, peace.' In the aria *'Dove Sei'* he calls on his love to console him:

> Where are you, my dear beloved?
> Come and comfort my heart.
> Come, come, beloved.
> I am overcome by torments, and by my sad lamentations,
> but with you there will be peace.

Coda

> I fear to wander in unbroken darkness
> even with those I love
> Geoffrey Hill, 'Coda'

The voice I fell in love with in May 1972, when James was 30, was not the same as the one I returned to in the late 1980s. It had changed, but was just as remarkable and beautiful, having developed greater plangency. It filled me with an even deeper yearning and ecstasy. During the time between those years, we had, in James' words, 'both had serious problems and suffered a terrible loss'.

When I listen to James Bowman's recordings, separated by thirty years, I am aware that the voice has undergone changes. During the Munrow period, James has described himself as 'Singing on a wing and a prayer'. He added that he gave insufficient respect to technique and interpretation. 'In retrospect, I was just singing the notes without having very much to say.' In later years, as his understanding developed, he looked at music from a more 'reflective' viewpoint, and gained 'a more interesting artistic perspective' from being slightly older. 'Nowadays, when I sing something particularly well,' he told me, 'I often think how I would have liked to have sung it like that twenty or thirty years ago – today it all feels much easier.'

In conversation with me, James also said, 'I think all voices sink and all voices get colours over the years. It's like an old painting fading. I feel like an old masterpiece hanging there. I think I've achieved different colours but my voice has certainly gone down and become a little rounder…The countertenor voice isn't a thing that lasts forever. It's always going to change a bit… I think it's just maturity setting in.'

Now that our correspondence is over, my information on James Bowman's career comes largely from Radio 3 and *The Times*. I've just come across a recommendation for his recital at Bowness-on-Windermere, in memory of the thirtieth anniversary of the death of David Munrow, and later on, in the autumn for his 65th birthday recital.

After almost forty years as a professional singer, James is still enjoying his work, but is not nearly as busy as he was. Tongue-in-cheek, he describes himself as a 'living legend', and adds, 'The work comes in sporadically.' He no longer sings every day, is clever at vocal deception, and chooses his repertoire carefully. Because he does not have an agent he does not feel pressured in any way, and can perform in interesting non-mainstream venues. He also gives occasional Master Classes and teaches 'on a selective basis'. These days he often likes to be a member of the audience, or so he says: 'I often think to myself – I'm not really enjoying this. I'd rather be in the audience.' In fact, James rarely listens to music other than his own; he prefers to listen to the spoken word when he is not working. 'Soldiering On', performed by Stephanie Cole, is his favourite among Alan Bennett's *Talking Heads*, revealing James' unexpected enjoyment of pathos in literature, like his surprising love of Brahms.

After all this time and an illustrious career on the world stage he has gone back to singing in a Chapel Choir, where he started, but this time as a Gentleman of the Chapel Royal, founded in the reign of Henry V. 'I've joined the Chapel Choir of her Majesty's Chapel Royal at St James's Palace, and I love it. It's a very small choir so you obviously can't sing flat out as a soloist, you have to listen to the others very carefully. But I love it and it's one of the most important things in my singing life at the moment…It's good to go back to that discipline again. I like singing at the great Festivals of the Church. I miss not singing at

Burning in Blueness

Christmas and Easter. I love that. I like the idea of being part of a choir. I love the repertoire; they sing Byrd, Tallis and Gibbons, which I adore. I like the ritual of the Chapel Royal – it's all the 1662 prayer book, and it's all very beautifully done. It has great dignity.' The Institution was formed as a body of clergy, musicians and singers (men and boys) serving the reigning monarch. Most of Elizabeth 1's (Gloriana) celebrated musicians, including Thomas Tallis and William Byrd, were gentlemen of the Chapel Royal. Vivat Gloriana! Henry Purcell's career began as a chorister of the Chapel Royal. Pelham Humfrey (1647-1674) was another chorister at the Chapel Royal, and spent his short working life entirely at the Chapel. John Donne's masterful 'Hymn to God the Father', reportedly written on the poet's deathbed, presented Humfrey with a wonderful text to set to music. James has recorded this piece; I heard him sing it live on many occasions. John Blow (1649-1708) succeeded Pelham Humfrey as Master of the Children of the Chapel Royal; he was teacher and good friend of Purcell. His 'Ode on the Death of Mr Henry Purcell' was recorded by James and Michael Chance in May 1987; because of its technical difficulties, James referred to it as ' Ode on the Death of Two Countertenors.'

Henrietta Maria, Charles I's music loving Queen, to whom James once likened me, had her own Royal Chapel in London, her image in pearls that he had given me an ironic reminder of our former empathy, now lost.

In a recent, autumn 2006, charity recital in Ottawa, James Bowman at the age of 65, again performed John Blow's 'Ode on the Death of Mr Henry Purcell'. On this occasion, his duettist was the young Canadian countertenor, Daniel Taylor. A member of a local amateur choir attended the concert and remarked that although she thought the sound coming from (the misnamed James Bauman) was amazing, it was Daniel Taylor who was the star. She added that the older singer should spend some money on a new suit, as the one he was wearing looked far too tight.

There was a more recent concert on April 6th, 2007, at King's College Chapel, Cambridge, an Easter Week performance of Bach's *St John Passion*, with the boys of the chapel choir and several eminent soloists, including James Bowman. Sonia Ribeiro, (now a convert to Bach's choral music), noted from a distance that in his two arias Bowman sounded to her a 'full-throttle countertenor', and at the end of the concert, as the soloists entered through the centre door, and walked up the nave to take their bows, Bowman in close-up looked unlike the godlike artist of the photographs on his CD covers: 'Nothing,' Sonia said on the telephone, 'to match your descriptions of him, Maxine.'

My own most recent glimpse of James Bowman was from my living room sofa. James, has recently, on the 31st August, 2007, taken part in the Service of Thanksgiving from the Guards' Chapel at London's Wellington Barracks, marking the Tenth Anniversary of the death of Diana, Princess of Wales. The music chosen aimed to reflect the Princess's tastes, and included some of her favourite pieces. James participated in Rachmaninov's 'O Virgin Mother of God Rejoice' from *The Vespers* and sung in its original Church Slavonic; he also sang in Mozart's motet '*Ave verum corpus*' and Faure's 'In paradisum'. The service was broadcast live on BBC1 and ITV. I noted that James, in his beautiful red and white robes, was very much singing quietly, as part of the choir, amidst flower arrangements that included growing English garden roses, and rosemary for remembrance. But, according to Bryan Appleyard in the September 2nd edition of *The Sunday Times*: 'This private yet public ceremony in the Guards' Chapel, a distinctly dodgy chunk of early 1960's concrete... is an odd occasion.' Princes William and Harry apart, most people would rather not have been turning up to Diana's memorial service 'to bow once more to her popular power'.

The Critics

> Against criticism a man can neither protest nor defend himself; he must act in spite of it, and then it will gradually yield to him.
> Johann Wolfgang von Goethe (1749 - 1832)

James always professed to ignore music critics, and treated them with contempt. 'Critics are horrible – always trying to dispose of people – they are all failed singers'. It was one of his typically sweeping generalisations with which I did not agree. In fact, although James has been locked in something of a long-running dispute with the music critic, Hugh Canning, he is hugely admired and respected by the academic and musicologist, Professor George Pratt. Canning regards the voice as a travesty, and in a *Sunday Times* article he denounced the countertenor sound as unauthentic and artificial, usurping the rightful place of women in Baroque opera. 'If you can't have a castrato', argued Canning, 'then get a mezzo instead'. In recent years Hugh Canning has softened his stance and given James rapturous reviews, even describing him as 'ageless', but Canning's misconception of the high male solo voice 'really gets up my nose' said James, and he bears him a grudge.

James' sole regret is his 1994 title role recording of Gluck's *Orfeo*, recorded live in France during a gruelling tour of Benjamin Britten's *A Midsummer Night's Dream*. He said that vocally it did not combine well with Britten's *Dream*, and also that his personal problems at the time were adversely affecting his voice. This has led critics to say that he was emotionally unsuited to the part of Orfeo, and uncommitted. One of them added, 'James Bowman seemed quite happy to leave Eurydice in the Underworld.' He sounded as if he couldn't be bothered to retrieve her, in Gluck's 'heterosexual' version of the myth.

Another French recording described by James as 'only adequate' is his title role performance of Handel's *Guilio Cesare*, recorded in 1995 with La Grande Écurie et la Chambre du Roy, under the direction of Jean-Claude Malgoire. He said he 'got by simply because of knowing the opera so well.' James had grave reservations about French Baroque instrumentalists; he regarded the English early music outfits as 'simply the best in the world.'

The broadcaster and ex-newsreader, Richard Baker, has always been an ardent admirer of James Bowman. Commenting on James as a Handelian in Handel's *Deborah*, live at the Albert Hall, he said: 'Countertenor James Bowman has one of the most startling voices of the century and, as I also love Handel, this concert performance of his early oratorio is quite unmissable... James Bowman's indecisive Barak was an affecting study in vulnerable authority.'

Of late some critics have been slightly negative about James' work, *The Times* remarking of a recent New Years Eve Concert at the Wigmore Hall, 'The veteran countertenor did...deliver some Handel arias – and rather touchingly. His voice is not the powerhouse clarion-call of old; these days, the highest notes tend to be artfully suggested rather than hurled out, and when the music went low he often disappeared beneath the accompanying violins. But his phrasing was exquisite, his tuning far more secure than was sometimes the case in his glory years, and – above all – he put over Handel's wonderfully gracious tunes (from *Alcina, Guistino, Solomon* and the *Choice of Hercules*) with immense character and charm.'

Even when a critic is full of praise for a performance from 'the veteran countertenor, James Bowman... still in fine voice', it is implied that his once brilliant career and dominance is now behind him; there is a note of surprise that he is still singing, along with an acknowledgement that James continues to excel in the quieter lute song repertoire. A review on Sunday, April 15th, by Fiona Maddocks of the Observer, described a Radio 3 broadcast of a concert for Holy Week, from the Temple Church, London. James Bowman was performing with Mark Levy and his viol ensemble Concordia; Dowland's cycle of *Seaven Teares* (1604), written shortly after the death of Queen Elizabeth 1, was interspersed with lute songs sung by James Bowman. In her review, Maddocks wrote: 'Dowland's highly chromatic harmonies in his *Seaven Teares* emerge as if through a shroud. Bowman's pure, bright voice offered perfect contrast.'

Although from a repertoire viewpoint, James is seen very much as a Purcell specialist, something he feels he owes to Robert King, he has always enjoyed working on earlier composers, especially Dowland. 'They [Mark Levy and his viol consort, Concordia] have an extra-lyrical, quasi-vocal manner that is very relaxed. I love that approach – it is certainly one I have tried to adopt myself and is one that I learned from Michael Chance. Above others, he taught me how to sit back and enjoy the sound I was producing – the more relaxed the singer is, the better the projection of the line.'

The most up-to-date review that I've come across is by Anthony Holden of *The Observer*, writing on Sunday, January 7, 2007. Holden gives James Bowman at 65, many compliments and recommends his 'clear diction' as an example to the next generation of singers, but it is nevertheless an account with caveats: 'Some performers past their prime seek to sustain their careers by sinking to the mercantile depths of *Celebrity Big Brother*; others simply continue to ply their trade in lesser venues – in the case of musicians, more modest auditoria with excellent acoustics, such the Central London Church of St Martin-in-the-Fields. This is where Thursday saw a packed house savouring a rare chance to hear the illustrious countertenor James Bowman singing Handel and Bach with the chamber group London Octave... The voice may be less resonant than in its golden days, not quite as rounded or robust, but its ethereal beauty can still raise the hairs on the back of your neck and its proprietor still knows how to pack quite a musical punch. After a graceful Bach Cantata, '*Wiederstehe doch der Sünde*', Bowman asked that no applause interrupt his progress through sombre songs reflecting what he considered a suitable post-Christmas "lack of merriment". After Pelham Humfrey's exquisite 'Hymn to God the Father', came three solemn Handel arias: '*Verdi Prati*' (from *Alcina*); '*He was despised*' *(Messiah)* and '*Ah! Si Morro*' (Admeto) . . . Bowman's consummate musicianship outshone any waning of his technical powers. Directing the ensemble himself often with no more than his shoulders, he even treated us to some delicate ornamentation in the repeats of 'He was despised'.... But this was also a master class in vocal control, the holding of a musical line and, above all, enunciation.'

It is somewhat ironic that the critic praises James' clear diction; whenever possible, I made sure that I was familiar with the libretto of a piece. After a performance James would always ask me with anxiety and great modesty, 'Could you actually hear the words I was singing, Maxine?', adding 'It is very difficult to hear sung words.'

James told me that he did not have perfect pitch (known as absolute pitch), only relative pitch. On the question of pitch, in the *Oxford Dictionary of Music*, Michael Kennedy writes: 'The sense of relative pitch may readily be acquired by practice, but the sense of absolute pitch much less easily. Absolute pitch is really an innate form of memory... Many good musicians possess this faculty, as many others do not. The possession of this sense is sometimes extremely useful, but may also prove an embarrassment, as, for instance, when a singer with absolute pitch is called upon to read music accompanied by an instrument tuned to what is to him or her "the wrong pitch", necessitating a conscious transposition of the vocal line.'

After his performances, James often said, 'How do I sound, Maxine? It is so difficult, sometimes impossible to hear myself. I hear only the resonating chambers within my face.' James quite often cupped an ear with his hand to shut out distracting noises and to improve his sense of his own voice. I noticed that he tended to do this when working with viol consorts like Fretwork; the viol consort Concordia has a much quieter sound.

Having told me some years ago that he would cease to make recordings after the age of sixty, it now appears that James is moving towards a further resurgence and new decade in his sixty-fifth year, although he has said that by the end of 1998 he was past his very best. Working with the young countertenor Daniel Taylor in a recital of Renaissance songs, James poignantly revisits Dowland's 'Flow My Tears'. This rare, late recording by James has been well received by critics: 'Bowman's perfect Elizabethan voice is matched in thrilling duet by the dazzling, if more conventional countertenor, Daniel Taylor... Bowman alone repeats some of the great Dowland Songs from the 1960's album; "Flow My Tears" is given extra melancholy by the passing of time.' From the Saturday *Times* Review, January 13th, 2006. James Bowman, Theatre of Early Music, 'Love Bade Me

Welcome', reviewed by Rick Jones. And more recently still, in November 2006, to mark his 65th birthday, working with his new piano accompanist, Andrew Plant, James has recorded a *Recital of English Song*. James returns to Purcell Odes and is joined by Daniel Taylor on August 4th, 2007, in what is described by the Canadian *Early Music Magazine* as 'his final appearance in Ottawa'. The programme takes place in the Dominion-Chalmers United Church, an historic venue renowned for its acoustic, as part of the Ottawa International Chamber Music Festival: 'Daniel Taylor and his theatre of Early Music and, in a terrific coup, the farewell concert of legendary countertenor, James Bowman.'

Thy Sun is Sinking

He who loves, he said, is more divine than the beloved, because the god is in the former, but not in the latter.
> Socrates, quoted by Thomas Mann, in *Death in Venice*

I used to imagine James seated at his desk reading my letters, resembling the painting *Portrait of a Gentleman in his Study*, by Lorenzo Lotto, from the Galleria dell' Accademia, Venice. I wondered if he had ever imagined me, pen in hand, all alone, bent with bated breath over my writing and listening to his work.

In the absence of his music and in the melancholy loneliness of a dream I entered his singer's house to be reunited with 'The Maxine Handy Library' and my private handwritten, letters. All was bathed in terracotta light, like the ruined tombs along the Via Appia Antica and the vanished Semitic civilisation of Motya. There, in his study, were the beautiful inscribed books: Michelangelo's *Love Sonnets* and *Madrigals to Tommaso de*

Cavalieri, front-covered by his 'Tityus'; Hervé Guibert *To the Friend who did not save my life*, Elie Wiesel's *Night* and *From the Kingdom of Memory*; Seamus Deane *Reading in the Dark*, and Primo Levi's collection of poems *Ad ora incerta, At an uncertain hour*:

> Dear James,
> I have traced the original Italian edition of Primo Levi's *Collected Poems*. They are published as *Ad ora incerta* and are coming from Italy. They will take about six weeks to arrive, but I'll send them to you as soon as possible...
> [1998]

The Marquis de Sade's *The One Hundred and Twenty Days of Sodom*, and Henry James' *Prefaces*:

> With their Baroque surface, their strange idiom, and their high seriousness, the prefaces have remained and will perhaps always remain closed to all but a few.'
> Leon Edel

Finally, Guiseppe Manfridi's *Cuckoos*, a black pearl:

> Dear James,
> I hope you enjoy Manfridi's *Cuckoos*, performed at the small fringe Gate Theatre in London and directed by Sir Peter Hall. At the centre of the two men and one woman triangle in this Oedipal tragicomedy is its poignant and humiliated Catholic heroine. The play ends with her suicide. I think it would make a marvellous piece for you and two others, in either the original Italian or Colin Teevan's formal and elegant English translation . . .
> Maxine

'Let's put an end to this. So we made a mistake. I made a mistake. I consented to sodomy. According to some this forever bars me from the kingdom of heaven. I have committed a sin, one which I had already committed in my youth. And my only justification can be that I was carried away by the all too human desire to return, however vainly, to that day long gone when a great love stirred ... But the past doesn't return.'

'I think your house did not love me, and I should not have come.' As I ceased to sleep and the dream was slowly fading, a blue night-light burned in the darkness and I heard James singing Solomon's paean to the rising and setting sun:

> When the sun o'er yonder hills
> Pours in tides the golden day,
> Or, when quiv'ring o'er the rills,
> In the west he dies away;
> He shall ever hear me sing,
> Praises to th' eternal King.

The poet John Clare, who all of his life hovered between sanity and madness, wanted his tomb to receive the morning and evening sun. He asked to be put into the earth on the 'North side of the Church yard just about the middle of the ground where the Morning and the Evening sun can linger longest on my grave.' His poignant wish was not respected.

Thy Day is at Evening

> One cannot start getting tetchy about wanting the voice to survive
>
> James Bowman

W. G. Sebald's subject is memory and its uncertain connection to the past. Atmospherically, we have to go back to his elusive documentary fiction of survival, *Austerlitz*, the last words of

Burning in Blueness

which are '...as evening began to fall'. Reading and writing are Austerlitz's favourite occupations and his primary interest is in writing about light and shade.

Everything for James Bowman seems to lose its intensity and interest after a decade. The pivotal association with Benjamin Britten and David Munrow's Early Music Consort was to last ten years from 1966-76, and in the case of the latter, have a tragic conclusion. Nine years later, in 1985, Bowman was introduced to Robert King, who 'resuscitated' his career, and has enjoyed a decade of working with a team again, making many of his truly outstanding recordings during this time. He regards David Munrow and Robert King as the two great mentors in his musical life. James continues to find new directions; each decade requires a different sound focus.

In 1997, James was awarded the CBE for services to Music.

'What do you think of my CBE, Maxine?' he asked me. I celebrated it with a special bouquet, card, and inscribed book for the Maxine Handy Library. The book, posted retrospectively in 1999, was a copy of *The Blackwater Lightship* by Colm Tóibín, author of *The Master* (2004).

After I had given James my formal congratulations, I said that I was already looking forward to his next honour, which would surely follow. As he seemed doubtful, I reminded him that this sequence had happened rapidly for Peter Pears, and James immediately brightened. 'Sir James sounds lovely,' I said, 'and is perfect for you.' But we both remarked that 'poor old Alfred Deller' had only made it to OBE. 'We are all in his debt,' said James.

In 2000 being appointed a Gentleman of the small and august Chapel Royal, in the service of the Queen, underlines James' position as one of England's elite musicians. I hope that when this great and unique artist retires from the Chapel Royal, after a decade of service no doubt, he will be given a knighthood. He has always said that he likes the idea of changing Persona.

Maxine Handy, March 2008

Postscript November 2010

James Bowman concerts 2010 – 2011

Special Announcement

21 May 2011:
  This concert at the Wigmore Hall London will mark James's very last appearance in London. Although he may from time to time sing outside London, it will only be very occasionally.
The concert features the works of Purcell and Handel with whose works he has been closely associated.

▲   ▲   ▲

Afterword 2011

'The outstanding countertenor James Bowman will give his final Wigmore Hall recital on May 21st. I have been listening to him there for half my life and I can't believe I'll never hear him there again, but James is pushing and that's a wise time to go. Oh, my veni, veni, venis long ago…With typical generosity he is sharing his farewell with the fast-rising Iranian-American harpsichordist, Mahan Esfahani. Purcell, Handel and Bach…mmm.'

Comments in reply: Maxine Handy says: May 8, 2011 at 5.40 pm:

'I am in entire agreement with your comments. For a decade I attended his every performance, and commissioned a Scena to celebrate his 50th birthday. I have all his recordings and have been listening to his unique voice for over three decades. This year I have at last completed two books on the great James Bowman; they have taken me more than ten years to write but were a labour of love…an offering to this divine artist. Yes, it is sad that he is leaving the London music scene, but James has enjoyed many different stages in his legendary career, and I think that this is just such another. He is not disappearing into memory alone; he will be singing in other, often charming venues. As I have said in my *Triple-Portrait of a Countertenor*, as James slowly fades with time, like an Old-Master painting, he becomes an ever more beautiful masterpiece.'

▲   ▲   ▲

James' tender and joyous farewell to his musical life and audiences in the capital celebrated the baroque composers with which he is so closely identified. His chosen repertoire of Handel, Bach and Purcell was a perfect expression of the beauty and vulnerability at the heart of his vocal genius. James took a little while to settle. When he first appeared on stage James admitted to being rather nervous – a touch of stage fright, he said! Some typically mischievous remarks to the audience helped him to relax – he expressed his satisfaction at the wisdom of his public, who had chosen to come to this very special evening at the Wigmore, rather than the abysmal production of *The Dream,* currently on at English National Opera. "Have you read the terrible reviews?" he asked with obvious amusement. "It is set in a boys' prep school. I have had quite enough of those in my life", he added pointedly. Amidst the scornful jokes, it was obvious that James felt much justified satisfaction that this new version of a role with which he had a lifelong identification, was a disaster. James' enchanted bank and magic wood had been replaced by a ghastly boys' school where unprotected children suffered abuse. Reaching for a glass of water to ease his dry throat, James emphasised that he did not want the occasion of his last London recital to be over-emotional, but it was clear that at times during the evening he was overcome, particularly when remembering David Munrow.

The recital brought to a close more than four decades of performance. It was a gentle goodbye, a graceful withdrawal from the Wigmore stage, which he had first stepped upon in 1967 with David Munrow's Early Music Consort. When the veteran Countertenor appeared on the platform, he was greeted with a heartfelt tribute to his supreme artistry. James had invited the brilliant young Iranian-born harpsichordist Mahan Esfahani to join him for his final bow in London, to accompany him, but also to perform solo. It was through a David Munrow recording that Mahan had first encountered Bowman and the countertenor voice. He produced from his pocket the very cassette he'd bought aged 10 – *Pleasures of the Royal Courts* – and asked Bowman to sign it, tucking the spilling spool back in his pocket as he did so. James highlighted the similarity between the harpsichord and the countertenor – both had started out in accompanying roles, but gradually transformed into solo instruments, which were now taken very seriously. James'

Burning in Blueness

decision to share his final London platform was both wise and typically generous. The presence of the thrilling Esfahani gave the evening a fresh excitement and energy, but the spotlight shone firmly on James Bowman. In the first half the capacity audience was treated to Purcell; after the interval James moved to Handel. He delighted us with the exquisite and little known 'Tacerò, pur che fedele' from *Agrippina*, caressed with delicate da-capo ornamentation by James.

Returning to his sole encore, Bowman playfully declined to name it! 'If you don't recognise this one you shouldn't be here'. I knew at once that it would be Purcell's *Evening Hymn*, hailing the setting of the sun. As James closed with the tenderest of legatos, weaving a rainbow tapestry, the audience closed with rapturous applause and a standing ovation.

This last London recital was intended to mark a significant moment in James' career. Although he intends to give recitals elsewhere, he will only perform infrequently. As he approaches his 70th birthday in November, he describes his voice as being 'in reasonably good shape', but in need of conservation. He talks about it as '… a friend – but a friend that can turn on you if it wants to. An alien living in your throat…It has a mind of its own. Quite uncanny.' It is live performance that he will always cherish, and not content with happy memories alone, there are many things still to come. On 25th June at Ely Cathedral he is performing in an evening programme of *Music and Memories*, with works by Tallis, Purcell, Handel, Vaughan Williams and Britten. James will also talk about his professional life and reflect on his time at Ely in the 1950s when he was a chorister. On 1st July 2011 he is singing with Catherine Bott, in an evening recital *A Midsummer Night with Bott and Bowman*, which will include settings of Shakespeare by Britten.

I left the Wigmore Hall with a number of photographs to treasure, including an image of James' final deep bow. As James sings with his entire body he is extremely difficult to photograph; blurred images are the usual outcome. At first I was disappointed by these hazy photographs, until I realised that the phenomenon of the out-of-focus image created its own seductive beauty. 'Unsharpness' presented James in performance as being in a state 'between apparition and dissolution between memory and forgetting'. Upon my return home I had the photographs professionally adjusted; an intricate process during which the boundaries between painting and photography were themselves blurred. This resulted in a complex and dynamic instability, which was at the heart of James' vocal agility in live performance. I felt that through these portraits his spirit was made visible and free. And as James has indicated, there is still plenty more to come from him, outside the capital; this he expressed in his programme notes. 'A philistine uncle of mine, now deceased, once said to me "When is your voice going to break?" Well, I hope not quite yet. I still enjoy singing and if I stopped completely I would miss all of my friends.'

James Bowman's farewell to the Wigmore Hall, May 2011

'I am grateful to have been able to record so extensively – to me, recording is essential for an artist.'

> The last London recital, 2011.

James Bowman
Complete Discography

Compact Discs

J S Bach	B Minor Mass	Collins 70322
	Solo Cantatas	Hyperion CDA66326
	St Matthew Passion	Teldec 2292-42509-2
	St John Passion	Philips 434 905-2
Biber	Requiem	Ricercar RIC081063
Blow	Ode on the death of Mr Henry Purcell	RCA Victor D134250
Britten	Midsummer Night's Dream	Virgin Classics VCD7 59305-2
	Death in Venice	London 425 669-2LH2
	Canticles	London 425 716-2LM
	Rejoice in the lamb	EMI CDM5 65111-2
	Purcell realizations	Hyperion CDA67061/2
Bruhns	Complete cantatas	Ricercar REC 8001/2
Burgon	Fall of Lucifer	Silva Classics SILKD6002
	Canciones del Alma	EMI CDC7 49762 2 or EMI CDM 5 66527 2
	Merciless beauty	ASV Classics CD DCA 1059
Buxtehude	German baroque cantatas vol 7	Ricercar RIC094076
Byrd	Consort songs, English Consort Music (I)	Ricercar RIC206442
David Cain	Play music by David Cain	BBC Records ZBBC 1925
Campian etc.	Elizabethan ayres and dances	Saga EC 3354-2

Cavalli	Calisto	Decca 436216-2DM02
Charpentier	Messe de minuit	EMI CDM7 63135-2
Couperin	Lecon de ténèbres	Hyperion CDA66474
Dowland	Lute Songs	Hyperion CDA66447
	Lute songs	Saga EC 3375-2
Dufay	Missa Se la face ay pale	Virgin Veritas 61283
Du Mont	Motets a deux voix	Ricercar RIC068053
Early Music Consort	Art of the Netherlands	EMI reflexe 64215
	The Medieval Experience	DG Archiv 449 082 2
	Monteverdi's contemporaries	Virgin Veritas 61288
	Art of courtly love	Virgin Veritas 61284
	Music of the gothic era	DG Archiv 415 292
	Music of the gothic era (2 CD's)	DG Archiv Produktion "Codex" 453 185-2
	Gregorian Chant, Perotin & Machaut	DG Archiv 4439 424-2
	Music of the crusades	Decca 430 264-2
	Ecco la primavera	Decca 436 219
	The pleasures of the royal courts	Nonsuch 71326
	The Triumphs of Maximilian I	Decca Serenata 436 998
	Adieu Madame - Music at the English Court	Deutsche Harmonia Mundi GD77 178
Gabrieli	Christmas motets	Hyperion CDA66398
Grier	12 Anthems	Herald HAVPCD177
Gluck	Orfeo ed Euridice	Astree E 8538
Handel	Admeto	Virgin Veritas 5 61369 2
	Ariodante	Phillips 442 096-2
	Athalia	L'Oiseau Lyre 417 126-

		2
	Belshazzar	Archiv 431 793-2
	Chandos anthems vol 3	Chandos CHAN0505
	Deborah	Hyperion CDA66841/2
	Giulio Cesare	Astree E 8558
	Julius Caesar	EMI CDMS7 69760-2
	Israel in Egypt	Decca 443 470-2DF2
	Joshua	Hyperion CDA66461/2
	Joseph & His Brethren	Hyperion CDA67171/3
	Judas Maccabaeus	Hyperion CDA66641/2
	Messiah	Erato 2292 45960-2 or Erato ECD 880503 or Erato 0630-17766-2
	Messiah	EMI CMS5 63784-2
	Messiah	EMI CDS7 49801-2
	Messiah	Pro Arte CDD 232
	Music for royal occassions	Hyperion CDA66635
	Foundling hospital anthem	L'Oiseau Lyre 421 654-2OH
	Occasional Oratorio	Hyperion CDA66961/2
	Orlando	L'Oiseau Lyre 430 845-2
	Ottone	Hyperion CDA66751/3
	Saul	Archiv 447 696-2
	Silla	Somm SOMMCD 227-8
	English Arias	Hyperion CDA66483
	Heroic Arias	Hyperion CDA66797
	Italian Duets	Hyperion CDA66440
	Tercentenary Concert	BBC Radio Classics

		15656 91522
Herbert Howells	Full moon and O my deir hert	Meridian CDE84158
Kerll	Missa pro defunctis	Ricercar RIC081063
Johann Kuhnau	Sacred Music	Hyperion CDA67059
Loussier	Messa Baroque du 21 Siècle	Decca 425 217-2 or Media 7 M7 856
Monteverdi	L'Incoronazione de Poppea	Virgin Veritas VCT5 45082-2
	L'Orfeo	Archiv 447 703-2AX2
	Vespro della Beata Virgine	Decca 443 482-2
Nyman	Time will pronounce	Argo 440 282-2ZH
Orff	Carmina Burana	Decca 444 591-2 or Decca 411 702-2
	Carmina Burana	Virgin Classics CUV 5 61262 2
Palestrina	Canticum Canticorum Salomonis	Hyperion CDA66733
Pergolesi	Stabat Mater	L'Oiseau Lyre 425 692-2
	Salve Regina	Meridian CDE84327
Praetorius	Dances from Terpsichore & Motets	Virgin Veritas 61289 2 7
Henry Purcell	Odes and Welcome Songs vol 1	Hyperion CDA66314
	Odes and Welcome Songs vol 2	Hyperion CDA66349
	Odes and Welcome Songs vol 3	Hyperion CDA66412

	Odes and Welcome Songs vol 4	Hyperion CDA66456
	Odes and Welcome Songs vol 5	Hyperion CDA66476
	Odes and Welcome Songs vol 6	Hyperion CDA66494
	Odes and Welcome Songs vol 7	Hyperion CDA66587
	Odes and Welcome Songs vol 8	Hyperion CDA66598
	Three Queen Mary odes	Virgin Veritas VC7 59243 2
	Birthday Ode for Queen Mary (1692 & 1694)	EMI Eminence CD-EMX 2134
	Queen Mary ode, Funeral Music & Organ Works	EMI Classics "Rouge et Noir" CZS 767 524-2 or EMI Classics 7243 5 69270 2 5
	Anthems and Services vol 1	Hyperion CDA66585
	Anthems and Services vol 2	Hyperion CDA66609
	Anthems and Services vol 3	Hyperion CDA66623
	Anthems and Services vol 4	Hyperion CDA66644
	Anthems and Services vol 5	Hyperion CDA66656
	Anthems and Services vol 6	Hyperion CDA66663
	Anthems and Services vol 7	Hyperion CDA66677

Burning in Blueness

	Anthems and Services vol 8	Hyperion CDA66686
	Anthems and Services vol 9	Hyperion CDA66693
	Anthems and Services vol 10	Hyperion CDA66707
	Anthems and Services vol 11	Hyperion CDA66716
	Anthems, Instrumental music and Songs	Teldec 9032 77608 2
	Te deum & Jubilate & Funeral music	Decca 430 263-2DM
	Secular Songs vol 1	Hyperion CDA66710
	Secular Songs vol 2	Hyperion CDA66720
	Secular Songs vol 3	Hyperion CDA66750
	Complete Theatre music (6 discs)	L'Oiseau Lyre 425 893-2
	Mr Henry Purcell's most admirable composures	Hyperion CDA66288
	Countertenor duets and solos	Hyperion CDA66253
	Vocal works	EMI CZS7 67524-2
	Dioclesian acts 1 – 4	Chandos CHAN0568
	Dioclesian masques & Timon of Athens	Chandos CHAN0558
	Dido & Aeneas	Chandos CHAN0586
	The Fairy Queen	Decca 433 163-2DM2
Alan Ridout	Epitaph for Amy Three sonnets of Cecil Day Lewis	Meridian CDE84158
Betty Roe	The Music Tree	Somm SOMMCD 208

252

Scarlatti & Hasse	Salve Regina	Hyperion CDA66875
Schütz	Symphoniae Sacrae	Chandos CHAN0566/7
Tavener	Akathist of Thanksgiving	Sony SK64446
Telemann	Cantatas	Meridian CDE84159
Various	Ikon	Hyperion CDA66928
	Great baroque arias pt 1	Allegro PCD 894 or MCA Classics MCAD-25213
	Baroque choral & string works	Arion ARN68026
	Italian cantatas	Arion ARN68046
	Recital	Meridian CDE84126
	Baroque vocal works	Meridian CDE84138
	Music from the Courts of Europe - London	United 88002 or Cala 88002-2
	German baroque cantatas vol 6	Ricercar RIC079061
	German baroque cantatas vol 8	Ricercar RIC103086/87
	Solo Alto Cantatas	Ricercar RIC101095
	Lo Sposalizio	Hyperion CDA67048
Vaughan Williams	Ten Blake Songs Linden Lea and other songs	Meridian CDE84158
Vivaldi	Sacred music vol 2	Hyperion CDA66779
	Stabat Mater & Nisi Dominus	L'Oiseau Lyre 414 329-2OM
	Nisi Dominus	L'Oiseau Lyre 443 199-2OM
	Nisi Dominus	L'Oiseau Lyre Double

			Decca 455 727-2
		Vespers for the nativity of the Virgin	Astree E8520
	Peter Warlock	My own country and other songs	Meridian CDE84158
	Weckman	Complete Cantatas	Ricercar RIC109097/098
	Compilations	Baroque beauties	Carlton ORCD11010
		Discover the classics – heroes & heroines	Carlton PCD894 or Pickwick PCD58
		Discover the classics - set 1	Pickwick BOXD21
		These you have loved Vol. 3	Classics for Pleasure CD-CFP4332
		Sacred Music	EMI EG764263-4
		Recital	EMI France 4 83086 2
		The Bach Family	Ricercar RIC92001
		The Music of the Kings Consort	Hyperion king1
		Essential Purcell	Hyperion king2
		The James Bowman collection	Hyperion king3
		The Kings Consort Baroque collection	Hyperion king4
		Portrait	Decca 436 799-2
		The world of sacred music	Decca 436 404-2DW0
		The world of Henry Purcell	Decca 443 393-2DW0
		The glory of Purcell	L'Oiseau Lyre 444 629-2OH

	England, my England (Film soundtrack)	Erato 0630 10700-2
	Le temps des Castrats	EMI CDC 5 55054-2
	La musique au temps des Castrats	Astree E8552
	Les Festes Champestres	Astree E 8631
	Fairest Isle	BBC Music Magazine BM 1
	The art of James Bowman	Meridian CDE 84332
	Intimate Baroque	Summit 118
	If music be the food of love	IMP 6801052

LPs

J S Bach	St Matthew Passion	Telefunken SAWT 9572/75
Bernstein	Chichester Psalms	EMI ASD 3035
Blow	Ode on the death of Mr Henry Purcell	Phillips 6575016
Britten	Rejoice in the lamb	EMI ASD 3035
	Canticle 2	EMI CSD 3772
	Canticle 4	Decca SXL 6608
	Death in Venice	Decca set 581-3
Byrd	Ceremonial Tudor church music	Argo ZRG 659
	Music of the English home	Turnabout TV 34709
Campian etc.	Elizabethan ayres and dances	Saga (number unknown)
Cavalli	Calisto	Argo ZNF 11/12

255

Charpentier	Messe de minuit	EMI S-36528
Desprez	Missa "L'Homme Armé"	Archiv 2533 360
Dowland	Lute songs	Saga 5449
Dufay	Missa Se la face ay pale	HMV CSD 3751
	Motets	Archive 2533291
Dunstable	Motets	Archive 2533291
Early Music Consort	Art of the Netherlands	EMI SLS 5049
	Art of courtly love	HMV SLS 863
	Music of the gothic era	DG Archiv Produktion 2710 019
	Music of the crusades	Argo ZRG 673
	Music of the Royal Courts of Europe 1150-1600	World Record Club ST 1108
	Henry VIII and his six wives	HMV CSD A9001
	The Art of the Recorder	EMI SLS 5022
	Monteverdi's Contemporaries	HMV SQ ASD 3393
	Love, lust, piety and politics Music of the English court from King Henry V to VIII	BASF/Harmonia mundi 25 22 286-1
	Elizabeth R - Theme and Incidental Music and song	BBC Records RESL 4
	Play music by David Cain	BBC Records REC 91S
	Ecco la primavera	Argo ZRG 642
	The Triumphs of Maximilian I	Argo ZRG 728
	Music for Ferdinand and Isabella of Spain	HMV CSD 3738

	Renaissance Suite (from the film "La course en tête")	HMV HQS 1415
Gretchaninov	Russian Creed Featured in "World of Your Hundred Best Tunes" series also "100 Greatest Classics" volume 3	TRX 103
Handel	Admeto	EMI IC 163-31 808/12
	Athalia	L'Oiseau Lyre 417 126-1
	The Choice of Hercules	EMI ASD 3148
	Julius Caesar	EMI EX-2702325
Di Lasso	Penetential Psalms	Archiv 2533 290
Machaut	La Messe de Nostra Dame	Archiv SAWT 9566-B
Monteverdi	Vespro della Beata Virgine	Decca SET 593040
	Selva Morale E Spirituale	Amadeus AMS 011-12
	L'Orfeo	Archiv 2723 018
Morales	Magnificat and Motets	Archiv 2533 321
Ockeghem	Requiem Mass	Archiv 2533 145
Praetorius	Dances from Terpsichore & Motets	HMV CSD 3761
Purcell	Birthday Ode for Queen Mary (1692 & 1694)	EMI/HMV ASD 3166
	Sacred Music at the English Court	Telefunken SAWT 9558-B
	The Fairy Queen	Decca SET 499-500
	Come, ye sons of art	Musicmasters MM 20005

	Ceremonial Music	Argo ZRG 724
Schütz	Voices and Brass	Argo ZRG 576
	Musikalische Exequien	EMI 065-03 828
	Christmas story	Argo ZRG 671
Tavener	Canciones Espanolas	RCA LRL1 5104
Vivaldi	Stabat Mater & Nisi Dominus	L'Oiseau-Lyre DSLO 506
Various	Songs in Shakespeare's plays	Archiv 2533 407
	Elizabethan lute songs	EMI HQS 1281 or EMI Eminence EMX2101
	Music from the 13th Century	Harmonia Mundi HMU 443
	Sacred music from the 15th/16th Centuries	Archiv 2533 361
	Anthems for the Chapel Royal	Argo ZRG 855
	The King's Musick	EMI C 063-30 119
	Motets by Monteverdi, Gabrieli & Schütz	L'Oiseau-Lyre SOL 333
	Christmas music	Abbey Records ABY 603
	Fantasies, Ayres & Dances	Rosetree RT 101

Videos

Britten	Death in Venice	(number unknown)
	Midsummer Night's Dream	Castle CV12008

Handel	Giulio Cesare	MCEG VVD383
	Honour, Profit, Preasure	1984 Number unknown
Soundtrack	Elizabeth R. part 4	BBC Video BBCV5641
Soundtrack	Zardoz	CBS/FOX No. 1298
Soundtrack	Rhapsody in August	A Kurosawa film Number unknown
Soundtrack	A corps perdu	Canadian film by Léa Pool Number unknown

Printed in Great Britain
by Amazon.co.uk, Ltd.,
Marston Gate.